C000261268

A FEW OF THE MANY

Previous titles by this author:-
> Spitfire Squadron
> The Invisible Thread: A Spitfire's Tale
> Through Peril to the Stars
> Angriff Westland

A sequel to 'A Few of the Many' is already in preparation. If you have any information, relics or photographs which you think may be of interest, or are a former wartime pilot interested in helping this young man further his extensive research, Dilip would be delighted to hear from you via Ramrod Publications on 01905 767735.

He is particularly interested to trace anyone, pilots or groundstaff, who served at Tangmere, Merston or Goodwood from March - November 1941 and have any recollections of Wing Commander Douglas Bader and his famous Wing.

Dilip Sarkar is also well known for speaking on the subject of his published work, and authoritatively presents slide shows relating to various projects at which he often chairs question & answer sessions with wartime pilots. At these unique events the Malvern Spitfire Team provides professionally presented displays of research and superb examples of restoration. Both Dilip Sarkar and the Malvern Spitfire Team can be contacted and booked for events via Ramrod Publications on 01905 767735. Presentations can be especially composed to suit your event's particular requirements.

Dilip Sarkar is also available for aviation historical consultancy work in respect of publishing projects, television and radio.

First published in 1995
by Ramrod Publications,
16 Kingfisher Close, St Peter's, Worcs. WR5 3RY, England.
© Dilip Sarkar 1995

All rights reserved. No part of this publication may be reproduced, stored in a retrieval system, or transmitted in any form or by any means without prior permission in writing from the publisher.

ISBN: 0-9519832-3-7

Designed and typeset by
Aspect Design, 89 Newtown Road, Malvern, Worcestershire WR14 2PD
and bound by Cedric Chivers Limited, Bristol.

A FEW OF THE MANY

AIR WAR 1939-45
A KALEIDOSCOPE OF MEMORIES

BY

DILIP SARKAR

RAMROD PUBLICATIONS

This book is dedicated to all of my family and friends
who help to make my ideas and ambitions become reality.

A Few Of The Many

Contents

Foreword

Flt Lt John Peters back in the cockpit of a Tornado GR1 after his Gulf War ordeal as a PoW.

Andrew Phillips

War is personal. Everyone involved experiences the extremes of emotion and has to face and overcome their own frailties. The majority receive little recognition, but their memories remain with them for life. In "A Few of the Many", Dilip Sarkar helps to set the balance and has captured the essence of some of these extraordinary experiences by allowing ordinary airmen to relate their fascinating tales in their own words. These now white-haired gentlemen describe the amazing events of their youth. If you want to understand, from a personal point of view, what it was like to have fought from a tiny cockpit during the Battle of Britain and afterwards, then this book is essential reading. "The Few" provide the benchmark against which "The Many" present and future Royal Air Force pilots must measure.

Flt Lt John Peters RAF, April 1995

Introduction

My personal fascination with the 1939-45 air war was, in the first instance and as described in the introduction to 'Through Peril to the Stars', stimulated by the moving stories of those young pilots who failed to return.

During the early days of my research I realised that it was fairly easy to write about the dead, their personal papers and diaries often having been made available by surviving relatives, but it was not so easy to write about the living. As my research progressed I met an increasing number of former RAF fighter pilots, and slowly, as we came to know and respect each other, the barriers came down and the memories came pouring out. Each of these men is possessed of a natural and genuine modesty and, understandably, an absolute reluctance to be seen as a 'line shooter'. Furthermore, and this is virtually without exception, each has said to me something along the lines of 'I was just one of hundreds of thousands of Allied airmen who were there and was just doing my job. My story is neither different nor interesting - go and talk to somebody else!' It has been a matter of convincing each in turn that the recording of their memories is essential to making as complete a history as possible of those now far off times, and indeed that the process could not be interpreted as 'shooting a line'.

Although some of the pilots in this book were undoubtedly great fighter pilots with impressive scores, like Wing Commanders 'Bunny' Currant and David Cox, my interest generally is not in the aces but in the 'unknowns'. What fascinates me is how 'ordinary' people were plunged into an extraordinary set of circumstances but responded so valiantly, presenting an anonymous mass of courage which went about its duties relentlessly until victory was achieved, and without which that end result would have been impossible. Few of these men received any official recognition for their service, and after the war faded into obscurity in civilian life. The fascination has been finding them today - all now men in their 70s and 80s, Old Age Pensioners in fact, and unlocking their memories. This has added another dimension to this book of 'where are they now?', which I hope the reader will find as interesting as I do. The Second World War was certainly the most dramatic event during their lives, and their memories of their part in it are often more riveting due to the modesty apparent in their telling.

In recent years several extremely commendable reference manuals have been published detailing biographical information concerning wartime pilots. However, in paying tribute to the unknowns, I did not wish to produce just the bare facts and figures, or even relate full biographical and service details in every case. Instead I wanted the pilots to tell their own stories, to breath life into records of their often traumatic experiences. I believe that this end result has only been made possible through my own personal relationship with each individual concerned. In some cases, however, it was still not easy to extract information, but in others once the flow started they were unable to stop as the memories literally flooded out.

There have been several inspirations which have culminated in 'A Few of the Many'. Firstly, in 1992 I had the great pleasure of meeting Squadron Leader Ron Stillwell DFC DFM RAF Retd with whom I had previously corresponded regularly for several years. When we met, however, Ron's memory and accounts of his flying days were excellent. I decided there and then that somehow I would have to put together a book that in some way reflected the memories of such men. Sadly Ron unexpectedly died soon afterwards. As I had not by then recorded his memories, my friend does not appear in this book, a tragedy indeed as he was an airman of great experience and popularity. Other friends, such as Wing Commanders Peter Howard-Williams and Roger Boulding, did help to record their memories, and so their stories are included in this book, but sadly they have not lived to see 'A Few of the Many' published. Secondly, whilst signing books at the launches of my previous titles, often with as many as 25 former pilots present, I have looked around me and realised the gift that I have been given, that of a special relationship with these men which makes such research possible. The initial idea was for 'The Last of the Few', but such a title would have limited the scope to just Battle of Britain pilots, although of course the survivors' experiences extended throughout the war and were not, therefore, just limited to 1940. Thus 'A Few of the Many' was born to include the entire spectrum of wartime fighter pilots.

The first man I ever met who was personally involved in the Battle of Britain was Bob Morris, a Fitter IIE on 66 Squadron. Since that first meeting I have been acutely aware of the contribution made by the essential, but often even more unsung, ground crews, so naturally wished to include the stories of both Bob and another ground crew friend, Fred Roberts, as a tribute to their contributions. I am sure that the reader will not find their stories any less fascinating than those told by the pilots.

To provide a balanced account, it is essential to offer a 'through the looking glass' view from the other side. Although this book is ostensibly a tribute, appropriately published in the 50th anniversary year of VE Day, to the RAF, one must nevertheless appreciate that the German aircrews also flew with great skill and courage. Several pilots in this book mention the common bond that undoubtedly exists between combat flyers, so for that reason I am delighted to present the stories of three no less gallant former enemy pilots. Their views and memories are equally essential to the history of the times.

Today, 50 years after the Second World War ended, Britain and Germany are now Allies. Their air forces are largely equipped with identical aircraft, in the form of the Panavia Multi-Role Combat Aircraft, better known as the Tornado. In the 1990s, the RAF and Luftwaffe, with other air forces of the Western

Alliance, remain prepared to fly into battle together whenever the call arises. Whilst the technology of today's weapons and fast jets is awesome when compared with the Spitfires and Me 109s of 50 years ago, essentially the spirit of their pilots remains the same. In fact, there are surprisingly many comparisons to be made between combat flying in today's high-tech world and the Second World War. In 1990, the RAF deployed Tornados to the Persian Gulf to join a Coalition air force poised to strike against Iraq after Saddam Hussein's invasion of Kuwait. Consequently, on January 16th, 1991, the Tornado went to war for the first time, and with it a new generation of combat pilots, many of them either my own age or even younger. Flight Lieutenants John Peters and John Nichol failed to return from their first sortie, having been shot down over Iraq, and were captured. Subsequently tortured and paraded on television in a counter-productive publicity stunt, their plight won the hearts of the free world. This XV Squadron Tornado crew later wrote about their experiences in a best-selling book, 'Tornado Down'. As in this book we are looking at Second World War combat flying across the span of half a century, I thought it appropriate to ask John Peters, with whom I share the same year of birth, to contribute the foreword to 'A Few of the Many'; I am honoured that he has kindly done so.

August gentlemen: former fighter pilots at the launch of 'Through Peril to the Stars' by Dilip Sarkar in September 1993. Such gatherings have not only been an inspiration, but have also provided unique opportunities for research. From left to right: Wg Cdr BJ Jennings DFM AFC, Sqn Ldr TA Stevens, Sqn Ldr RM Pugh AFC, Flt Lt AW Minchin, Sqn Ldr LH Casson DFC AFC, Wg Cdr GC Unwin DSO DFM, Flt Lt KA Wilkinson, Flt Lt T Dzidzic, Flt Lt DH Nichols, Flt Lt R Rayner DFC, WO CD Spruce, Sqn Ldr I Hutchinson, Flt Lt WLB Walker, Flt Lt RL Jones & Grp Capt GR Edge OBE DFC.

The reader will be the judge as to whether I have succeeded in my two aims in respect of this book: firstly to make a contribution to history, and secondly to provide some long overdue recognition in an appropriate year to the 'average' squadron pilot - but how can anyone describe these people as average when they were heroes all?

To conclude I can only say that so long as wartime fighter pilots draw breath, my research will be both intense and ongoing. If you were a wartime fighter pilot and are reading this, or have any other information regarding their whereabouts, I would be delighted to hear from you via Ramrod Publications. There is an enormous amount of work yet to be done, so we need all the help we can get.

Dilip Sarkar, Worcester, February 1995.

Chapter One

Wing Commander Christopher Currant DSO DFC

Flight Lieutenant CF 'Bunny' Currant pictured during 1940.

Christopher Frederick Currant was born in Luton on December 14th, 1911, and joined the RAF in 1936. In the service he was inevitably known as 'Bunny', and indeed still is today by his many friends. Bunny first flew Gauntlet biplanes with 46 Squadron in 1937, followed by Hurricanes with 151 during 1939. Commissioned in April 1940, Pilot Officer Currant, a regular officer, joined the Auxiliary 605 'County of Warwick' Squadron at Wick in Scotland. On May 21st, 1940, 605 Squadron's Hurricanes flew to Hawkinge, just inland of Folkestone and the closest RAF station to France. From there the squadron flew daily patrols over France to supplement the hard-pressed squadrons of the Advanced Air Striking Force. In March 1991, Bunny reflected on the dramatic events of over 50 years before:-

'On May 21st, 1940, the squadron was ordered off from RAF Wick to RAF Hawkinge to be directed on offensive patrols over Northern France as the German army attempted to over-run Dunkirk. I was ordered to patrol the Arras area with Flying Officer Hope as my Number Two. As we prepared to take off, Squadron Leader Teddy Donaldson, the CO of 151 Squadron, landed from a patrol over France and was rather pessimistic about the outlook over there. From our airfield I could see smoke on the horizon over France and could hear the rumble of bombs dropping in the distance. We took off, climbed away heading for the scene of the battle clearly visible as we climbed south. At about 15,000' in the Arras vicinity I saw He 111s dropping bombs. Saw them explode along the road and in the woods as I opened the throttle and dived towards the Heinkels. Gunsight on, straps tight and locked firm as I raced in with a quarter deflection from behind the Heinkel. Got it well in the sight and opened fire. Saw hits on the port engine and fuselage. Smoke, steam and flames appeared and it banked left in a fairly steep dive. The next thing was extraordinary. I saw and heard no enemy fire striking my aircraft but suddenly there was silence as the engine seized, the propeller stopped. There it was in front of my nose - just a stationary airscrew. The cockpit filled with fumes hissing noisily. Steam and glycol but no smoke. I opened the hood, undid my straps and climbed out on to the wing intending to jump. I then did a very stupid thing. I changed my mind. My mind said "I can put this thing down!" I climbed back in and glided down and with wheels up slid into a field. I had no time to do up my straps and as the Hurricane skidded rapidly to a sudden stop I hit the side of the cockpit with my nose and broke it (the nose!) and cut my face. I clambered out, looked up to see Flying Officer Hope circling round and fly off back to Hawkinge. I grabbed my maps, parachute and Sidcot flying suit and made my way to a farmhouse where the folk very kindly bathed my cuts and we conversed quite ineffectively in pidgin French and English. I was aware of them pointing eastwards and could easily distinguish amongst the gabble of French words "Les salles boches", which I took to mean the bloody Germans. So I was eager to head north towards Calais hoping to catch a boat back to England. I walked a long way still carrying my parachute, maps and Sidcot. I was bloody hot. It was a warm, sunny day. Eventually I walked into a small French town. Found the town hall and an official, and begged for a car to take me to Calais. Miracle, he did, and we drove past miles and miles of civilians in carts, bicycles, lorries, prams, old folk, young folk, kids and hundreds of French soldiers heading west. What a terrible depressing shambles. We made Calais and I went aboard and at 10 pm that evening was back in the Officers' Mess of RAF Station Hawkinge. Next day I found myself in Folkestone hospital where they put me to sleep and fixed my nose. Rejoined 605 Squadron about 3 weeks later at RAF Drem near Edinburgh. I was to find myself in the same Folkestone hospital several years later having a German bullet removed from my skull'.

During the Battle of Britain 605 Squadron operated from Croydon, and during that time Bunny accounted for nine enemy aircraft destroyed, which made him officially an ace, and shared in the destruction of several more. On October 8th,

1940, he was awarded a DFC, and a Bar a month later. With the death of 605's CO in action on November 1st, Bunny took temporary command of the squadron. In early 1941, Flying Officer Currant DFC & Bar was rested as an instructor. His return to operations in August 1941 saw him given command of 501 'County of Gloucester' Squadron at Ibsley in Hampshire. During that period the morale boosting film about the Spitfire's designer, Reginald Mitchell, entitled 'The First of the Few', was made at that station. 501 Squadron supplied the Spitfires for the film. The opening scene showed David Niven talking to a group of fighter pilots on 'an airfield somewhere in England'. Those featured really were Spitfire pilots, from the Ibsley squadrons, including Bunny Currant himself. In June 1942 he was promoted to Wing Commander and led the Ibsley Wing, the following month receiving the DSO for his work with 501 Squadron.

Pilot Officer David Fulford of 118 Squadron, and Squadron Leader Bunny Currant (CO of 501 Squadron), at Ibsley in 1941 during the making of the film 'The First of the Few'. At centre is actor Leslie Howard who played the part of Spitfire designer RJ Mitchell.

Wing Commander Currant later commanded 122 Wing of the 2nd TAF based at Gravesend and comprising 19, 65 and 122 Squadrons flying Spitfire Mk IXs and then Mustang IIIs. Officially his final 'score' of enemy aircraft destroyed was 15, and he shared in the destruction of at least five others. He remained in the post-war RAF and eventually retired in 1959. In 1945, whilst reflecting on his time as a fighter pilot, Bunny wrote a number of poems, two of which are reproduced here. After each poem are Bunny's memories of those particular events, written in 1994.

Croydon - September 1940.

Once again he took to the air, and Croydon was the base
To fight it out in fear and sweat so many times each day
To smell the burn of cordite flash, to see the flames of war
High above the fields of Kent the dive, the zoom, the soar.
Returning from a clash of foes one day he came across
A sight which burnt deep in his soul and never can be lost.
A pilot dangling from his chute towards the earth did drift
He circled round this friend or foe so hopelessly alone
To keep away whoever dared to fire on such a gift.
It was a useless gesture, though, as round and round he flew
He saw as in an awful dream first smoke and then flames spew,
Curl up his back as arms he waved and burn the cords of life
Snapping the body from the chute, snatching him from war's strife.
With sickening horror in his heart, he landed back at base.
He cried himself to sleep that night in thanks to God's good grace
That he was spared yet once again to live and fight this fight
Against the things he saw as black, for things he believed were right.

'At the time of this event the battle over London and south-east England was in full flow. We were busy. Oh boy were we busy! There had been reports from RAF pilots of being shot at as they floated down in their parachutes by Me 109s. I was racing back to Croydon having expended all my ammunition in a great big mêlée of Heinkel and Dornier bombers, Me 109s, Me 110s, Hurricanes and Spitfires. I had attacked a number of bombers from above, from the side, from below and head-on. It was a frantic whirl of in-fire-break-down or up-and-in again and again. And then there was no ammunition, all gone, head for home like mad. As I flew westwards south of London I came across this pilot in his parachute, yellow Mae West prominent. Ours or theirs I could not tell. I knew about the attacks by Me 109s and so flew round and round to stop any swine from attacking this pilot. I was determined that no bugger would get this lad. No-one did. They'd got him already as he had almost certainly baled out of his plane on fire. Clothing wet from petrol, embers glowing, fanned by the air as he floated down. Yes I wept myself to sleep that night, who wouldn't?'

Redhill - March 1942.

Until in 1942, high over Northern France
They hoped to lure Germans up to try their skill and chance
They used some bombers as a bait to bring them closely in
The trap worked well and on they came black crosses set on wing,
And in the fight that filled the sky he found himself alone
With three Focke Wulfs upon his tail, their guns ablaze with lead.
As bullets smashed his instruments and one went in his head

He felt the warmth of blood and sweat run down his hair and neck
And down he dived in swifter plunge to get close to the deck
As down and down he hurtled on he looked back to his tail
To see the flash of German guns pour out their deadly hail.
The earth rushed up to put a stop to screaming howling dive
He bent in two and pulled her through to zoom up and survive.
He weaved and jerked in desperate thought and prayed to God aloud,
And looking back he saw the grim black crosses of the foe.
They let him be, to get back free to cross the Channel grey.
With fearful heart and sickly pain he headed west for home
He turned the tap on oxygen pack to breathe and hope and pray
That engine sound would keep him bound for distant friendly coast,
For pure white cliffs that always seemed like splendid welcome host,
For waves of green that nature's scene would turn to fields of hay,
For native soil which gave such joy in which to live and play.
It seemed an age ere pilot caged in Spitfire's lovely shape,
Saw chequered earth of his own birth in patterns down below
Revealing there the larger square where airfield's shape did show.
Throttling back with lowered flap he circled in a glide
Locking tight the shoulder straps that held him safe inside,
Fingers flipped selector switch and wheels dropped into place
As airfield hedge slid underneath and grass rode up in grace
To meet the final flattening out of aircraft's slowing pace.
But bullet-punctured rubber tyres caused wheels to bite in deep
And in a flash there came the crash of somersaulted heap.
All was silent save the hiss of liquid on hot metal,
Something which to weary nerves meant only deadly petrol
Spilling out from smothered wreck of Spitfire upside down
Holding taut the pilot caught who struggled like a clown,
Terrified that trapped inside he'd be flame's hungry meal
Before the crews who rushed to help could lift the wreckage clear.
But powerful arms with heave and strain gave him the room to move,
He crawled away and felt strong hands his elbows firmly steer
To guide him to a stretcher close, to speed him on his way
To hospital in Folkestone to wait and think. He lay,
With thoughts that death was near to hand, to ponder on his wound
Would he survive or would he die? He prayed and felt much moved
As white clad figures wheeled him in to operate and probe.
On table top so still he lay as needle pierced the flesh
And anaesthetic washed his mind from all its fears so fresh
From all the vivid coloured strains that bit into the soul,
From all the longings in his heart, for life and victory whole.

'Here comes Folkestone Hospital for the second time in two years. The scenario was this. Air Chief Marshal Leigh-Mallory, then Commander-in-Chief of Fighter Command, decided to operate large numbers of Spitfire squadrons over Northern France daily for weeks and months. Using small sections of RAF bombers as bait for the Luftwaffe to be drawn into battle with the dozens of escorting Spitfires. I was leading 501 Squadron escorting six Boston light bombers at 22,000'. In the kerfuffle that followed I found myself alone with three FW 190s and in the fierce scrap that followed I found to my cost that the Spitfire Mk V was no match for those vastly superior fighters. However, I was only hit once. At the same moment as some of my instruments disappeared in dust one bullet entered my skull - and STUCK. It passed through the cockpit canopy, through my helmet and into my skull and stopped, or I would not be writing to you now 52 years later. I rolled over and opening the throttle wide dived vertically for the ground 22,000' below. As I dived I looked back to watch each FW 190 sit behind me and fire - the Germans always used a lot of incendiary bullets which could easily be seen. As the first one broke away the next one took up the attack and then the third one. Not a single bullet hit the aircraft. When I got to tree-top level and below, I kept turning violently left, then right, missing trees and buildings by inches. They gave up as I neared the French coast, formed into a vic formation of three and flew off inland. The poem tells the rest. Today I still have seven tiny bits of a German bullet inside my skull. The hospital gave me the bullet which years later I threw away - clot! I am now 83 and have no right to be alive'.

In the lapel of my suit jacket is a tiny, brass coloured Spitfire brooch. I wear it with great pride for it was given to me by Bunny Currant himself. Anyone having read the foregoing will understand why that tiny Spitfire means so much, a gift from a brave man my senior by half a century.

Wg Cdr Bunny Currant DSO DFC RAF Retd pictured at the launch of 'Through Peril to the Stars' *in September 1993.*

Alan Bray

Chapter Two

Squadron Leader Harry Welford AE

Pilot Officer Harry Welford pictured in 1940.

In this book are told the stories of many RAFVR pilots, but the pre-war Air Force also comprised Auxiliary Air Force squadrons, their pilots reputedly young men of wealth who flew for pleasure at weekends, often in their own aeroplanes. But was this the case in reality? Harry Welford was a member of the Auxiliary Air Force:-

'During July 1939, my cousin Robert got permission to take me up to the Auxiliary Air Force base at Usworth to give me a trip, "flying experience". It was a fine day and ideal to get the feeling of "no longer being earthbound", as my cousin put it. However, I knew that what goes up must come down again. I was nervous. I was strapped in the front cockpit of an Avro dual control trainer with Robert in the rear. This seemed odd to me as I had expected the passenger to sit behind. Anyway we taxied out and Robert spoke to me through the intercom, swung into wind and took off. After a circuit of the airfield we did a trip over the local countryside pointing out such landmarks as Penshaw Monument, the River Wear, and, of course, Sunderland and Newcastle further north. All these will long remain in my memory as pointers to the aerodrome itself. My cousin asked how I liked it and my response was enthusiastic, whereupon he suggested performing the odd aerobatic. Before I could respond he dived steeply and performed a loop followed by a slow roll. My stomach was not feeling so good and I was quietly sick over the side. Robert must have seen my distress because he went down to land, by which time I was alright again. We joked about it but when we got in one of the senior officers must have spotted the mess in the cockpit and gave poor Robert a ticking off for doing aerobatics during an air experience exercise. He then made him clean the cockpit.

'607 Squadron of the Auxiliary Air Force was formed on March 17th, 1930 as a day bomber unit. However it was not until September 1932 that personnel were able to move into the site at Usworth for training. In December the first Wapitis were received and were operated by the squadron until September 1936 when it re-equipped with Demons. The squadron's role then changed to fighters. Soon after the Munich crisis in 1938, the Demons were replaced by Gladiators. The latter type was actually being used for operational training when I started my elementary training on Avro Tutors. The squadron went over to the continent for the Battle of France actually flying Gladiators, but fortunately these were then replaced by Hurricanes. When the squadron returned to England after Dunkirk it reformed at Usworth on Hurricanes.

'It was on December 4th, 1938, my 22nd birthday, that I was very pleased to be accepted for training with 607 "County of Durham" Squadron. In fact I had already flown a couple of instructional flights. In the early part of 1939, I was at the works during the day getting in as much time as possible to complete my apprenticeship. During the evenings it was a case of working on the college subjects. At the weekends I was spending more time at the aerodrome having lectures and dual flying instruction, and undertaking Link Trainer work.

'607 Squadron had the services of a regular RAF adjutant and assistant adjutant, who not only did the routine duties of adjutant but had also the responsibility of instructing training officers and NCO's who would become Auxiliary flying personnel. There were of course regular airmen and other personnel on the staff, in charge of whom was the Station Commander, "Tubby" Mermagen. He was a

Pilots of 607 'County of Durham' Squadron of the Auxiliary Air Force pictured at Abbotsinch during summer camp 1939. Pilot Officer GHE Welford is standing, extreme left.

great character, completely unflappable, and quite awe-inspiring to likes of lesser mortals like me. In the evening or on a "Dining-in Night" he was always impeccably dressed and would drink all night without batting an eyelid until he passed out and was carried to his room by his faithful Batman. Even "In Vino Veritas" he looked dignified without a hair of his head ruffled and next day he was bright as a button.

'The squadron's annual summer camp in 1939 was actually a prelude to war. None of us would be out of uniform for the next six years. Many would not survive for one year, let alone six. The summer camp was at Abbotsinch near Glasgow which was the home base of 602 Squadron, another Auxiliary unit which was holding summer camp elsewhere. We pilots flew our machines up there whilst the ground crews were transported by road in advance of our arrival, erecting tents and marquees for service and messing facilities. The Gladiators took off in squadron formation and were a sight to be proud of, whilst we trainees followed in our Avro Tutors in open order led by the instructors. I was very proud to be flying solo on the longest cross-country I had done, although I was following the leading instructors, and wished that some of my fancied girlfriends could see me now! We all arrived at our destination and landed without mishap.

607 Squadron summer camp 1939, Abbotsinch. All are pilots, from right to left: Stuart Parnell, JBW Humpherson, Francis Blackadder, Harry Radcliffe, Harry Welford, unidentified, Lancelot-Smith (CO), Jim Bazin, George White, Peter Dixon, Monty Thompson & Tony Forster.

'I was commissioned in May 1939 and called to full-time service on August 24th. In October I started my service flying training and then went to 6 OTU Sutton Bridge to learn to fly Hurricanes. There we became familiar with all aspects of our Hurricanes and concentrated on aerobatics and more unconventional versions of them to avoid enemy attacks. We also did a lot of formation and simulated attacks and fighter tactics. A favourite exercise was to go up in pairs with an experienced pilot and then he would tell you over the R/T to follow him in all the manoeuvres he carried out. He aimed to lose you, and generally did, then got on your tail and the situation was reversed. Afterwards you discussed the different tactics of defence and attack and the instructor would advise you according to his experience.

'Having previously only flown biplanes with fixed-pitch airscrews and no flaps, I required instruction on these additional facilities. I was therefore given dual in a Harvard aircraft which had most of the Hurricane's refinements, but not all, and nowhere near the power of its 1,280-HP Rolls-Royce Merlin. It was in the air when I started worrying how, in the name of heaven, was I going to get this thing called a Hurricane down again. I did a few manoeuvres and a couple of circuits, got my wheels and flaps down, my God, how the speed dropped and how the attitude changed. I was coming down too steeply, I opened up the throttle and she assumed a more gentle engine-assisted approach. I touched down and throttled back but then realised that I had not got much more aerodrome to pull up in. Hell, I was on the ground and intended staying there. It being a grass field I did not roll too far but far enough, even with judicious braking to be just short of chopping the far hedge with my propeller. Nobody worried very much because I was sent off formation flying for the very next trip on the same day.

'I very soon built up my confidence in the Hurricane with which a relationship akin to love blossomed forth. After all, it was upon the performance of this aircraft that my future life or death would depend, presuming the development of the right skills in its handling. We were all very apprehensive of how we would make out in our new role as aggressive fighter pilots. Would we press home our attacks? Was our attitude of mind going to provide the right stimulus to use our aircraft and skills to seek and destroy the enemy? This is where our instructor and guide came in, Flight Sergeant Soper DFM who was on rest from 1 Squadron having already completed a tour of operations in France. He was quietly spoken with a classic "Handlebar Hank" moustache with eyes that flashed enthusiasm when he expounded his theories and tactics. One would imagine that his heart must have dropped each time he viewed a new intake of half-baked trainee fighter pilots, some raring to go like mad fools and others scared through lack of knowledge of what they were going to be up against. However he took them all in his stride warning one lot of overconfidence and imbuing in the others a full understanding of their capabilities. How can you instil a sense of cool and calculated aggression with every nerve sprung tight in anticipation of your opponent's move in a bunch of inexperienced greenhorns who will, in a matter of a few weeks, be pitched headlong in front of an experienced and highly efficient enemy? Flight Sergeant Soper however had a gift for doing just that, and under his leadership we would all have gone out there and then and tackled any number of Me 109s. About a year later I heard that he had got a commission and was flying as a Wing Commander when he was lost at sea. Though an extensive search was made Soper was never found, another tragic loss of a born leader.

'After six hours on Hurricanes some of us were put on stand-by to be flown over to France as replacements for the squadrons over there suffering losses, including 607. A Rapide and a Bombay were already on the aerodrome waiting to take us when a signal came through cancelling the flight. This was on June 6th, 1940 when the capitulation of the French was about to take place. We therefore resumed our training until June 15th.

607 Squadron pilots at Usworth immediately prior to participating in the Battle for France. From left to right: Harry Radcliffe, Robert Pumphrey, Jim Bazin, 'Humph' Humpherson, unidentified, Dudley Craig, Joe Kayll, Alan Glover and Tony 'Nit' Whitty.

'Upon completion of this training I was pleased to be posted back to 607 Squadron, the remnants of which had returned from France to our home station at Usworth. I was delighted to be back with 607 and also to be at our home station where we could renew our contacts and relationships with friends and family. The sad thing was the gaps in the ranks of those lost in France and coming across from Dunkirk. Of the 20 or so pilots that I had known, six were killed including our CO, Lancelot-Smith. Three were of such seniority that they were posted to command other squadrons and of whom one was killed later. My cousin was shot down over France and made a prisoner of war, another, Peter Dixon, was shot down near Dunkirk and managed to get on board one of the "Little Ships" on the troop evacuation run when it received a direct hit and everyone was lost.

'Replacements started coming in but far from being "on operations" we had to do another month of practice flying, repeating what we had already done at OTU. It was tedious but did bind us into a team, and of course we became more proficient in handling the Hurricane. There was a young officer, a South African called George Drake, who seemed even to us to be just a boy, although we were not much older. A Sergeant Pilot called Burnell-Phillips also joined us; he had lost his commission for disobeying specific instructions regarding low flying. He was an intrepid flyer and won a DFM but was later killed doing formation aerobatics with two Polish pilots after the Battle of Britain. A terrible waste, but such is the mentality of many fighter pilots who not having combat to fight in have to tax their skill by challenging danger in every other way possible. I can hardly profess to be of that school myself, but after scoring my first kill off the Newcastle-Sunderland coast, I flew down Northumberland Street at rooftop height - nothing to brag about but if a bloke like me can do that, what could a man with fire in his belly? I had actually thought of flying under the Tyne Bridge but the low-level and high-level railway bridges were a bit too close for comfort, and anyhow I hadn't got that much fire in my belly!

'Apart from aerobatics we did a lot of formation flying and development of Fighter Command No 1 attacks which were from astern as opposed to the quarter. Squadron formations were practised with simulated interceptions and "Battle Climbs" which were used to get a squadron to a specific height, i.e. 25,000', on a timed basis. We flew down to Catterick for target practice and Prestwick for night-flying. Sometimes we would do air firing in quarter attacks. Another exercise was to do "quick getaway" and rapid re-arming and refuelling which would be very necessary when under continuous attack from the enemy.

'By mid-July we were operational. Though we continued to practise formation, aerial combat and No 1 & 3 attacks, we also flew patrol duties along the NE coast providing aerial cover to the merchant vessels and fishing boat convoys. On August 7th we spotted a Ju 88 weather plane in the distance and flew 100 miles out to sea but could not intercept as he flew into cloud just as we came within firing distance. In fact it was a bit stupid of us to go so far out, but in the excitement of the moment one gets carried away even though strict instructions had been dished out to you not to stray too far from the coast. These convoy patrols covered from Acklington to Scarborough but only 5-10 miles out to sea. About this time I had my first flight in a Spitfire which was a lovely aircraft to fly, not all that different from a Hurricane except that in taxying the nose seemed to rear right up in front of your line of vision and you had to swing from left to right, this being rather heavy on the brakes with the danger of burning out the brake shoes.

'On Thursday, 15th August, 1940, we were to have our first big encounter with the enemy, and one considered on a par with those attacks that 11 and 12 Groups were experiencing in the south. At 12.30 pm we were going off duty for 24 hours leave when the whole squadron was called to Readiness. We heard from the Operations Room that there was a big "flap" on, that is a warning of imminent enemy action up and down the NE coast. We waited out at dispersal points, at "Flights", for half an hour, then we were told to "Scramble" in squadron formation. I was in a feverish state of excitement and quickly took off and climbed up to our operational height of 20,000' ready to patrol the coast. We kept receiving messages on the R/T of 40 or 50 plus "Bogeys" approaching Newcastle from the north. Although we patrolled for over half an hour we never saw a thing. Just as I was expecting the order to "Pancake" I heard the senior Flight Commander shout "Tally Ho!", and "Tally Ho!" it was! There on our port side at 9,000' must have been 120 bombers, all with the swastika and German crosses as large as life, having the gross impertinence to cruise down Northumberland and Durham's NE coast. These were the people who were going to bomb Newcastle and Sunderland and our friends and relations who lived there.

'I'd never seen anything like it. They were in two groups, one of about 70 and the other about 40, like two swarms of bees. There was no time to wait and we took up position and delivered a No 3 Attack in sections. As only three machines attacked a line of 20, I could not see how they could miss us. However, we executed our first attack and in spite of the fact that I thought I was being hit all over the place, it was their machines that started dropping out of the sky. In my excitement during the next attack I only narrowly missed one of our own machines doing a "split arse" breakaway. There couldn't have been more than two feet between us. Eventually, spotting most of the enemy aircraft dropping down with only their undercarriages damaged, I chased a Heinkel and filled that poor devil with lead until first one, then the other engine stopped. I then had the sadistic satisfaction of seeing the aircraft crash into the sea. With the one I reckoned to have damaged in the first attack, they were my first bloods and I was elated, especially to later discover that the squadron had not suffered any losses. 607 claimed six He 111s and two Do 17s destroyed, five He 111s and one Do 17 probably destroyed, and four He 111s and one Do 17 damaged'.

On August 15th, 1940, all three Luftflotten on the Western Front made concerted attacks on targets from Northumberland to Dorset. The Luftwaffe planners wrongly believed that their attacks in the north would meet with little opposition due to the British having been forced to make good losses suffered in the south by reinforcing with those squadrons from northern England. The most northerly part of the raiding force, consisting of 63 He 111s of I & III Gruppen KG26, escorted by 21 Me 110s of I/ZG76 (there were no Do 17s), was intercepted east of the Farne Islands by Flight Lieutenant Ted Graham and 11 other Spitfires of Acklington's 72 Squadron, the first of five RAF fighter squadrons to attack the raiders from bases between Catterick in Yorkshire and Drem on the Firth of Forth. It was this formation too that provided Pilot Officer Harry Welford of 607 Squadron with his first glimpse of a massed 'Valhalla'. The southerly part of the raid, directed against the airfield at Driffield, and comprising 50 Ju 88s of KG30, was engaged by 616 Squadron's Spitfires and the Hurricanes of 73 Squadron's 'B' Flight. Those Spitfires and Hurricanes claimed eight enemy aircraft destroyed in what became known as the 'Junkers Party' to the RAF and, more ominously, 'Black Saturday' to the Luftwaffe. It was a salutary lesson to the Germans that Fighter Command was far from beaten, and far from being down to the 'last Spitfire'. It also indicated the folly of sending bombers on raids against England without an adequate fighter escort. For 607 Squadron the action was to be invaluable combat experience, as in early September the unit was posted to Tangmere in 11 Group:-

'I shall always remember September 8th, 1940, because this was the day after the evening that Betty Elise and I became engaged, but our move to Tangmere was confirmed that day. We were to relieve 43 Squadron whose CO, "Tubby" Badger had been shot down earlier in September, since when the squadron had been led by Flight Lieutenant Tom Morgan with barely half the complement of pilots left capable of operational duties.

'Of course it was a tragedy so far as my fiancée was concerned and, though I felt the same, there was a war to be fought and we were trained fighters. This was the beginning of the end, and as we all climbed into our Hurricanes having bid our adieus that fine September day, I wondered how many of us would see Usworth or Newcastle again. Strange as it may seem, dirty, smoky old Newcastle was to seventh Heaven compared with the clean, green fields of southern England.

'We arrived at a completely blitzed aerodrome and were greeted by the remains of 43 Squadron, some with crutches, others with their arms in slings and yet another with his head swathed in bandages having had his face torn by an exploding enemy cannon shell. Though they had so many casualties it was quite amazing to see them walking about. Needless to say, they were very pleased to see us having just been up on the third sortie that day and waiting for news of the latest victims. We only had time to refuel when we were called out to an operational trip that evening. There was no interception on that occasion and no casualties. The next morning I was, to my great disappointment, not called upon to fly and later the squadron went off. In a way I was fortunate as six out of 12 were shot down, three Sergeants were wounded and three Officers killed. One of them was my best friend, Stuart Parnall, and the others, Scotty and the young South African George Drake, were all lovely people, people like Alex Obelenski and Ching Mackenzie with whom I would have flown to hell in glorious comradeship. Somehow we could not believe it, no-one talked about it and we all hoped for news filtering through from some outlandish pub or perhaps some hospital. No news came and we hardened ourselves to the worst, "killed in action". We bit back our tears and sorrow. It was "You heard about Stuart and Scotty, rotten luck wasn't it?" Someone would add, "And young George, bloody good blokes". After that epitaph the matter would apparently be dismissed with the ordering of another round of drinks to avoid any further trace of sentiment'.

It must be appreciated that Auxiliary squadrons were raised from areas local to certain airfields, for example 607 being the 'County of Durham' with its home base at Usworth, 616 'South Yorkshire' at Doncaster, and 609 'West Riding' at Yeadon. The members of the squadron were possibly old school friends, business associates, friends of the family - even relatives. Understandably losses hit these squadrons very hard indeed.

By September 17th, 1940, 23-year-old Pilot Officer Harry Welford had become a veteran. On that day 'B' Flight of 607 Squadron ('A' Flight already being aloft) was scrambled from Tangmere at 1505 hrs on the squadron's fourth sortie of the day, Harry flying as Blue 2. This occasion saw the Hurricanes patrolling the Biggin Hill/Gravesend line at 17,000'. The commander of Luftflotte 2, Generalfeldmarschal Kesselring, launched a single but multi-wave fighter sweep which crossed the Kent coast from 1500-1600 hrs. Each formation consisted of two Gruppen of Me 109s, some 60 plus aircraft in total. In the main, the RAF controllers preferred to avoid combat for obvious reasons. Only II & III/JG53 'Pik As' were intercepted in any numbers at about 1525 hrs, but the Me 109s shot down two 501 Squadron Hurricanes (including Sergeant Eddie Egan, see Tony Pickering's story). 41 Squadron's Spitfires then attacked, followed by the Duxford Wing. Over their allotted patrol line, 213 Squadron's Hurricanes, also from Tangmere, acted as rearguard to 607 Squadron's 'B' Flight. Suddenly the Hurricanes were bounced from above and behind by a horde of Me 109s:-

'When attacked we were warned to break formation. I broke and took evasive action as a result of which I lost the squadron. As we had instructions to reform rather than fly alone, I saw a group of fighters ahead and intended joining up with them when I saw that they were Me 109s! I took a quick burst but then an unseen 109 fired a cannon shell which hit my air intake. I did a quick flick roll which dropped me below cloud. Again no 109s about and just a lone Hurricane which guarded my tail as I forced landed. The engine had seized and looking down I saw a field into which I thought I could land. As I made the approach glycol and smoke streamed from the engine and when I opened the hood the fumes were sucked through the cockpit and impaired my vision. The field was smaller than I thought but there was a wattle fence which acted like an arrester wire and the plane skidded across the second field, and was brought to an abrupt stop by a tree at the far end, making me crack my head on the reflector sight and blood poured from my face. Thinking that the plane might catch fire, I undid my belt and jumped out only to fall flat on my face because my leg, which had been injured by shrapnel, collapsed on me. Two farm workers rushed over and picked me up and put me on a wattle fence telling me that there was a German plane down in the next field with the pilot in it, very dead. I regret now that I declined their offer to show me, but at the time I felt pretty dicky. I gave my report to Flight Lieutenant Jim Bazin in hospital and he acknowledged that I had shot down the German aircraft in the field next to mine, although now I am not so sure as neither Dilip Sarkar nor I have been able to identify a possible candidate from the information available concerning German losses. I was consequently in hospital with "Tubby" Badger, 43 Squadron's former CO. He was very brave, always laughing, but sadly succumbed to his injuries'.

The Me 109s had shot down one Spitfire and damaged two others, and shot down four Hurricanes, including the great ace Sergeant 'Ginger' Lacey of 501 Squadron who baled out safely near Ashford. Two Fighter Command pilots were killed. Three Me 109s were destroyed in response, all pilots being killed, two of them by Sub-Lieutenant 'Admiral' Blake, a Fleet Air Arm pilot serving with 19 Squadron. One of his victims was Oberleutnant Jakob Stoll, Staffelkapitän of 9/JG53 and therefore an expensive loss to the Germans.

It is believed that 607 and 213 Squadrons were bounced by elements of JG27, and that Harry Welford was shot down by Hauptmann Eduard Neumann, Gruppenkommandeur of I Gruppe. Neumann's *flugzeugbuch*, or flying log book, indicates that he actually shot down two Hurricanes in this combat, so it is possible that he also attacked 607 Squadron's Sergeant Landesdell who was killed. Neumann was an experienced *jagdflieger* who had fought during the Spanish Civil War. He later became Kommodore of JG27 and led the unit in North Africa during the time that Hans-Joachim Marseille, who achieved 158 victories before his death, was with the unit. Neumann did much to encourage the young Marseille who destroyed more British aircraft than any other German *experte*. Neumann's own final score was 13. As an Oberstleutnant he became Jagdfliegerführer, or Jafü (leader of the fighter forces), in Italy and survived the war.

After his brush with Hauptmann Neumann, Harry Welford was hospitalised but returned to the squadron on October 20th, 1940. By that date 607 had been itself withdrawn from Tangmere to rest at Turnhouse in Scotland. During the Battle of Britain the squadron had lost a total of nine pilots killed. For the next two months it was Harry Welford who found himself passing on his combat experience to new replacement pilots.

Harry Welford, right, pictured with other 607 Squadron stalwarts, Francis Blackadder, left, and Joe Kyall, centre, at Durham Cathedral on November 14th, 1993.

Lance Henderson

Having been posted away from 607 Squadron on December 16th, 1940, after a long spell instructing, Flight Lieutenant Welford returned to operations with 222 Squadron based at Maldeghem, flying Spitfire Mk IXs, in November 1944. The squadron returned temporarily to the UK whilst it converted to Hawker Tempests but was back with 2nd TAF in February 1945, remaining on the continent until June. Squadron Leader Welford left the RAF later that year, the war over and the enormous number of trained service pilots no longer required by the RAF.

Now retired and aged 78, Harry Welford and his wife Betty live in picturesque Devon somewhat more peacefully than Harry was able to during the summer of 1940!

Chapter Three

Flight Lieutenant William Walker AE

Pilot Officer William Walker pictured in 1940.

William Walker is a true gentleman, and at the launches of three of my four previous books has been a most welcome guest, friend and supporter. I have enormously enjoyed opportunities to sit and sign books with such remarkable line-ups of wartime fighter pilots, and indeed the chances provided by these rather special occasions to further research by talking to survivors on a one-to-one basis. William Walker and I have consequently enjoyed many such conversations, not least about his recent globe-trotting visits to the Salinas airshow in America - at the age of 81! I am therefore delighted to include his story in 'A Few of the Many':-

'I was lucky to join the RAFVR in September 1938 as in those days one had to be under 25. My 25th birthday was in August but I was accepted as my application had been submitted some weeks before my birthday. At the time I was working for Halls Oxford Brewery and attached to Kidlington aerodrome for flying lessons. They only had 26 pilots and I was number 26. I remember my instructor saying that it was a very lucky number being twice 13! As a survivor I think that his prediction was about right. I was enrolled as an AC2, but because no airman below the rank of Sergeant was allowed to fly an aircraft, I was promoted to Sergeant the following day.

'With so few pilots the instructors were a bit short of work during the week so I used to motor out in my lunch hour for flying and actually did my first solo in a Magister during a lunch break on September 28th, 1938. The following day, the Prime Minister, Mr Neville Chamberlain, returned from Munich after his meeting with Daladier, Hitler and Mussolini. After landing he proudly waved his piece of paper signed by himself and Hitler guaranteeing never to go to war. Had my patriotic response been premature, therefore? No matter, I wished to fly and the RAF were teaching me for free and I was enjoying all the delights of a private flying club and the company of several other enthusiasts. I was then moved to Ind Coope's brewery at Romford and was transferred to fly from Stapleford Abbotts where I flew Tiger Moths, perhaps the best aeroplane I ever flew for sheer exhilaration.

'When the war started I had clocked up enough hours to have completed my elementary flying and so was sent to ITW at Cambridge to await a posting to an Advanced Flying School. I was eventually sent to Brize Norton where I completed my training on Harvards.

'I had my first night flight of 45 minutes duration on March 30th, 1940, in a Harvard from Brize Norton with Flight Sergeant Holman as instructor. After a further 45 minute flight with Flight Lieutenant Sykes on April 1st, I was despatched on my first solo night flight. I took off into complete darkness after leaving the flarepath. There were no ground lights during the wartime blackout and there was no moon. I must have become completely disorientated and in a matter of minutes crashed into a field. The plane was utterly smashed but by some miracle of fate my starboard wing had hit the ground with such force, about 200 mph, that the entire engine had broken away from its mounting and had spun off to finish some distance away. This had not only saved my life but had prevented the aircraft from catching fire. I climbed out of what remained of the cockpit and walked with my parachute across several fields back to the aerodrome and into the locker room where several pilots were hanging about, night-flying having been abandoned. They were astonished when I walked in as all thought that I had "bought it" - several ambulances and other vehicles had been despatched to find the wreckage and recover my remains. Somebody produced a flask of whisky and suggested that I must need some, but I said "better not in case somebody smells my breath." I scarcely had a scratch and no bones were broken. I then returned to the Mess and went to bed.

'The following morning I was given a medical check-up which revealed nothing untoward and I was then told to report to the Chief Flying Officer, Squadron Leader Jarman. It was with some apprehension that I approached his office in the control tower having just smashed up one of his £10,000 Harvard aircraft. I noticed several instructors with him when I entered. He greeted me with a smile and said "let me rub your back, you have a charmed life!" He then asked whether I wanted to go on an extended leave, but I declined as I wanted to complete the course. He said that I could do so provided that I accepted the crash as being due to my error and that there were no funny little men playing about with the controls. He added that planes could be replaced, but pilots were in short supply.

'I was then given many hours in the Link Trainer and another three hours and 50 minutes dual night flying before being allowed off on another solo night flight. This occurred on May 9th when I made two landings without damaging the aircraft!

'In retrospect it was probably rather crazy to send me solo after only 90 minutes night flying, but as many other pilots had about the same night tuition and flew without mishap, I must have been slow to adjust to this alien environment.

'My spectacular crash was to benefit one enterprising airman in the photographic section - he took photos of the crash and, selling them at 6d a card, made quite a sum'.

Once William Walker's Advanced Flying Training with 'Course 45' was successfully completed, he was commissioned as a Pilot Officer and awarded his 'wings' on April 25th, 1940. He then went not to an OTU, but, on June 18th, straight to his squadron; No 616 'South Yorkshire' Squadron of the Auxiliary Air Force flying Spitfires at Leconfield:-

'The early days of war were interesting in so far as we were so unprepared for what was to come. It is my lasting regret that I did not have more operational training - trying to pick it up with the squadron straight from flying school was a pretty haphazard affair. For instance, I flew my first Spitfire on June 23rd, 1940, and was made operational on July 1st'.

Flying from Leconfield, 616 Squadron was engaged largely on convoy protection and general patrol sorties over the North Sea. It was a repetitive chore, the monotony only occasionally broken; on June 26th Pilot Officer Donald Smith destroyed an He 111 bomber at night, and three nights later Pilot Officer Roy Marples had shot down a second raider.

616 Squadron, however, did not have to await its posting to southern England for its first major clash with the enemy during the Battle of Britain. The squadron was also in action off the north-east coast on August 15th (see Squadron Leader Welford's story). The squadron engaged 50 Ju 88s and several Me 110s at 15,000' and 10 miles out to sea off Flamborough Head. By the time the Spitfires broke off the engagement and returned to Leconfield, eight bombers were believed to have been destroyed, four probably destroyed and two damaged. 616 Squadron had suffered no casualties in the fight, which became known as the 'Junkers Party'.

Just a few days later, however, the squadron was posted south to 11 Group. At 1410 hrs on Monday, August 19th, 1940, 616 Squadron's Spitfires landed at Kenley airfield in Surrey which had been badly damaged in the heavy Luftwaffe

The Three Musketeers: Flg Off Jack Bell, Flg Off Teddy St Aubyn and Plt Off Bill Walker, pictured immediately before 616 Squadron took off for Kenley on August 19th, 1940. All three pilots were to be shot down on August 26th, both St Aubyn and Walker being wounded whilst Jack Bell was reported safe after a forced landing. Bell was killed in action just four days later, however, and St Aubyn in 1943.

attack of the previous day. On Thursday August 22nd, the squadron experienced its first clash with the Luftwaffe since the 'Junkers Party'; Green Section were patrolling in line astern over the white cliffs of Dover when 12 Me 109s bounced the Spitfires from above. Pilot Officer Hugh 'Cocky' Dundas was shot down in flames, only narrowly escaping the confines of his doomed Spitfire's cockpit, and Pilot Officer Lionel 'Buck' Casson's aircraft was hit in the wing by a cannon shell. The Me 109s failed to escape completely unscathed, however, as Sergeant Wareing destroyed one of their number.

Saturday, August 24th 1940, saw Manston airfield in Kent heavily bombed, but although 616 Squadron were scrambled and patrolled Deal, the squadron did not encounter the enemy.

The following day the squadron intercepted a raid consisting of 15-20 Do 17 bombers and their fighter escort, which consisted of a similar number of Me 109s. Again the Spitfires were almost immediately bounced and broken up by the German fighters. After the ensuing combat, Flying Officer George Moberley claimed an Me 109 destroyed, Flying Officer Jack Bell one probably destroyed, and Sergeant Marmaduke Ridley a Do 17. However, Sergeant Westmoreland was shot down and killed, and Sergeant Wareing was missing, only much later being reported as being a prisoner of war.

Monday, August 26th, saw three major German aerial assaults which pursued the current strategy of attacking airfields and industrial targets. The first of these raids headed for the Fighter Command Sector Stations at Kenley and Biggin Hill. Amongst those squadrons scrambled to meet the enemy was 616 Squadron. At 11.05 am seven Spitfires of Blue and Yellow Sections took off from Kenley to intercept an He 111. Blue Section sighted the Heinkel just above cloud at 7,000', but the enemy aircraft disappeared in the all enveloping mists. Yellow Section was ordered to pancake and Blue Section was vectored to Dungeness to look for a stray barrage balloon at 10,000'. Not having found the offending balloon, Blue Section received a second vector from the ground controller, this time to intercept two raids, each consisting of over 40 enemy aircraft. At 'Angels 17' 100 Me 109s were sighted 3,000' above Blue Section's puny formation; the odds were over 30 to one in the Luftwaffe's favour. Whilst the section hastily formed up in a defensive circle, Yellow Section desperately climbed flat out to reach their comrades. Before their arrival the Germans pounced.

In the vicious attack that followed, Blue Section was swiftly despatched from the fight, three Spitfires spiralling down from the battle; Flying Officer Jack Bell managed to forced-land at Bekesbourne, Sergeant Copeland likewise at Wye, and Pilot Officer Roy Marples crash-landed at Adisham having been wounded in the leg by a cannon shell.

William Walker remembers that day:-

'It was still dark when the orderly awoke me with a cup of tea at 3.30 am that morning, just two days after my 27th birthday which had passed unnoted amid the excitement of summer 1940.

'616 Squadron had arrived at RAF Station Kenley, Surrey, on August 19th, from Leconfield aerodrome in Yorkshire to which I had been posted after getting both my "wings" and a commission. The Mess at Kenley was a rather sombre building and far removed from the modern, light and cheerful Mess at Leconfield. Kenley had been bombed on several occasions prior to our arrival and many scars bore witness to the damage and loss of life. An atmosphere of purpose prevailed and the squadron was having to respond to a life of far greater activity than at Leconfield where only a few raids had disrupted our lives.

'I drank my tea slowly and gradually awakened to another day. It seemed such a short while since we had been "stood down" the previous evening at about 9 pm, after which a few beers had refreshed our spirits before bed. I dressed and went down to breakfast, always a quiescent occasion at the unearthly hour of 4 am. In the distance the sound of aero engines could be heard indicating that the groundcrews were already busy. One was so accustomed to the drone of engines that it passed almost un-noticed amid the clatter of cups and plates.

'Following breakfast I joined other pilots outside the Mess. We all climbed aboard a lorry and were driven to dispersal to be at "readiness" where a hut and a few tents comprised the squadron's base. A few days earlier the Duke of Kent had paid a visit to our modest location and had wished us well.

'I was allocated Spitfire R6633, and was to fly with Yellow Section led by Flying Officer "Teddy" St Aubyn. The plane stood within 50 yards of our hut and so I walked over and placed my parachute in the cockpit with the straps spread apart and ready for wearing immediately I jumped in. Two of the ground crew stood by the plane with the starter battery plugged in. I walked back to the hut as the sun rose and added a little warmth to a chilly start. Pilots sat about either reading or exchanging the usual banter which was now routine. We had spent many months in this way and it was now a way of life. At 8 am our second breakfast arrived at dispersal. This was just as fulfilling as the breakfast of four hours earlier with coffee, eggs, bacon, sausages and toast to replenish our undiminished appetites'.

At 11.46 am, five Spitfires of 616 Squadron's 'A' Flight took off from Kenley. After orbiting base they went on to patrol Dover and Deal at 17,000'. William

Walker:-

'The telephone rang in the dispersal hut and a shout of "Yellow Section Scramble! Patrol Dungeness/Dover Angels 20!" sent me running to my plane. I leapt onto the wing and was in the cockpit, parachute strapped on, within seconds. I pressed the starter and the engine fired immediately. The groundcrew removed the plug from the cowling and pulled the remote starter battery clear. I waved the chocks away and taxied the aircraft, following my Section Leader and Sergeant Ridley to the end of the runway for take-off. Within minutes Yellow Section was airborne. We headed east, climbing quickly and passing through cloud, reaching our patrol course in some 15-20 minutes. We flew in wide formation and had been airborne for about an hour without sighting any enemy aircraft when suddenly several Me 109s appeared'.

Over Dungeness the flight was bounced by the marauding German fighters. Flying Officer 'Teddy' St Aubyn's Spitfire was hit and caught fire, and Flying Officer George Moberley's Spitfire plunged into the sea, killing the pilot. Also fatally hit was Sergeant Ridley who crashed near Dover. The Spitfires had suffered the enormous misfortune to have encountered all three Gruppen of JG51 on a Geschwader strength *Freie Jagd*. Moberley and Ridley are believed to have been killed by the Staffelkapitän of 4/JG51, Hauptmann Josef 'Joschko' Fözoe, whilst St Aubyn was the 15th kill of Oberleutnant Josef 'Pips' Priller, Staffelkapitän of 6/JG51.

Sgt Marmaduke Ridley, pictured here at Leconfield in early 1940 adjacent to a petrol bowser and with Flg Off Jack Bell. On August 26th, 1940, Ridley was shot down and killed over Dover by Hauptmann 'Joschko' Fözoe, Staffelkapitän of 4/JG51.

Hauptmann Joschko Fözoe recounts a successful combat over England during summer 1940. Before his recent death, Fözoe's recollections of the action on August 26th, 1940, were sent in a detailed letter to historian John Foreman and have significantly contributed towards the accurate reporting of this engagement.

Dr Alfred Price

Only one British pilot managed to bring his sight to bear: Flight Lieutenant Denys Gillam attacked an Me 109 which was firing at a Spitfire. The two opposing fighters dived from 11,000-4,000', Gillam firing all the way. Like a terrier, Gillam pursued his victim through cloud, emerging to see the Me 109 crash into the sea.

Oberkannone: Major Werner Mölders, the 'Father of German Air Fighting' and perhaps the greatest fighter ace of them all. On August 26th, 1940, he shot down Plt Off William Walker; fortunately the 616 Squadron Spitfire pilot lived to tell the tale, albeit wounded.

Chris Goss

JG51 was being led by its famous 27-year-old Kommodore, Major Werner 'Vati' Mölders, the so called 'Father of German Air Fighting'. Awarded the *Ritterkreuz* on May 29th, 1940, for 20 aerial victories, this experte of experten was eager to reach 40 and receive the *Eichenlaub* (Oak Leaves). Major Mölders must have seen the handful of Spitfires below as easy pickings, and led his Me 109s down in a perfect ambush. His personal tactics were to attack from behind and slightly below, in the 'blind spot'. He selected a Spitfire and opened fire from such an attitude which resulted in his 27th kill - Pilot Officer William Walker was the target, and now recalls those 'rather traumatic events':-

'When the Me 109s bounced us I banked sharply to port, towards an Me 109. Suddenly my Spitfire was raked with bullets. The one that got me had attacked from behind, in the "blind spot", and I never even saw it. The controls ceased to respond and a sudden pain in my leg indicated that I had been hit. Baling out seemed to a sensible option. My two colleagues had completely vanished.

'I pulled back the hood and tried to stand up but realised that I had not disconnected the radio cord which was still plugged in, and had to remove my helmet before I was free to jump. The aircraft was still banking to port so jumping out was easy. I was still at 20,000' and pulled the ripcord immediately. A sudden jerk told me that all was well and that I was on my way down. I looked around but could not see a single aircraft. Below there was 10/10ths cloud. I had no idea where I was. It seemed to take ages to reach the clouds and passing through I realised that I was still over the Channel. Thinking that I would soon land in the sea prompted the thought that I had better remove my heavy flying boots. I did this and let them fall. I watched them spiral down for what seemed like ages and I then realised that I was still much higher than I thought. I inflated my Mae West and eventually landed in the sea. I easily discarded my parachute and could see the wreck of a ship sticking out of the water a few hundred yards away and swam to it. I reached it and climbed on, sitting there for about half an hour when a fishing boat came alongside and I clambered aboard. I was now extremely cold from my immersion and wet clothes. The fishermen gave me a cup of tea well laced with whisky as we headed for land. When about two miles offshore, an RAF launched came alongside and I was transferred to it. By this time the tea concoction had worked quite disastrously on my cold stomach. Fortunately there was a loo aboard to which I retired with some relief. I was still enthroned when we reached Ramsgate harbour. An aircraftman kept knocking on the door and enquiring whether I was alright - it was some time before I was able to emerge! I was carried up the steps to a waiting ambulance. Quite a crowd had gathered and gave me a cheer as I was put in the ambulance. A kind old lady handed me a packet of cigarettes. I was driven to Ramsgate hospital which had been badly bombed. The doctors there had a go at removing the bullet in my leg but realised that it was too great an undertaking in view of the prevailing conditions. I was put to bed under an electric-light frame. I was absolutely frozen and it was some five to six hours before I could feel my circulation returning.

'Breakfast the following morning consisted of only a cup of tea and a few slices of bread and butter, which was all the hospital could provide following the bombing. I realised for the first time what terrible conditions people in the south-east were living in whilst at the same time having to cope with existence.

'It was decided that I should be transferred to the RAF hospital at Halton, Bucks, and so I was collected at 8 am. The journey was eventful. Firstly the driver had no clue as to the route, and secondly this shortcoming was not assisted by the fact that all road signs had been removed in anticipation of a German invasion. Luckily I had a slight knowledge of the way and by lying sideways on the stretcher was able to look through the glass behind the driver and give directions. We had been detailed to collect from Manston a shell-shock case who was to be delivered to Mill Hill hospital. This accomplished we set off for Kenley to enable me to collect my belongings. Whilst there I told the driver to take me to dispersal so that I could say farewell to any remaining pilots. It proved a sad occasion, however, as the squadron had suffered severe losses and very few pilots actually remained operational.

'It was mid-afternoon when we resumed our journey with the prospect of getting across London where several roads were closed due to bombs. We eventually arrived at Mill Hill and deposited a rather woebegone airman who had scarcely uttered a word throughout the entire journey throughout most of which he had spent trying to light a cigarette with a pair of very shaky hands.

'We then resumed our journey to Halton. I knew the road intimately as I had used it frequently when working at Aylesbury during the early 1930s. It was reassuring to see old and familar landmarks again. It was now past 8 pm and I had had nothing to eat since the meagre breakfast at Ramsgate. I was dying for a pint of beer and told the driver to pull up at a pub where a couple of pints of best bitter did much to restore lagging spirits. The last proper meal I had eaten was the breakfast at dispersal before take-off some 36 hours before. The two pints on an empty stomach therefore made me feel quite light headed.

'It was almost 10 pm when we arrived at Halton and I was put to bed. Sadly, by this late hour, the kitchens had been closed for some hours but a wonderful night nurse produced a wonderful and perhaps appropriate meal - scrambled eggs!

'After breakfast the next morning, doctors appeared and attended to the many officers in my large ward of some 20 beds. Nobody came to me, however, and, apart from my leg getting rather painful, I was beginning to worry about gangrene. The previous 48 hours had been rather traumatic to say the least, so my concern was not entirely unjustified.

'At noon the head doctor, a Group Captain, did his rounds. As he passed my bed he asked what I was in for. I told him that I had a bullet in my leg. He said, "Oh yes, and who is looking after you?" When I told him that I had yet to see a doctor despite having arrived the previous night I thought that he was going to have a convulsion! He literally exploded and his wrath remains a vivid memory. Never were so many doctors torn off a bigger strip. It was action stations from thereon and within just 10 minutes I was in the operating theatre.

'When I regained consciousness the surgeon was by my bedside. He said "I think you may like to have this", and handed me an armour-piercing bullet. He then told me that as he was prising open the bone in my leg to extract the bullet it shot out and hit the ceiling of the operating theatre! I still possess it as a cherished souvenir.

'My entire leg was now encased in plaster. After a few months at Halton my leg began to heal and I was transferred, with my leg still in plaster, to the Palace Hotel at Torquay which had become an RAF hospital.

'Fortunately my sense of humour never quite left me and later a doctor asked how my accident had happened; I told him that it was no accident but a deliberate attempt on my life by a German fighter pilot!'

It is not surprising that William Walker's visit to the 616 Squadron dispersal on August 27th, 1940, was depressing. In the fight of August 26th, 616 had lost seven of the 12 Spitfires which flew on operations that day. Four pilots had been wounded and two were dead. The squadron clerk, obviously a master of the understatement, recorded in the Operations Record Book that the action was 'a very unfortunate engagement'.

On Tuesday, September 3rd, 616 Squadron was relieved at Kenley by 64 Squadron. 616 Squadron, now comprising just eight of its original members, flew north to Coltishall in Norfolk.

An analysis of the Battle of Britain casualty list reveals that 71 fighter squadrons and other appended units took part in the conflict, 22 of which lost 10 or more pilots, the highest number of losses being the 19 casualties suffered by 501 Squadron, an Auxiliary Hurricane unit which was in the front line throughout the duration of the battle. A further 18 units suffered more casualties than 616 Squadron, although not reaching double figures, whilst six suffered no losses at all. The 'South Yorkshire' squadron flew from Kenley for just 15 days. During that time a total of 11 Spitfires had been destroyed and three damaged. In addition to the five pilots killed, six were wounded and one was taken prisoner of war (one more 616 Squadron pilot was to die in action before the end of the Battle of Britain). These statistics are almost identical to the claims made by the squadron in respect of casualties inflicted upon the enemy: 10 enemy aircraft destroyed, three probably destroyed and six damaged (of the squadron 'bag', seven destroyed, two probably destroyed and three damaged were all claimed by Flight Lieutenant Denys Gillam AFC, who was subsequently awarded the DFC).

It is perhaps excusable, in view of various inaccurate films and publications, to form the impression of Spitfire and Hurricane squadrons sallying forth into battle with bravado, wreaking great havoc upon the dastardly 'Hun'. In reality this was not the case. Whilst the combat records of some squadrons are outstanding, the majority are comparable with each other, and indeed with the enemy. The same could be said of individual pilots: the high personal scores of some make them stand head and shoulders above the 'average' squadron pilot, Denys Gillam's Battle of Britain claims being an ideal example, but these men were very much a minority. Most fighter pilots enjoyed comparatively mediocre success, but these combined statistics, when absorbed into Fighter Command's overall result, illustrate the enormous collective effort made by these young pilots during the summer of 1940. The late Lord Dowding summed up the situation perfectly when he said 'think not of us as individuals or personalties, but as a Battle of Britain team.' In short, the home team's score had been adequate to keep Hitler at bay and provide the world with evidence that Germany was not invincible.

Who can reason why some pilots survived whilst others died in those dangerous skies? Research indicates that Pilot Officer William Walker was shot down on August 26th, 1940, by Major Werner Mölders. Two young men of similar age, but flying and fighting in such different circumstances; Mölders perhaps the ultimate wartime fighter ace and Kommodore of his battle-hardened Jagdgeschwader, Walker a junior pilot and, by his own admission, inadequately trained and in a squadron with comparatively little combat experience. Perhaps surprisingly, it was not Mölders who survived the war as he was killed when the He 111 in which he was flying to Ernst Udet's funeral crashed on landing at Schmiedefeld in November 1941. By that time the 28-year-old had become Hitler's General der Jagdflieger and, with 115 victories, was a holder of the Oak Leaves with Swords and Diamonds to the Knight's Cross of the Iron Cross.

After recovering from his injuries received at the hands of Major Mölders, William Walker returned to 616 Squadron on May 1st, 1941. By then the squadron was a part of Douglas Bader's Tangmere Wing, but three weeks later Pilot Officer Walker was posted as attaché to No 1 Aircraft Delivery Flight (ADF), Hendon. There he was to remain until joining 116 Squadron at Heston early in 1942. An anti-aircraft co-operation squadron, 116 exchanged its Hurricane Mk Is for Tiger Moths in July 1942, by which time William was a Flight Lieutenant and commanding 'E' Flight. Two years later he was posted to the Gunnery Flight at Redhill, and then in October 1944 returned to 1 ADF, by then at Gatwick. Flight Lieutenant Walker remained with that unit until being demobbed on September 1st, 1945.

Clearly the highspot of William Walker's war was his time with 616 Squadron, particularly at Kenley when he was lucky to survive an encounter with one of the greatest fighter aces of all time. It is fitting to allow this fine old gentleman, now retired as chairman of the Ind Coope brewery, the last word: 'Looking back to the time when so many of us on Course 45 had such high hopes and felt invulnerable, it is terribly sad that some would not survive a year, would never see the enemy and all their hard work and training should prove fruitless. Whilst they were just casualties of war in the records, they are a reminder to me of many happy days of friendship that are well worth recalling and should be remembered. They were the most exhilarating days, but one lost so many friends who were all so young. It is sad that the best pilots seemed to get killed whilst the "hams" like me survived'.

Flt Lt William Walker (left) and Sqn Ldr Iain Hutchinson (222 Sqn, summer 1940) reminiscing at the launch of 'Through Peril to the Stars', *September 1993.*

Alan Bray

Chapter Four

Squadron Leader Tony Pickering

*Tony Pickering pictured whilst a Flight
Lieutenant serving in the desert.*

Tony Garforth Pickering was an RAF Volunteer Reserve pilot who had joined
on July 30th, 1939, and learned to fly at Ansty. When the country mobilised for
war, Tony was called up immediately and after an initial period at No 3 Initial
Training Wing at Hastings, commenced his service flying training. Upon
completion, he did not go to an OTU but was posted straight from flying Harvard
trainers to a fighter squadron:-

'I was a Sergeant Pilot during the Battle of Britain. First I was posted to 32
Squadron but had never flown a Hurricane. The CO sent me and some others
to an OTU to learn how. We returned to be told that the squadron was moving
north for a rest, but as we didn't need one we would be posted to 501 'County of
Gloucester' Squadron, an Auxiliary unit which was flying Hurricanes at Kenley.
The ace "Ginger" Lacey was also an NCO pilot with 501 at the time.

Sgt Eddie Egan of 501 Squadron, killed in action, aged 19 years, whilst flying over Kent with Sgt Tony Pickering on September 17th, 1940. The photograph was captioned by his sister, Mrs Jane Somerville, 'Eddie's last spring'. The family has upheld the RAF tradition, however, as Sgt Egan's nephew has been a member of the Red Arrows aerobatic display team.

'I was flying with Sergeant Eddie Egan when he was killed. I did not know Eddie terribly well but I suppose he was my friend and he was a nice lad, he really was. We were flying along, just the two of us, looking about all the time for trouble, and I saw four Spitfires behind us. We were talking to each other on the R/T, monitoring the movements of the "Spitfires". Suddenly one of them zoomed forward, just left the others standing, and shot Eddie down. I turned towards his assailant but the old Hurricane was just too slow, the Hun just shot Eddie and flew off with the others, they just climbed high and left us. I looked over the side and saw Eddie going down, the aircraft in flames. Eddie went in in a wood outside Ashford in Kent. After I landed I filed a report on the incident, giving the location of where Eddie had crashed. Six months later I had to see the Air Ministry and pin-point the site as Eddie had never been found. The next I ever heard of Eddie Egan was when I happened to read an article in the Sunday Express a few years ago in which it said that Eddie's bones had been discovered by an aviation archaeology group at the very spot that I had advised the Air Ministry

A 501 Squadron Hawker Hurricane Mk I pictured at Kenley during September 1940.

that he had crashed all those years ago. I got in touch with them and told them what I knew, and through them contacted Eddie's sister, a very nice lady whom I still see occasionally. There was an inquest but I was amazed not to be called as a witness, I did see him go in after all! Incidentally, the plane that shot Eddie down did not look like an Me 109. We thought that they were "He 113s" at the time, but we now know that the type was merely a propaganda ruse by the Germans. The Hun involved definitely had elliptical wings.

The way it was: pilots of 501 Squadron at readiness, Gravesend, August 1940. From left: Sgt Tony Pickering, Sgt RJK Gent, F/Sgt PF Morfill, Sgt PCP Farnes, Sgt A Glowacki (Polish), unidentified, Sgt WB Henn, Sgt SAH Whitehouse, Sgt JH Lacey (in tunic with cigarette), Plt Off RC Dafforn.

'I was shot down on September 11th, 1940, in Hurricane P5200, SD-W. The CO, Squadron Leader Hogan, had ordered us to perform a head-on attack on a large formation of German bombers heading for London, I cannot recall whether they were Dorniers or Heinkels, but they were definitely not Ju 88s. Anyway, we dived head-on at the Huns and I pressed the gun button and shut my eyes! One of the nose gunners gave me a squirt and hit the sump. I started smoking and managed to spiral down away from the fight. It was a lovely day and I could see Kenley below quite clearly. As there was no-one about I thought that I could just come down quite slowly and make a nice landing. At about 3,000' the petrol caught fire and I was over the side pretty sharpish! The Hurricane went down and crashed and I landed in a Guards depot where I was given a couple of whiskies. I was wearing ordinary uniform trousers, shoes, an open neck shirt with no tie as it was hot, and that was it. I hadn't had a shave that morning and I remember being a bit singed about the face and hair but was otherwise uninjured.

'Another time I came across a lone Ju 88 somewhere over Kent, heading back

Pilots of 501 Squadron at Kenley, September 1940. From left: Sgt Tony Pickering, Flg Off DAE Jones, Flg Off VR Snell, Sgt SAH Whitehouse, unidentified, Sgt RJK Gent, F/Sgt PF Morfill, unidentified, unidentified, Plt Off RC Dafforn and Plt Off S Witorzenc (Polish). Both Gent and Dafforn lost their lives on active service during the Second World War.

to sea. I thought it would be no problem to catch up the Hun, press the button and that would be it. I slotted in behind and ran flat out to catch him. Suddenly he just pulled away from me, just left me standing, had at least an extra 50 mph on me, and that was the last that I saw of him. The Hurricane just wasn't fast enough, we even used to bend the throttle levers in flight trying to squeeze a bit more boost out of the Merlin. A Spitfire would have caught that Ju 88. In the Hurricane's favour was that it could take a terrific amount of punishment, the Spitfire not quite as much.

'I was 18 during the Battle of Britain. I came from a small village where everyone knew everyone else, we went to school, did our homework in the evenings and went to church on Sundays. We were innocents really, the RAF was a bit of a shock,

501 Squadron Battle of Britain survivors at Colerne, 1941, from left: Plt Off 'Ginger' Lacey DFM, Plt Off KW Mackenzie DFC, Plt Off SAH Whitehouse, Plt Off RC Dafforn & Plt Of VH Ekins. Of this group, only Dafforn was killed during the war, Lacey died in 1989 and Ekins in 1993.

all these chaps who were going around night clubs and girls, it was something to touch a girl's arm at a dance then, not like it is now!'

Tony Pickering was lucky to survive the Battle of Britain. 501 Squadron was in the front line throughout the entire 16 week battle and suffered the highest number of pilots killed by any fighter squadron during that time - 19. He later left behind the lumbering Hurricane and, having been commissioned in December 1941, became a flight commander on 113 Squadron with which he served until January 1944. A year later he was posted overseas and commanded the Bombing and Gunnery School at El Ballah before leaving the RAF in December 1945. I found his story greatly inspiring, to be an 18-year-old flying Hurricanes in 1940...! He is now aged 73, an active campanologist, and, not surprisingly, amongst the youngest members of the Battle of Britain Fighter Association, the membership of which is unique as it comprises the Few themselves.

Tony Pickering pictured with his flying log books, 1988.

Chapter Five

Flight Lieutenant Richard Jones AE

Pilot Officer Richard Jones photographed at Fowlmere, September 1940, whilst serving with 19 Squadron.

Readers familiar with my previous works will know that my first book was 'Spitfire Squadron', published in 1990, and which told the story of 19 Squadron during the Battle of Britain period. During the course of my research for that title I traced and obtained tremendous co-operation from every surviving 19 Squadron pilot from that period, or so I thought. Somehow, however, I had managed to completely overlook one of their number, Flight Lieutenant Richard Jones. To cut a long story short we finally made contact during mid-1991, which led to me motoring the short distance to spend a day with Richard and his truly charming wife Elizabeth. I am delighted, therefore, to include Richard Jones in 'A Few of the Many'.

Richard was another Volunteer Reserve pilot who had learned to fly at No 8 Elementary Flying Training School at Woodley, Reading. There the embryonic fighter pilot flew Hawker Hart, Hind, and Audax biplanes, before the Miles

Magister monoplane trainer. In September 1939 he was mobilized and undertook advanced training on Harvards at RAF Ternhill. Then in June 1940 Pilot Officer Jones learned to fly the Spitfire at 5 OTU, Aston Down. The following month, with the opening clashes of the Battle of Britain being fought, Richard was posted to 64 Squadron which was engaged in the defence of London and flying from Kenley in 11 Group:-

'My memories of joining 64 Squadron after leaving Aston Down are slightly hazy. However I remember being met by the CO, Squadron Leader ARD MacDonell, who immediately made us new pilots feel at home. He referred to all new intake pilots from the OTUs as "his chicks".

'To give us battle experience as quickly as possible whenever the time allowed, we were paired off with a senior battle-experienced pilot to practise dog-fighting and yet more dog-fighting to give us both experience and confidence in the Spitfire and in battle conditions. We were lucky. Had I been posted to 64 Squadron later in the summer of 1940 there just would not have been the time for such extra-curricular training.

'Squadron Leader MacDonell was first and foremost a gentleman, quiet, determined and an excellent pilot and leader who looked after the interests of all under him in the squadron. He had the respect of all of us.

'I well remember my first operational engagement with the enemy. We were about nine Spitfires against 30-40 enemy fighters. Before meeting them I had butterflies in my stomach wondering what to expect. When they were spotted we waded into them and once engaged all fear disappeared - we immediately realised it was either them or us - all hell appeared to be let loose with aircraft everywhere. The next moment we were all on our own, everyone else had disappeared.

'In fact, in the panic of my first engagement I don't think I even fired a shot as it appeared to take all of my time to just avoid a collision. I felt it was the most valuable experience that I had ever received in my life. I returned to base a more mature individual and felt extremely lucky to have survived to tell the tale.

'Another thing that I remember are the three states of Readiness. One state was "Readiness" with all pilots kitted up and ready to go, another was at 15 minutes state, which meant that you had to be in the Mess and ready to be called on duty immediately, and finally 30 minutes state which meant that you could relax, perhaps go to the local cinema or play billiards. From that state you could be called up onto 15 minutes and then Readiness as the cycle went. If you were on Readiness, then that day you would get up very early in the morning, around 4 o'clock, so that you would be at the aerodrome and ready before dawn in the event of an emergency. Immediately, however, you had a remarkable breakfast and I must admit that the attention which we had from the staff was amazing. After breakfast we used to get into what we called was the "Cattle Truck" to be driven over to the dispersal point and the aircraft. If we were on Readiness then we got kitted up, excepting our helmets and parachutes, and waited in the crew room for something to happen. If you were not flying then you were always waiting for something to happen. Most people spent their time either playing cards, reading or sleeping, waiting, and suddenly the tranquillity was shattered by a telephone's bell. Immediately everyone was tense because the telephone brought news of a scramble, or possibly something less traumatic, but I think that it was the telephone that started your senses quicker then anything else.

'If it was a scramble then you were into the Spitfires, engines started and away. We would be given immediate instructions, say "Scramble 8-10,000' over Dungeness". We knew that because of our radar system of early warning, wherever we were sent there would be a good chance of meeting the enemy. If we did meet them then of course we would engage them to the best of our ability.

'When we came back, anybody that had been successful, perhaps in shooting down an enemy aircraft, might do such a thing as a victory roll, but those were not encouraged because we did not always know whether our aircraft had been damaged. Immediately you landed the Intelligence Officer took full details from each pilot of what had happened whilst the groundcrew did a fantastic job in preparing the aircraft for immediate take off again. We then waited again until such time as we were either scrambled again or taken off Readiness when we would be relieved by another squadron. We would then drop back to 15 minutes, then 30, until the cycle went round again. Actually we were always ready for any eventuality.

64 Squadron, Hornchurch, November 1940. From right: Plt Off T Gray, Plt Off P Beare, Plt Off JG Pippett, Sqn Ldr J Rankin, Plt Off RL Jones, Plt Off E Watson, Sqn Ldr ARD MacDonell, Flt Lt R Gittens (Engineering Officer), Plt Off JH Rowden, Flg Off EG Gilbert, Plt Off AR Tidman, Plt Off A Towers (Adjutant), Flt Lt DM Taylor, Plt Off K Hawkins, Flt Lt JA Thomson, Plt Off AG Donahue (American).

'An incident - one of many - was the visit to our 64 Squadron of 11 Group early in August, 1940, by the Air Minister, Sir Archibald Sinclair.

'We were all lined up to meet him, standing in front of our Spitfires. He congratulated us on the work that we were doing and in his opening words thanked the **Hurricane pilots of 12 Group!** Obviously, I thought to myself, he did not know the difference between Spitfires and Hurricanes!'

On September 20th, 1940, Pilot Officer Richard Jones was posted from 64 to 19 Squadron at Fowlmere in 12 Group. The latter unit was by that time commanded by Squadron Leader Brian Lane DFC, another exceptional fighter pilot and leader of men, and the squadron was a part of Squadron Leader Douglas Bader's Duxford Wing. On September 28th, a single Gruppe of Ju 88s headed for London, protected by three Me 109 equipped Jagdgeschwader. 19 Squadron were up, Pilot Officer Jones flying Spitfire P7432:-

'When patrolling the Tenterden area at 29,000' the controller informed us that as there were apparently no enemy aircraft in the vicinity we could return to "pancake", or return to base and land. I was "Arse-end Charlie" and relaxed slightly as we dived to 20,000'. Suddenly about four feet of my starboard wing just peeled off - my initial thought was that it was a poor show on a new aircraft. Then a loud bang and a hole appeared above the undercarriage. I was obviously the target of an enemy fighter up sun. Immediately I took evasive action, simultaneously my engine cut out for good and I was suddenly in a high speed stall and spin. My radio was U/S so I was unable to inform the squadron who returned to base blissfully unaware that I had been shot down.

'I recovered from the spin at about 10,000' - the aircraft was not responding to the controls - I realised too that the hood was completely jammed. I subsequently crash-landed with a dead engine in one of only two suitable fields in a heavily wooded area just outside Hawkhurst. Unfortunately I did so amongst a flock of sheep and I regret that several were killed. I was rescued by the army and first taken to the Hawkhurst doctor who treated a flesh wound to my leg, then to their Mess prior to returning me safely to Fowlmere.

'My Spitfire had a broken propeller and radiator, a few holes and some missing parts, but was otherwise relatively undamaged'. For some reason, and this was in fact quite common regarding aircraft not too badly damaged, the incident was not recorded in any official records. Therefore no record of Richard Jones being shot down in P7432 appears in any Battle of Britain history - not even 'Spitfire Squadron'! In his flying log book, Richard wrote 'Shot down and crash-landed at Hawkhurst, Kent. Killed three sheep. What a bloody mess!!!' On November 15th, 1940, Richard Jones returned to 64 Squadron with whom he remained until April 1941. That month he was seconded to the Ministry of Aircraft Production, and 'lent' to the de Havilland Aircraft Company as a test pilot. Richard consequently test flew Hurricanes and Spitfires which had been repaired at the factory, a job which he retained until January 1946 when he left the Air Force. After a long post-war career in the motor industry, Richard Jones, now a very fit and active 73, is semi-retired and still working part-time as an usher at a Magistrates' Court in Oxfordshire. In 1988, he attended a dinner at RAF Abingdon as a guest there of No 6 Air Experience Flight. Also dining was Herr Günther Domaschk, an Me 109 pilot flying with JG2 'Richthofen' during the Battle of Britain, who had expressed a wish to meet a Spitfire pilot whilst he was in the UK. Deep in discussion about their wartime experiences, a fellow diner was overheard describing them as being 'like long lost brothers'. If you knew Richard Jones with his gentle manner and kindness, that he so warmly greeted a former adversary would be no surprise.

Richard Jones pictured at home, 1992.

Chapter Six

Squadron Leader Peter Brown AFC

Pilot Officer Peter Brown, 1940.

Some 10 years ago I visited the Aerospace Museum at Cosford, and there saw, amongst a pile of rusting aircraft wreckage recovered from local wartime crash sites, the virtually complete Merlin engine of Spitfire P7304. Many other major components from the aircraft were also on show, but no research material relating to the aircraft's 'life' and demise were exhibited. The yellowing, typed caption peeling off the engine merely read 'Spitfire P7304. Crashed Hinks Plantation, 22/8/43. The pilot was killed'. It concerned me that both the demise and historical background story of this superb exhibit was accorded so little attention. When I arrived home my archive was checked, and information was forthcoming that Supermarine Spitfire Mk IIA P7304 was the 24th Spitfire built at the Castle Bromwich Aircraft Factory, having been test flown by Alex Henshaw, the Chief Test Pilot himself, on July 26th, 1940. The Spitfire then went to 611 Squadron, the first to receive the Mk II, and on August 21st was damaged by a Do 17. Further checks revealed that the pilot on that occasion was Pilot Officer

MP Brown whose section actually destroyed the raider concerned. Enquiries made of Wing Commander Pat Hancock, Honorary Secretary of the Battle of Britain Fighter Association, quickly confirmed that Maurice Peter Brown, or 'Sneezy' as he was more commonly known in RAF circles, was still alive. A letter was soon on its way to Squadron Leader MP Brown AFC RAF Retd, and the response was both immediate and positive. Peter and I met shortly afterwards. I have since come to very much appreciate his friendship and efforts on my behalf, the story of the P7304/Do 17 episode having been related in my third book, 'Through Peril to the Stars'. After leaving the RAF, Peter mainly worked in the plastics industry but also became a journalist for three years. When I invited him to write a piece for this book, his response was enthusiastic, as I anticipated, and Peter chose to wrote about his time with 41 (Fighter) Squadron, 'an inside story of the Squadron at war 1940/41'. That he was once a journalist is reflected by the quality of the following:-

'When Dilip Sarkar invited me to write about my memories of 41 Squadron in 1940/41, I wondered how I could approach such a daunting task.

'The Squadron's achievements and its pilots' personal fighting records have been well documented over the years, so I have decided therefore to write about the pilots - not as the helmeted young men behind reflector sights - but as individuals that were always part of the squadron.

'I have included some events in the air that have not previously been written about and which I hope therefore will be of interest.

'I trust that the reader will quickly see the thread running through the pages that whether in the air or on the ground 41 was always a Squadron. We had a mixed team of young men, including regular officer, NCO and VR pilots. They came from all parts of the world, with different backgrounds and educations. Everyone, even the newest pilot, as I personally experienced, was at once accepted into the team and treated as a friend and colleague. There were no select groups or cliques.

'In spite of 41 Squadron's great achievements, dedication and sacrifices, its leaders and pilots never received the awards and recognition that they deserved and that other squadrons received during this period. The pilots, however, considered, quite rightly, that they were professional fighter pilots and took on the tasks and dangers for which they had been trained. At times casualties were very serious but the Squadron's morale always remained intact.

'I joined 41 Squadron at Hornchurch on September 28th, 1940, as a replacement pilot. I had previously served in 12 Group for a year as a regular pilot with 611 Squadron which was also equipped with Spitfires. My experience included convoy patrols, Dunkirk, North Sea X Raids and Wing operations from Duxford. I had flown several times with the five squadron Duxford Wing, including September 15th. We had been well aware in 611 Squadron that a tremendous battle was being fought by 11 and 10 Groups, and wanted to play our part in it. Nothing of any real significance, however, was happening in the

12 Group Sector. In July, August and September, for reasons tactical possibly, but more likely political, we (611 Squadron) were kept in 12 Group. During this same period, 41 Squadron carried out two tours in 11 Group.

'When I was posted to 41 Squadron I considered myself to be quite an experienced pilot and looked forward to the "Great Adventure"'. The change to the tempo of fighting in 11 Group was traumatic. The war immediately became very personal and a fight for survival against greater odds. Much faster reactions were required in order to survive. Fortunately for me I had been posted to 'A' Flight and flew as No 2 to Flight Lieutenant Norman Ryder. I note from my log book that on my first patrol with 41 I damaged a Do 215. This is a surprise as I know that it took me three or four sorties to gradually become aware of what was happening, where the enemy aircraft were and what action we were taking. It is not surprising that many pilots were shot down on their first, second or third flights. Few pilots actually saw the aircraft which shot them down.

'On my third day with the Squadron I note that I took part in five sorties. I had certainly moved up into another and more deadly dimension. For days the patrolling and fighting was almost continuous with several sorties per day, intercepting the enemy and often finding the Me 109s above. The pilots in 11 Group were fighting to the death. Generally 15 minutes after landing they were expected to be ready to take-off again, often with depleted numbers. In contrast, the fighter pilots in 12 Group led a more relaxed life, which was totally frustrating for those pilots who wanted to go south and fight.

'Some ground controllers seemed unaware of the crucial importance of height to fighters. If you had it you could win. If the Me 109s had it you were in serious trouble. After a number of serious casualties due to having been jumped by 109s whilst the squadrons were climbing to intercept, some flight commanders in 11 Group ignored the course instructed and instead flew one which would at least ensure that they would be at the same height as the 109s at the time of interception. I believe that one flight commander was threatened with a Court Martial for doing this, an action described as "failure to carry out operational orders".

'The Spitfire was undoubtedly a beautiful aircraft designed to fly and fight up to 30,000' and even higher. But the designers and RAF engineers had failed to consider the air temperature at 30,000', and therefore the cockpit temperature. In winter, this could be as low as -40 degrees F. So the Spitfire and Hurricane were designed without any cockpit or gun heating. Most of us wore three pairs of gloves. Frostbite was not uncommon. When we complained about this, Fighter Command supplied us with flat packs which had to be wetted before take-off and then inserted into the knee pockets of our Sidcot flying suits to keep our knees warm! However, we were much more grateful for the submarine sweaters and seaboot stockings that were also issued. At high altitude some of our guns froze up and failed to fire. This not only reduced our effectiveness as fighters, but made the aircraft slew to one side if the frozen guns were in one wing only.

Another problem was the continued icing up of the bulletproof screen when diving down to lower altitudes. This was a serious handicap. Being of an inventive mind, I decided to take a large cloth soaked in glycol - an anti-freeze - with me in the cockpit. On the first flight we dived from height and the windscreen duly iced over. I grabbed the cloth to clear the screen. Alas the cloth was as stiff as plywood! This gives an indication of the cockpit temperature on that and indeed many other flights.

'At take-off time most pilots would face the aircraft's tail and pass water, most of which went over the tail-wheel. A full or half-full bladder for $1^1/2$ hours at 30,000' was something to avoid. By the time the pilots had finished, the fitters

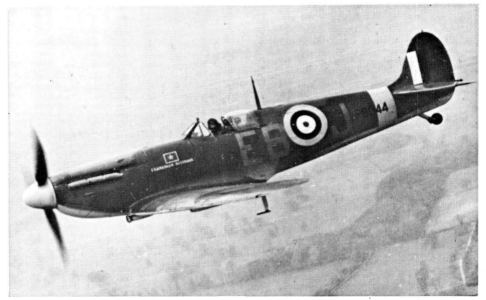

Above: Peter Brown airborne in a 41 Squadron Spitfire Mk IIA, early 1941. This is a presentation aircraft named after its donor, the 1st Canadian Division. The inscription was in yellow.

Left: Spitfire P8044, '1st Canadian Division' is presented to the RAF at Hornchurch, early 1941.

had started the engines and we were ready for take-off. The unusual facet of this story is not that it happened quite regularly, but that towards the end of 1940 a formal letter was sent out by Fighter Command's engineering department giving strict instructions that urinating on the tail-wheel must cease forthwith as it was causing corrosion damage. The letter was treated with great hilarity - we wished they had spent their time putting some heat into the cockpit instead!

'In October the pilot of one of the Me 109s I claimed baled out and landed near West Malling aerodrome. As Fighter Command had previously almost always refused to accept my claims I decided on this occasion to get evidence. I landed at West Malling and went with the Intelligence Officer to see the German pilot who was in the lock-up. After introductions we had a friendly chat through our interpreter. Finally we shook hands and I wished him the best of luck. Why? Well, he was obviously not a Nazi, but he was a fighter pilot and for some reason this made for a common bond. I took as a souvenir his survival jacket which was superior to our Mae Wests, and wore it for the rest of my time on 41 Squadron. Group allowed this claim to be considered as confirmed!'

The particular day in question was Sunday, 20th October, 1940. Exactly one month previously the Luftwaffe had commenced 'tip'n run' raids executed by single-bomb carrying Me 109s. The RAF ground controllers had to mount

Left: Flt Lt Peter Brown pictured at Hornchurch after the Battle of Britain and wearing the Schwimmveste of Feldwebel Bielmaier whom he shot down on October 20th, 1940.
Right: 41 Squadron's Guy Long and Peter Brown pictured at Hornchurch, early 1941. Peter is wearing a Sidcot flying suit and his captured German lifejacket. This snapshot was enlarged from a one inch square original, hence the quality.

constant patrols to guard against this new threat, as when formations of Me 109s crossed the English coastline they all had to be intercepted as no-one could tell which contained fighter-bombers and which were pure fighter sweeps. On October 20th, strong formations of Me 109s made five attacks on the south-east and London, although due to their extremely limited bomb carrying capabilities little damage was actually caused. Flying Officer Peter Brown's victim was an Me 109E-7 of 5/JG52 which was flown by Feldwebel Bielmaier. Peter still has both Bielmaier's *schwimmveste* and his pilot's qualification badge, and at the time of writing enquiries are underway in Germany to ascertain whether Herr Bielmaier is still alive - what an interesting meeting that would make over half a century later!

Peter continues his memories:-

'During November 1940, each fighter squadron was stood-down one day a week for rest and recuperation. This was an opportunity eagerly seized by many squadrons to disappear in all directions and especially to London and the bright lights. Our CO, Don Finlay, had been an Olympic hurdler and had a fanatical interest in personal fitness - not shared by anyone else in the squadron. However, the CO decided that we should all go on a cross-country run as we all needed to be physically fitter. Someone said that we were expected to fly to the enemy, not run after them! As almost none of our pilots smoked or drank more than a few beers, we all felt that we were fit enough for action. The CO, however, was adamant, and we were instructed to report to the main gate for a six mile cross-country run. What a motley crowd assembled in every variety of athletic dress. I don't remember who led, but the pace could only be described as reluctant. Finally our athletic CO took over the lead. Within a few minutes he misjudged the jump and fell into a stream. I don't know who won, I finished in the middle order, but the CO, in spite of his fitness and strenuous efforts came in 6th - the pilots were fitter than he thought! We were never ordered to participate in a cross-country run again.

'41 Squadron's home base was at Catterick in Yorkshire, and also in that county lived Lord Guisborough who had been a pilot during the Great War. He was appointed our Intelligence Officer and became totally dedicated to the pilots. To every pilot in 41 he was known as "Gissy", a term of affection enjoyed by all. To everyone else in the Mess, no matter what rank, he insisted on being rightfully addressed as Lord Guisborough. After every trip Gissy would rush to interview the pilots. After a few exaggerated stories the pilots would then give him the true report of the action. We teased him because we were fond of him. I heard that once Gissy was posted from the squadron, but he simply refused to go. It would have required either a courageous or foolhardy Group officer to threaten to Court Martial a Noble Lord for refusing to obey an order. Yes, Gissy, the Lord Guisborough, was definitely one of the Squadron.

'Our Squadron Medical Officer was Flight Lieutenant Ernest Anthony. The "Doc" had been a very popular GP in Upminster, near to Hornchurch, but when he joined the Squadron he immediately became involved in caring for the pilots. He gave hospitality at his home and arranged other social occasions which were a welcome relief from the fighting. To him the pilots were young men that he was privileged to care for. After the squadron moved to Merston in 11 Group during late 1941, they were engaged in sweeps over Northern France. After a period of continuous activity, Doc became very concerned that some of the pilots were showing increasing and serious signs of stress. He rightly wrote a formal note to Group expressing his concern and suggested that the pressure be eased. Within 48 hours he was posted to the Middle East. Loyalty to the Squadron appeared to be an undesirable characteristic in 11 Group.

'In the evenings we would quite often frequent a favourite pub in Upminster. We liked its atmosphere and it also had a very good pianist who was known as "Georgie". He was undoubtedly a homosexual and his scarlet fingernails left us in no doubt! But we pilots liked Georgie, he was happy and friendly and could play any tune. He contributed to many relaxing evenings for us. We took care of his drinks. His sexuality was not an issue, indeed it was never considered. When we were at the pub he was one of us. One evening a rather drunken sailor went up to Georgie when he was playing and called him a "Bloody Pansy". Georgie stopped playing, stood up and with one blow felled the sailor. He then sat down, picked up the tune and continued playing for us for the rest of the evening as though nothing had happened. Yes, Georgie was a man after our own hearts.

'After the Battle of Britain was over, Fighter Command asked for pilots to volunteer for postings to Malta which was having a pretty tough time. We offered to go as a complete squadron, but no-one would volunteer on their own. Our offer was not accepted.

'In writing personal notes about the pilots I am reminded of Shakespeare's "We few, we happy few, we band of brothers", from Henry Vth.

'I think that the one great strength of the Squadron was that the flight and section leaders had all been with 41 for a long time, and so were well bonded before the Battle of Britain. Serious in the air but great friends with lots of humour off duty.

'The first I must write about is Pilot Officer George "Benny" Bennions DFC, who was shot down and badly injured in October 1940, just three days after I joined, in fact. I did not, therefore, have time to get to know him well personally, but I soon learned that he was a 41 Squadron legend. As a very experienced former NCO pilot he frequently led the Squadron as a Pilot Officer in some of the darkest days. His loss and serious injuries were felt personally by all the pilots - something that rarely happened. He was accredited with eight confirmed victories during the Battle.

'Flight Lieutenant Norman Ryder DFC was a very experienced fighter pilot and flight commander. When the CO, Squadron Leader Hood and the other flight commander were both killed in action on September 5th, 1940, Norman de facto took over leadership of the Squadron, which he shared in the air with

Pilot Officer Bennions. All the pilots hoped and expected Norman to be given command of the Squadron. He had those personal qualities that all leaders desire but very few achieve. He was respected, liked and trusted. But it was not to be, and Squadron Leader DO Finlay became our new CO.

'I flew many times with Norman Ryder, and his tactics were always to put the flight or squadron in such a position that all pilots could engage. This was different from the headlong rush led by the leader I had experienced in 12 Group. We were all disappointed to lose him, but delighted for Norman himself when he was given command of 56 Squadron at Northolt in January 1941. His qualities of leadership were soon recognised as within five months he was given command of the Kenley Wing.

'Although Norman had led his flight and squadron in both the Battle of Britain and afterwards in an outstanding manner, he received no decoration or recognition from Fighter Command.

'Pilot Officer Eric Lock DSO DFC & Bar became the second and "unsung" legend of 41 Squadron. He was basically a loner and was one of the "hunters" during the Battle. He personified the Squadron crest, "Seek & Destroy", although it often seemed to be a one man battle! Although he took off with the squadron he often disappeared, landing later on his own to report another victory. As the son of a farmer he no doubt used a shotgun from an early age; his keen eyesight, shooting ability and personal courage enabled him to shoot down at least 20 enemy aircraft. As a new and young pilot, however, Fighter Command were suspicious of his claims and refused to confirm some of them, especially as there were often no 41 Squadron witnesses. This total has now, I believe, been confirmed by post-war researchers and probably makes him the top scoring British pilot of the Battle. Fighter Command, however, only gave him his first decoration after the destruction of 16 enemy aircraft - during 1940, five destroyed usually earned a DFC! Eric Lock was eventually seriously injured when attacking an Me 109 on November 17th, 1940. He returned to operational flying, with 611 Squadron, but was killed on a Sweep over France.

'Flight Lieutenant Tony Lovell DFC was Commander of "B" Flight. He was a very special person and a "gentle man" in the nicest possible way. He was a first-class flight commander and a friend to us all on the ground. He had a strong religious faith but was always ready to join in the Squadron fun. We were lucky to have flight commanders of this calibre. Tony had five victories confirmed during the Battle and got his DFC. After a distinguished war record, which included awards of not only the British DFC but also the American version, and our DSO & Bar, he was killed in a flying accident when a Wing Commander.

'Flight Lieutenant John "Mac" Mackenzie DFC, a New Zealander, was a tough fighter in the air but on the ground showed the more youthful side of his nature. He was liked by all. He flew more than 200 sorties with 41 Squadron and won a DFC for his work in the Battle. As a personal friend, I was sorry to see him posted as a controller to Catterick in April 1941.

'Squadron Leader DO Finlay had been appointed CO of 54 Squadron on August 26th, 1940, having previously held an engineering post. He was shot down and wounded on his second sortie. In mid-September he was posted to command 41 Squadron. DO was still very much a peacetime regular officer with no experience of either fighting or leading a squadron at war. Both he and 41 Squadron might have been better served if instead he had been posted to command a squadron in either 12 or 13 Group where he would have had more time to become acclimatised. He found it difficult to relax and become integrated into the team of pilots. I feel that for quite a while he lived in the shadows of Norman Ryder and George Bennions, a difficult situation for any leader.

'A team has many players. Not only did we have "aces", but many more Red Twos, Blue Twos and Top Cover pilots who often just gave protection without the opportunity to engage the enemy themselves, despite personally being in a position to be "jumped". One of these was my friend Flying Officer Dennis Adams who was with me in 611 Squadron - we both drove to 41 Squadron in his MG. Pilot Officer Bob Beardsley was another, he survived three tours on fighters and received his DFC in 1941. Pilot Officer EP "Hawkeye" Wells, a New Zealander, had outstanding eyesight, often being able to identify an aircraft before the rest of us even saw it! Needless to say, he was always a welcome member of the flight.

'Myself, Flight Lieutenant "Sneezy" Brown, was proud to serve with 41 Squadron, many times as Red Two, and am now fortunate to write about my friends and colleagues of those critical months.

'In my records I have the programme for a carol singing service at the Hornchurch Station Church on December 21st, 1940. I remember that 'A' Flight had been persuaded to attend by the Flight Commander, Norman Ryder, as he felt that we should go and share the occasion with all of the other personnel on the Station who we rarely saw but contributed to keeping our aircraft serviceable, and the controlling and administrative staff who all played their part. The pilots attended, mainly I believe because it was seen as a "Flight occasion".

'In December, as an early part of the new plan for aggressive action against the Luftwaffe over France, someone devised "Rhubarbs" in which pairs of aircraft, using low cloud for cover, flew over to France and dived down to attack suitable targets. As many of those targets were Luftwaffe airfields with their notorious anti-aircraft defences - duly warned - the sorties were fraught with some danger. My only pleasant memory of Rhubarbs was practising with Norman Ryder and beating up the Southend bypass at 20'. It was great fun - no-one was shooting back! Although we trained in pairs, mainly beating up the Southend Road, weather conditions led to the cancellation of our planned trips even up to the stage of sitting in the cockpit. I don't mind too much about missing out on Rhubarbs!

'One of the offensive sweeps that we undertook in January 1941, was to Walcheren Island in Holland. We were despatched as a single squadron to fly at 15-20,000' to the island. The pilots were concerned that the straight line distance was 140 miles and mainly over the sea. We were totally unaware of the flight's purpose, but as we reached land and flew round the Dutch island, I certainly felt that we could only be acting as a diversion or even as bait. The Luftwaffe had ample warning of our progress and if we had been attacked by 109s from above we could have taken serious punishment - and for what? We thought that this was a useless trip, putting the Squadron in needless danger. It was perhaps part of Group masterplan. I have often wondered at what level of command senior officers in the RAF forget that pilots are people, and merely regard them as aircraft that can be converted to disposable numbers with acceptable losses. I wonder who it was who sent us to Walcheren Island ?

An oft used photograph of 41 Squadron pictured at Hornchurch sometime between late November 1940 - mid-January 1941, but rarely are all identified. From left, standing on Spitfire: Plt Off HC Baker, Plt Off DA Adams, Plt Off FJ Aldridge, Sgt EV Darling, Plt Off JN Mackenzie, Flt Lt ADJ Lovell: Standing in front of aircraft, from left: Plt Off DE Mileham, Flt Lt EN Ryder, Sgt RA Angus, Sqn Ldr DO Finlay, Sgt TWR Healy, Sgt JS Gilders, Plt Off EP Wells, Plt Off RC Ford.

'With the appointment in November of Leigh-Mallory as the replacement for Keith Park, 11 Group decided to go onto the offensive with a series of sweeps across Northern France. As this originally involved several squadrons forming up with six Blenheims carrying a few bombs, they were hardly offensive in reality. The Luftwaffe had ample time to get into position if they wished to fight, or to stay above or even on the ground if they chose not. Even if we shot down one for one we were the losers. We lost both pilot and aircraft, the enemy pilot could bale out and fight another day. However, fighter sweeps were the order of the day, whatever the merits or demerits. My experience of sweeps was limited as we moved north. But in the sweeps we lost some very experienced Wing and Squadron Leaders, and many other pilots - and for what? I hope that this aggressive spirit and the losses inflicted on the Germans justified the loss of these pilots. Were the sweeps we carried out tactical or political or both?

'During February 1941 we continued with patrols and X raids but the tempo of the fighting was much slower than in 1940. One sad event to record was the loss of two of our pilots, Sergeant J McAdam and Sergeant RA Angus, one of them killed by Mölders, one of the German aces. On that day I was leading a patrol of six Spitfires in the Dungeness area at 25,000'. Control warned me that there were bandits in our immediate vicinity at 6,000'. Spitfire No 6 had developed engine trouble and returned to base, and No 5 should have taken over as top cover. With the enemy so far below us we were obviously searching beneath us. After a short while I looked up and saw a group of Me 109s way above and diving down on us. I shouted a warning and led the squadron upwards to meet them head on. We were broken up and two of our five were shot down. When I was circling one of our injured pilots on his parachute and then after he splashed into the sea, to direct Air Sea Rescue, I was attacked by four 109s. I returned fire but without any obvious effect. As Flight Leader I must accept responsibility for the disaster. But how well can we be expected to fight with information that was so utterly misleading? Without the controller's highly inaccurate information on height we could have fought on equal terms'.

The combat described above between 41 Squadron and JG51 occurred on Thursday, 20th February, 1941. It was Sergeant McAdam descending by parachute whom Flying Officer Brown tried to protect. During that descent, however, the unfortunate pilot was seen to burst into flames. When his body was later picked up by a patrol boat, he was found to have been shot in the back. In a dogfight there was much stray ammunition being flung about the sky and it is likely that McAdam was so hit, Peter Brown possibly having been the intended target. The views of Major Mölders on pilots strafing parachutes were well known in the Luftwaffe - had he witnessed such an incident an immediate court martial would certainly have followed. Sadly, Sergeant Robert Angus was also missing; he baled out into the sea but could not be found. Both 41 Squadron pilots, in fact, were victims of Major Mölders, the Luftwaffe's 'Oberkanone'.

'The following day John Mackenzie was also leading a flight of six Spitfires on patrol, and feeling rather apprehensive after our losses of the previous day. Without any warning Sergeant JS Gilders dived his aircraft and in spite of calls from John there was no reply from Gilders. At first the Flight thought he had seen some enemy aircraft but he continued his dive straight into the ground. It was probably oxygen failure. Either he had failed to turn on the supply correctly or there had been a mechanical failure. Several of us had experienced oxygen supply problems but had recovered in time. It is probable that some of the inexplicable crashes in the Battle of Britain could well have been due to oxygen failure. The oxygen bottle was stored behind the armour plating which protected the pilot. It had only a small knob to turn and was difficult to operate especially with three pairs of gloves and being behind our backs. The Command engineers fortunately soon came up with a practical answer in the form of a capstan about six inches in diameter which gave much easier control'.

Sergeant Gilders was destined to remain buried with the wreckage of his Spitfire until hitting the international headlines during the summer of 1994 when his body was illegally recovered by amateur, so called aviation archaeologists. For a variety of reasons, a number of casualties were not recovered from their crash sites at the time, but have since been found by those whose fascination is the collection of parts of crashed wartime aircraft. The practice of such excavations, however, is restricted by the Protection of Military Remains Act, 1986, and before the first spade is turned a licence must be obtained from the Ministry of Defence. Such permission, however, will not be forthcoming either in cases where pilots remain 'missing', or where live ordnance can be anticipated. Regarding the former circumstance, the Government's policy, rightly or wrongly and for a variety of reasons, is to 'let sleeping dogs lie'. In many cases this has appeared somewhat unreasonable when particular crash sites have been identified beyond doubt and the families of those concerned have requested an exhumation. Whilst the Ministry's response is generally a refusal, it is possible to comply with the law and obtain co-operation. For example, in recent years the Prince of Wales intervened in such a case which resulted in the RAF recovering a Spitfire pilot for burial, and in February 1993 the Malvern Spitfire Team, Ministry of Defence and RAF mounted a joint operation to search the Severn Estuary for a missing Canadian Spitfire pilot (see 'Through Peril to the Stars', also by this author). However, others, such as those concerned with the Gilders recovery, although no doubt as deeply moved by what is an emotive topic, have irresponsibly sought not to comply with the law but instead to openly proceed with an unauthorised recovery, presenting the Ministry of Defence with a body and veritable public relations minefield. No-one, least of all myself, would argue that brave young men like Sergeant Gilders et al. do not deserve a Christian burial in hallowed ground, but the point is that the exhumation of human remains is neither a matter to be taken lightly, nor undertaken by amateurs. It is my firm belief that, to avoid further scandals like the Gilders saga, the circumstances of which many readers will be familiar, the Ministry of Defence should be urged to organise an operation to clear the remaining questionable sites, and those recoveries carried out only by the professionals of the RAF Aircraft Salvage Team. This should be done, in my view, without delay.

Peter Brown continues, and returns us to 1941:-

'The Squadron was ordered to move north to Catterick on February 19th but their runway was snow-bound, a twist of fate that resulted in us being on patrol on both February 20th and 21st with their disasters. Catterick was in 13 Group and was considered to be a rest area. Many of our senior and experienced pilots were now being posted away and we were receiving replacements fresh from OTU who needed a great deal of training. The sector was quiet but Group demands for night patrols put a great strain on the few experienced pilots left. For a period I was on duty all day followed by the night standby or patrol, followed by the next day's flying. I managed alternative nights off as my only time not on duty. So much for rest and recuperation. There were a few X raids but generally only with low cloud and single enemy aircraft; however, Squadron Leader Pat Meagher, seconded to the Squadron, shot down a bomber on a night patrol.

'A' Flight of 41 Squadron pictured at Catterick, June 1941. Flt Lt Peter Brown third from left, wearing black pre-war style flying suit and captured German lifejacket, Sqn Ldr DO Finlay (CO), centre.

'In March 1941 I was confirmed as 'A' Flight Commander. It was quite a comfort to us to find that Al Deere, formally of 54 Squadron fame, was one of the Catterick controllers. Catterick had a single short runway and was surrounded by hills - not ideal for either bad weather or night flying. My main memory of late March is that we very nearly lost the CO and both Flight Commanders within 10 minutes after take off without any enemy aircraft in the Sector. It was dusk with very low cloud. Group asked for a section of three aircraft to be sent after an X raid. Mac and I as flight commanders were totally opposed as it was almost night and the weather was impossible. However, Don Finlay the CO insisted that we should carry out Group orders, but that he, Mac and I should make up the section. Squadron Leader Finlay took off on the flarepath followed seconds later by Mac and me. As soon as he was airborne Finlay realised that conditions were impossible for any flying and reported that he was landing at once - which he did. He overshot the flarepath, went across the Great North Road at high speed and finished up 200 yards away in a field with a badly damaged aircraft but was himself unhurt. Mac and I were watching this whilst circling on the circuit lighting. Suddenly without warning ALL the lights went out.It was like being enclosed in black velvet. I went on to instruments ready to climb up to get height and bale out, but fortunately Mac's outburst of "Colonial" language on the R/T assured flying control that there was still two more aircraft in the air. The circuit and runway lights came on again - what a relief. Mac landed next knowing that there was probably no wind or even down wind. Using all his experience he landed safely except that his Spitfire was firmly embedded in the hedge at the far end of the runway. The night was the blackest I have ever known. I was still orbiting having seen two crashes. The Spitfire is not good for night landings and even less so for a slow drag-in approach. Looking out from side to side as the only way to see the runway lights, I landed at the lowest possible speed, braked desperately and switched off. I finished close to Mac's aircraft, not in the hedge but only 20-30 feet short. Mac and I said very little to one another but we both knew we had shared a traumatic experience that we would never forget. What a terrible waste and how close to a terrible disaster on a sortie against which we had protested so strongly. There could have been no possible benefit from any flying at such a time. I wonder if Squadron and Group records show this as three sorties? Whenever Mac and I met, even 50 years later, we never failed to talk about this event. It had made an indelible impression on us. Finlay's refusal to listen to good advice from both his Flight Commanders had nearly cost three lives and three Spitfires.

'In 1941, it would take about 20 minutes to get a telephone call from London to Yorkshire through the operators. About 20 minutes after Don Finlay crashed over the Great North Road the phone rang in Catterick station sick quarters. It was Don's wife who said "I know my husband has had an accident, will you get the Squadron Doctor to tell me if he is safe, injured or killed." Doc was able to reassure her as at that moment Finlay walked out of the ambulance into sick quarters and spoke to her at once! Mrs Finlay lived in the suburbs east of London and must have asked for the connection within seconds of the crash - and she was 200 miles away. A confirmed case of ESP I would say - one of hundreds during the war.

'As life was rather quiet in April someone organised a Squadron shoot in the local woods. When the members of the squadron making up the party assembled, their miscellaneous garments were a sight to behold. As for the guns, or should I say weapons - any weapon that fired and could be found or borrowed was in use. Anything in the woods that flew, moved or just sat still was fired at. I am delighted to report that there were no casualties amongst the pilots. Also that the wood life and bird life were probably more frighted than damaged.

'Throughout my story of the squadron it will have been seen that I have on occasions been critical of controllers, Groups and Commands. This is intended. The years have confirmed that whilst the young men in the squadrons were giving their lives and fighting under great danger, the battle was put in jeopardy by the personal jealously and ambitions of the heavily braided. It is fortunate that the loyalty and dedication of our pilots overcame not only the Luftwaffe but also the effects of such ambitions.

'In his book "Tattered Battlements", Wing Commander Tom Johnston wrote about Battle of Britain pilots and their standards. I think it is very profound and correct, and I am sure he would have given me permission to quote from it:-

"A man was not judged by any of the old standards, race, birth, religion, wealth or membership of the best clubs, but according to his personal integrity. If he passed the test the other things did not matter - if he failed then they would not help him. It followed naturally that a service (squadron) which applied a universal standard should command a universal loyalty".

'This is how I remember the pilots, my friends and colleagues, of 41 (F) Squadron with whom I was privileged to serve.

'There were only four 41 Squadron pilots decorated in 1940. The first in 1941 did not occur until October'.

Peter Brown flew some 200 sorties during his time in Fighter Command, and made a number of combat claims, but for him there was to be no recognition of his service; yet another unsung hero. On June 28th, 1941, Flight Lieutenant Brown left 41 Squadron and became an instructor on Spitfires at 61 OTU, firstly at Heston, then at Rednal. On October 14th, 1942, he graduated from the Empire Central Flying School. Then followed a period instructing on Hurricanes before transfer to Flying Training Command on July 21st, 1943. On New Year's Day 1944, Peter was promoted to Squadron Leader and retained that rank when he left the RAF in 1945. Whilst there was to be no DFC, Squadron Leader Brown was awarded the Air Force Cross for his extensive work training pilots. In 'Civvy Street', Peter Brown entered the plastics industry, firstly as a jounalist, then as a technical manager and he was made a Fellow of the Plastics Institute for his contribution to the industry. He eventually retired from business in 1989. For the past 13 years, some of them overlapping his busy business life, Peter has also applied his gift as a healer to cancer sufferers in both clinics and hospices. He is undoubtedly yet another fine and remarkable man whose story should be told.

In addition to the fascinating account of his tour with 41 Squadron, Peter also sent some interesting observations regarding the Big Wing controversy. He is certainly well positioned to comment, and therefore this material is surely essential reading for any student of summer 1940:-

'For 50 years the informed and uninformed have been arguing the merits and demerits of Big Wings. Having flown in the Bader Wing on several occasions, including twice on September 15th, 1940, and having also served during the Battle of Britain in 11 Group, I feel I can offer a balanced view of the fors and againsts.

'The Battle of Big Wings versus Squadrons in the Battle of Britain was never in my opinion a tactical issue. The issue was essentially one of politics and based upon personality problems between personnel of air rank. The commanders of 10 Group and 11 Group, however, collaborated most effectively. The animosity between the commanders of 11 and 12 Groups might have lost us the Battle. How often have bad tactical decisions with high casualties been made in all three services because of personal pride and ambition.

'In August 1940, when the Battle of Britain was beginning to take shape, Lord Dowding should have enlarged 11 Group northwards to include Duxford and Fowlmere. He should then have transferred the five squadrons to 11 Group to be used as it wished, but probably as two or three squadron wings. Who can doubt the tactical advantages to the 11 Group commander of having an additional five squadrons at instant command in his own sector. 12 Group could have easily been protected by Hurricane squadrons. The only aircraft that could have reached even the sector coast would have been twin-engined bombers or Me 110s, against which the Hurricanes could have had tremendous success. In the event of a major raid on the Midlands the five Duxford squadrons could then have been sortied north to defend.

'We sat in 12 Group Spitfire Mk IIs at readiness from July to September, chasing the occasional X raid and flying later in the Duxford Wing. During that period of time 41 Squadron with Spitfire Mk Is, and indeed many others, were fighting to the death, going north for a short rest and then returning to fight again against desperate odds. Where are the tactics in using Spitfire squadrons in two adjoining Groups in such a different way? In 12 Group we were utterly frustrated. 12 Group had many squadrons at readiness. What a tremendous boost to Park if he had five of them in his direct control. But there was little chance of that. Leigh-Mallory wanted his aircraft used to shoot down enemy aircraft in 12 Group. But there weren't many enemy aircraft over 12 Group so we remained sitting at readiness.

'The major and most often voiced criticism of the Big Wing is that it took too long to form up. This is totally without foundation. Bader led the first Hurricane squadron out of Duxford, taking off into the prevailing SW wind. His two other Hurricane squadrons then followed in correct order within minutes. After two or three minutes flying SW, Bader executed a slow climbing turn to direct south - exactly where the Wing had been despatched, and enabling the following squadrons to cut the corner. The two Spitfire squadrons were based at Fowlmere, three miles to the west. We therefore took off parallel with the third Hurricane squadron which we could see, and on the flight south we climbed up to 15.000' as top cover. The Wing was already in formation except for height which we achieved en route. When London was reached each squadron was in its pre-arranged position. There was no wasted time in formal forming up. Of course there should be no confusion between the Duxford Big Wing of 1940 and the Wings used later in the sweeps over France. Their assembly procedures and functions were quite different. London would certainly be in our sight within 15 minutes after take-off.

'My main criticism of the five squadron Wing was that it was not possible for the Wing Leader to control five squadrons effectively under Battle of Britain conditions when the enemy were met. There were too many of our own people milling about and too many attacking one enemy aircraft. I would suggest that two or three squadron Wings would have been more effective, although not as prestigious of course, and would have shot down more aircraft. The two smaller Wings would have given the controllers a double chance at an interception. My view is that the significant contribution of the five squadron Wing was that on September 15th, and by the grace of God, we made interceptions with the two main German raids of that day. For days previously, the German aircrews had been told by their chiefs that on the basis of their claims and general intelligence RAF Fighter Command was finished, with only a few aircraft left. Imagine the psychological effect on those German aircrews over London to see 60, and probably looking like 100, RAF fighters diving out of the sky and attacking them, after they had been harried all the way in. The psychological effect was doubled when on the second main raid they were again attacked by a Wing of 60 aircraft. They were not to know, of course, that they were the same aircraft! I believe that with the heavy losses inflicted by 11 Group and the two interceptions by the five squadron Wing, that it became obvious on September 15th to both the German aircrews and their commanders that the RAF was in fact far from finished and that there was no hope for a German aerial victory over England in 1940.

'I believe that the Big Wing concept, which had a natural place later during the sweeps over France, was deliberately built up and publicised by 12 Group during the Battle of Britain as a means of trying to create 12 Group prestige and belittle the efforts of the squadrons in 11 Group. Park of 11 Group did magnificently. If Dowding had given him a further five squadrons under his own direct sector control he would have had the reserves he desperately needed. That would have been the correct tactical decision.

'In conclusion I would say that the Battle was fought in the south of England and over London. Tactically that is where all our best squadrons, well rested, and the best aircraft should have been. Our forces should not have been split by an out of date black line on the Group plotting table.

'The Battle of Britain was one of the most important battles in history and was fought over England in 1940 and won against superior odds. During the Battle, the serious problems caused by jealously and ambitions at air rank level should have been resolved resolutely and instantly. When the Battle ended in victory one would have expected that the Commander-in-Chief and the 11 Group Commander would have automatically received high honours, not only for themselves but as a reflection of the sacrifice of the many young pilots of Fighter Command. Both were, however, removed from office without any major recognition. Air Vice-Marshal Park was replaced by Air Vice-Marshal Leigh-Mallory who had battled against him and had helped create the myth of the Big Wing. The pilots who fought in the Battle of Britain never forgave the RAF and felt that the treatment of their leaders was only another sign of the political jockeying at high level which took place away from the dangers of the Battle'.

As Peter says, the controversy surrounding the Big Wing has already raged for over 50 years - I have little doubt that it will long continue to do so.

Peter Brown today.

Chapter Seven

Corporal Bob Morris

Corporal Bob Morris.

Bob Morris was the first person I ever met who had actually been involved in the Battle of Britain. During that time Bob was a Fitter IIE with a Spitfire unit, 66 'Clickety Click' Squadron. Bob's enthusiasm for the Spitfire remains as keen now, over 50 years later, as on the day that he caught his first glimpse of 66 Squadron at Coltishall as an impressionable 19-year-old. That enthusiasm has always been an inspiration to me personally. Not surprisingly in view of his great interest, Bob was amongst the first members of the Malvern Spitfire Team, which was formed in October 1986, and has served as vice-chairman for most of his membership. We have been delighted to welcome Bob at our various activities, aircraft recoveries, exhibitions and the like, and his input has always been invaluable, particularly in advising Dennis Williams on the aeronautical engineering aspect of our interest. Our friendship with Bob Morris certainly made me aware of the groundcrews' role and the dangers and deprivations that they too faced and which are all too often passed over by authors and historians.

In the 50th anniversary year of VE Day, I believe it only right that in addition to paying tribute to the pilots - our heroes all -we should also remember those like Bob Morris who served in a far less glamourous but no less essential role. Every pilot I have spoken to has only the highest regard for such men. Reproduced below is a transcript of a tape which Bob Morris recorded for me in late 1994. It is certainly an eye-opener:-

'How much I appreciate what you are doing in giving the groundcrews who served in squadrons during the Battle of Britain some recognition in your new book. I have noticed that when you tell people that you were there, they only want to speak to you if you were a pilot. They forget that without us the pilots would not have got off the ground! So I think that it is to your great credit that you are now going to put this right.

'I joined the RAF before the war started. I was more interested in the technical than flying side so studied aeronautical engineering at the RAF Technical School at Halton in Buckinghamshire. I was an apprentice being trained as a Fitter IIE (engines). I was still on my course when war came. Because of the urgent need for more personnel thereafter, other activities such as time off and sport were cancelled to get us trained quickly. In May 1940 I passed out as an Airman 1st Class, looked at the list pinned on the board and discovered that along with Cadman, Briggs and Elliot, I had been posted to 66 Squadron at Coltishall in 12 Group. I knew neither the location of Coltishall or what aircraft 66 Squadron had.

'Coltishall was in Norfolk, and my first glimpse of 66 Squadron was from the bus which travelled alongside the airfield for a short distance - what a thrill to see Spitfires! This was a young man's dream!

'In 66 Squadron I found that the set-up was that there were two groups of technical people who looked after the aircraft. The trades in the RAF were subdivided into five, the technical people being in the first and we did all the major work on the aircraft. Group Two were flight mechanics, the semi-skilled, and their job was to look after the aircraft's daily requirements, like the daily inspection: oil, petrol, tyre pressures, etc. In our group there was a Fitter Engines and a Fitter Airframe, likewise in the second there was a Flight Mechanic Engine and a Flight Mechanic Airframe. The latter two always remained with the same aircraft. The Flight Mechanic Engine would start up the aircraft's engine first thing in the morning, so that when a scramble call came the engine was already nice and warm. We Fitter IIEs, however, never had an aircraft of our own as there were less of us, so we could be called upon to work on any of the Squadron's Spitfires. We used to do the 30, 60 and 90 hour inspections. When each aircraft had done the maximum amount of flying hours per its particular type of engine, it had an engine change - we would also do those.

'My first jobs were mainly inspections, as opposed to repair work. I remember a pilot getting into the cockpit and I helped him to get going, pulled the chocks away and set him up to fly. As he taxied out I thought to myself "I bet he doesn't know that this is my first attempt!" Perhaps he wouldn't have taken off so confidently had he known!

'We shared Coltishall with the Hurricanes of 242 Squadron, but we were not there for long as we were moved to Kenley in 11 Group, right down in the thick of it, the Battle of Britain having started by this time. When we arrived at Kenley on September 3rd, 1940, it was an absolute shambles, there was hardly a building left standing. As we drove around the aerodrome to our assembly point, I saw a car park full of vehicles - but there was not one which hadn't been riddled by gunfire or shrapnel. There were shelters destroyed, buildings flattened. We were only at Kenley for a week, but that short time was absolutely devastating. During that week I think we lost eight pilots, so at the end of it we were practically out of action.

'From a ground viewpoint we had to learn very quickly about air raids which were incoming thick and fast. Once I looked up and saw five parachutes descending. We were now dispersed around the edge of the airfield with plenty of space between each aircraft. We could not put the aircraft either in a hangar or in a group for fear of them being wiped out together. However, it meant that we had to work on them out in the open, often without any cover when a raid occurred. They had built some blast pens at Kenley, but nowhere near enough, so you could be a quarter of a mile away from any shelter. It is perhaps surprising but you do get used to it, almost blasé about it, in fact. We used to carry on working after the siren had gone, right up until the Germans were practically overhead. If you then left your aircraft and lay down on the ground some distance away from it, the chances of being killed by a bomb were remote. Strafing was a bit more hazardous, but the greatest problem was bomb-blast, i.e. what it actually threw into the air. If it exploded near a road, building or runway then huge slabs and chunks of concrete and masonry could come falling down on you. You therefore tended to lie there and keep your fingers crossed that when all the rubbish thrown up came down, none of it hit you.

'On September 10th, 1940, 66 Squadron moved to Gravesend, which was no more than a civilian flying club airfield. We were the only squadron there, at what was Biggin Hill's satellite. At Gravesend we looked down on the River Thames, opposite Tilbury, and I remember bombs hitting large floating oil tanks in the river there. I always admired the sailors of the little boats, tugs and the like, that used to pull out those tanks which were on fire, to stop the flames spreading. However, we were not bombed at Gravesend. There was only one hangar there, our dining room, a small hut for flying control and a pilots' crew room and that was it. Without much to hit on a grass airfield, we would have been hard to put out of action anyway.

'By this time though we were finding the living conditions at Gravesend a bit trying. We had a half day off every 10 days. We used to spend that half day fast asleep. We were exhausted working such long hours, from dawn to dusk. At Gravesend there were no billets, so a restaurant about 3/4 mile away, called

"Laughing Waters", adjacent to a big lake, was commandeered. We were taken there in our usual mode of motorised transport - a Bedford three-tonner. The building was just a shell, nothing on the floor and all we had to sleep in was two blankets. It was a mighty cold place just with two blankets and the floor, on the edge of a lake! The only thing that had not been taken away were the rowing boats, so every morning to get warm we rowed around the lake.

'Fortunately we were not in "Laughing Waters" for very long before they decided to move our billets again, this time to Cobham Hall, the Earl of Darnley's estate. We slept in the servants' quarters, but at least we had beds. We were quite near Cobham village, and it was strange, wherever we were the officers would find a restaurant or similar for their evening drinks whilst we other ranks would find a pub or similar. We never went into theirs and they never into ours.

'As we had lost so many pilots at Kenley, we now had replacements arriving at Gravesend, although we still lost several more pilots at Gravesend. However, one of the young pilots that got killed there I had actually got to know quite well, Pilot Officer Reilley, he was an American who got into the RAF through a Canadian connection, as of course the USA was still neutral at this time. He was shot down and killed. By this time we were quite accustomed to losses, it sounds terrible to say that now but I think that you can get used to anything. I was on my half day, fast asleep on my bed at Cobham Hall as we usually were on our half days off, when the Sergeant stuck his head round the door and said "Everybody on Half Day - outside, best blue, best greatcoat, webbing belt round your waist and get on the lorry!" He did not tell us what for but we got dressed and piled onto the lorry - it took us to a church near Gravesend, and it was then that we realised that we were going to be Guard of Honour at Pilot Officer Reilley's funeral. As he was from overseas, there were no family there, but we sat in the church for the service. A four-wheel trailer was hitched up to our truck and the coffin was put on this trailer and we had to march behind it through the middle of Gravesend to the cemetery where the burial took place. Afterwards we piled on the lorry to go back to Cobham Hall. On the way back someone said that since he had arrived in the UK, Reilley had got married and his wife had recently given birth to a little baby boy. The end of this story is that in 1983 I attended a 66 Squadron reunion at Kenley - there I met a man in his 40s, a family man, who was Reilley's son!

'At Gravesend we got a new CO - Squadron Leader Athol Forbes replaced Rupert Leigh, and we lost Pilot Officers Mather and Corbett, and Flight Lieutenant Gillies.

'Our entertainment was to walk to Rochester or Strood to the pictures, then walk back again. We also went to dances at the Co-op Hall in Gravesend.

'During the day it was long hours, work, work, work, and then more work. Non-stop. It is surprising, however, how you can get used to a new routine. I remember being at Gravesend on what was considered at the time to have been the great day - September 15th, 1940, now celebrated as Battle of Britain Day.

At Gravesend we used to watch the German aircraft coming in, heading for London or elsewhere, the trails in the sky, and how relieved we were when they passed overhead and went straight on! During that September, as we were so close to the river, there would often be a ground mist which lasted all day. You may have a day with absolute thick fog in which no aircraft could take-off, or no bombing could take place because the Germans could not see us, we used to get all our work done by early afternoon and then, inevitably, a football always seemed to appear from somewhere, and a game would start on the edge of the aerodrome. We never used to pick a side, you just joined in with whichever side appeared to be winning, and that was the way you kicked! On one occasion we were busy playing in thick fog - you could only see about half-way across the airfield - when we heard these German aircraft circling round above us looking for something to bomb. Suddenly, right through the fog came a parachute flare which landed on our football pitch - someone kicked some dirt onto it and we just kept on playing - the Germans then flew off. No-one ran for shelter, that was how used we had become to it all.

'You never heard anyone talk about defeat. Of course we were not conversant with all the facts, though occasionally we would get some air force "Bigwig" come down and give us a pep-talk.

'It was towards the end of our time at Gravesend that we began to see the DFCs and DFMs being awarded to the pilots. And of course I remember the aircraft damaged in combat. I remember Pilot Officer "Bogle" Bodie coming back with his port mainplane knocked about by a cannon shell, and I had to rip part of the aileron off for him which he proudly took as a souvenir. I always remember a Spitfire coming in making a horrible whistling noise - it had a bullet hole right through a propeller blade! We did not have a new propeller, however, so we smoothed out the hole and drilled corresponding holes in the other two blades - it then flew for another fortnight with that same airscrew! We had to drill the other holes as when the propeller is assembled it is very finely balanced to prevent vibration.

'66 Squadron must have been about the first squadron to fly a clipped wing Spitfire, that was at Kenley actually and by accident - a Spitfire came in with a badly mangled wing-tip and other damage, so it had to go back to the maintenance depot as it could not be repaired on the squadron. We took off the damaged wing-tip, put doped canvas on the square-ended wing-tip as it now was, and did likewise with the other wing. That aircraft flew back to the depot as a clipped wing Spitfire, the actual official modification not coming out, of course, until 1942.

'On October 30th, 1940, we moved from Gravesend to West Malling, although I could never understand why they moved us such short distances. A squadron move is a very complicated business involving a great deal of men, engineering equipment and spares. West Malling is about two minutes flying time from Gravesend, so I could never understand the logic behind moving the squadron there, about 12-15 miles. Someone said that it was to confuse the enemy - it certainly confused us! We were there no more than a couple of weeks before abandoning West Malling as the airfield was like a bog - the aircraft would land and then sink up to their axles in mud. We were then moved to Biggin Hill on November 7th. Upon arrival we found that station to be a shambles too. There were very few buildings still standing. There were no billets etc., so the military commandeered a Women's Institute hall - no beds, nothing - so we were given white linen sacks. A farmer gave us a load of straw, so we filled up our sacks with straw, so you just walked in, found a little bit of empty floor, plonked it down with your two blankets, and that was where you lived. Our washing facilities were fire buckets. The only time you had hot water was when a fire bucket was heated over the stove. Because of the conditions under which we were both working and living, we were getting very tired. You can stick this kind of thing for a while, but after a while the strain begins to tell. However, we soldiered on.

'So far as the aerodrome was concerned, it was another hard slog, no buildings to work in so again always working out in the open. We were sharing the aerodrome with 92 and 74 Squadrons. Once again it was a case of scrambles, sirens telling us to take shelter, carry on working, inspection procedures, just the hard, unromantic slog. We did have some raids and bombs dropped, but what can you say about it? One raid in the end tends to be just a repetition of the foregoing. We used to watch the Germans going over, heading for London, which was a relief for us. I saw some dogfights over Biggin Hill, we were in an aircraft bay and saw a German aircraft on fire, and four parachutes come out, two of which were on fire. We saw these two German aircrew falling faster and faster until the parachute had completely burnt away and they fell to their deaths. Although you knew that enemy aircraft were being shot down, you rarely saw one as they were regularly collected by the Maintenance Units. At Biggin Hill, however, I had the chance to look over an Me 109 which was on the station and virtually complete. I looked in the cockpit and by our standards it was nowhere near up to the Spitfire's instrumentation standards, it was very bleak.

'There was a tradition at Christmas where airmen were waited upon by senior NCOs and Officers. So it was that at our Biggin Hill Christmas Dinner 1940 we were so waited upon. We had worked the whole day without any scrambles, so we assumed that it was the same on the other sides, a kind of unoffical ceasefire.

'We moved from Biggin Hill and left 11 Group to join 10 Group at Exeter on February 24th, 1941. From Exeter we provided protection for the docks at Plymouth and Bristol. 504 Squadron's Hurricanes were also at Exeter. We were still well within the action. Once again no billets, so a house was commandeered for us to live in. Because we were living outside the camp, we devised a system whereby a team of us fitters would take it in turns to sleep on the aerodrome, in a wooden hut, every third night. The German bombers soon paid us a visit. It happened when we were sleeping in the wooden hut, we were bombed quite heavily. The Sergeant in charge and myself, I was an LAC, got out of the hut,

Members of 'A' Flight, 66 Squadron, at Exeter photographed by another pilot, Plt Off 'Duke' Collingridge, sometime between February and April 1941. From left: Sgt Thompson, F/Sgt DAG Hunt, Sgt DCO Campbell, Sgt Reid, Plt Off Clements, Sgt Stephens (Armaments NCO), and Sgt WJ Corbin. The Spitfire Mk IIA is P7843 LZ-C, 'Aldergrove' which was one of many presented by the Belfast Telegraph. The aircraft is having its guns harmonised.

but as there was no shelter we jumped down into a ditch which had running water. We got into it and crouched down with bombs and incendiaries showering down all around us, it was quite frightening. It is strange, but by the note of a bomb's whistle you can accurately estimate the distance from you it is going to hit. Eventually we heard one coming down and the Sergeant shouted "Heads down! This is ours!" It was close enough - that next morning I measured from where I was to the edge of the crater and it was only 25-30'. We had been showered in rubble and mortar, and the bomb blocked up the stream so that the water started rising so that we had to get out. Our hut had completely collapsed. We had to get out and find somewhere else to shelter, but the problem with negotiating an unlit airfield at night is that there are many obstacles in the shape of equipment left lying about, like hand-pulled oil bowsers and racks of oxygen bottles. Fortunately the bombers soon disappeared, so we soon went around putting incendiaries out, using the sand that had been left in piles at various locations on the airfield. Unfortunately they had not put any anti-freeze in with the sand so at first the tumps were frozen solid! I spent the next couple of hours with a big piece of timber breaking up the sand whilst others rushed around with spadefuls. Several aircraft were damaged on the ground. By morning it was obvious that as a squadron we were going to be non-operational for a while. I

remember going back and
looking at where I had been
crouched in the ditch and
around that position there were
about a dozen incendiaries
sticking out of the ground, and
some in the water even closer to
where I had been. If one of those
hit you you would have been
dead. We got them all out before
being relieved by the daylight
shift.

German bombs dropped on Exeter airfield but which failed to explode - since defused!

'Shortly after this they moved us to a billet on the aerodrome. If the night
bombers came over we would get under our beds, which was also protection if
the hut came down on top of you. One night it was quite moonlit and I went
outside to see the German bombers going over. Incendiaries had been dropped
and there were fires everywhere. We ran down to see what we could do. There
was a Wellington that had landed for an overnight stop and it was well alight.
We had to go close to it when we were running to help our own squadron, but an
officer shouted to us to get some fire extinguishers. We had to do what he said,
so we got a couple of hand-held extinguishers, and this officer had us standing in
front of the mainplane of this Wellington which was blazing madly all over,
squirting two hand-held fire extinguishers on to it! The silly sod stood there
guiding us where to squirt them - frankly it was like peeing in the Thames to
raise the water level! At the same time there was .303 ammunition going off
from the aircraft's machine-guns, and we did not know whether there were any
bombs on board. This daft so and so just hadn't got a clue. Soon the extinguishers
ran out, so he ordered us off to get some more, so off we went - we knew he didn't
know who we were because he was not one of our officers, so once we got out of
sight we just carried on to our own squadron. There we had the job of putting
out incendiaries which had also started a lot of fires on the headquarters brick

buildings. As the firemen proper
were committed there, we had
to look after ourselves. We later
went up to the cookhouse to see
if there was any cocoa going, so
we filled our mugs full and went
back to our billets to sleep. Next
morning we were working flat
out again. Strangely in all the
nights we were bombed, 504
Squadron   was   always
untouched.

The burnt-out wreck of the Wellington at Exeter.

Amongst those 66 Squadron Spitfires damaged at Exeter during the bombing was X4036, LZ-X. This was a famous Battle of Britain aircraft having been the regular mount of 234 Squadron's ace, Plt Off Bob Doe. Coded AZ-D, this aircraft was painted by master aviation artist Frank Wootten in his 'Down on the Farm'. X4036 later perished in a fatal flying accident.

A 66 Squadron Spitfire Mk IA apparently having suffered a landing accident at Exeter during early 1941.

'On another night we were bombed again, as we ran for cover a friend of mine tripped straight over a bomb that was half sticking out of the ground! He just picked himself up and carried on whilst I gave it a very wide berth!

'One morning our pilots were supposed to be on stand-by, but did not arrive at dispersal by the appointed hour. 66 Squadron was then sent to Perranporth in Cornwall as a punishment. We were right on the cliffs - when the Spitfires took off they were almost immediately over the sea. Again there were no billets so we lived at the "Atlantic Hotel", but again there was no furniture so it was back to the floor. "Ginger" Finch and I found a little place nearby that did bed and breakfast, so we stayed there one night - what a treat to sleep in a real bed!

'By and large we groundcrew were all quite young - I was 19, indeed the pilots were often only in their early 20s. Being young was an advantage because then you do not see the dangers. Now, over 50 years later, I look back and think that I would be much more frightened if I had to do it all again. Being young you tended to take it all so much lightly.

'Whilst at Perranporth my time with the Squadron came to an end and I was posted overseas, so that is the story of my life with 66 Squadron. Now I look back on those times with great pride and affection'.

Despite having studied the Battle of Britain since childhood, I was unaware, prior to listening to Bob's tape, just how hard and long the groundcrews did actually work, and of course during the bombing there were also casualties amongst their numbers. I was perhaps most surprised by the appalling living conditions, if they could be called that, that these men were expected to exist in; shocking, desperate though the hour undoubtedly was.

Bob Morris left the air force after the Second World War and became an engineer. He retired in 1986 and now lives close to Shobdon airfield in Herefordshire, where Mike Bush once instructed, his story also being told in this book. I hope that Bob's friendship and enthusiasm are around for many years yet to come.

Bob Morris, right, pictured at the Malvern Spitfire Team's excavation of Spitfire R6644 in September 1987. The excavation was organised by the Team to raise money for both the RAF Association's 'Wings Appeal' and the Polish Air Force Association, the Spitfire having been flown by Plt Off Franek Surma of 308 (Polish) Squadron on the day of the crash at Madresfield, May 11th, 1941. Here Bob discusses the identification of some recovered items with the Polish representatives present, Battle of Britain pilots Sqn Ldrs 'Gandy' Drobinski DFC and Ludwik Martel. Bob's enthusiasm for the Spitfire remains undiminished more than half a century since he first saw the Spitfires of his beloved 66 Squadron.

Chapter Eight

Flight Lieutenant Keith Lawrence DFC

Pilot Officer Keith Lawrence pictured in 1940.

In addition to the British and those free pilots from the occupied lands who fought in 1940, we must also remember those who came from the Commonwealth countries. For example, some 4,000 New Zealanders served with the RAF during the Second World War; many perished, but one survivor is Keith Ashley Lawrence.

Born on November 25th, 1919, and educated at Invercargill, Keith Lawrence applied to join the Royal Air Force via the Direct Entry Commonwealth Recruiting Scheme in 1938. In March 1939, he was amongst a contingent of New Zealanders sent to train with the RAF in England. After flying training he was granted a Short Service Commission in the air force with the rank of Pilot Officer and posted to 234 Squadron in November. The squadron was equipped with Bristol Blenheim Mk IF fighters, but received Spitfires in March 1940. During the Battle of Britain, 234 Squadron was a part of 10 Group, initially flying from St Eval in Cornwall, and then moving east to Middle Wallop on

August 14th. The 11 Group controller frequently called upon 10 Group for assistance during the Battle of Britain, and so it was that the Middle Wallop Spitfire squadrons, including 234, often found themselves in action over south-east England during that fateful summer.

Pilot Officer Lawrence was an experienced fighter pilot by the time he fired his guns in anger for the first time. On July 8th, 1940 - two days before the official start of the Battle of Britain - he shared a Ju 88 destroyed with two other pilots 25 miles south-east of Land's End. Four days later he was allowed half a Ju 88 damaged over St Eval itself. On August 24th he destroyed an Me 110 near the Isle of Wight. On September 7th, Goering launched the major aerial assault against London, and 234 Squadron was called into action by 11 Group over the capital. On that day, Pilot Officer Lawrence damaged a Do 17 and destroyed an Me 109. When 234 Squadron returned to St Eval on September 9th, 1940, Pilot Officer Lawrence remained in the battle zone and joined 603 Squadron at Hornchurch. On September 15th - now celebrated as Battle of Britain Day - 603 Squadron's Spitfires clashed with Me 109s south-east of Maidstone; Keith Lawrence destroyed one and damaged two others.

Pilot Officers Mortimer-Rose and Lawrence of 234 Squadron during the Battle of Britain. 'Morty' was killed in the desert during 1943, aged 22 Years. The latter is wearing an armband indicating him to be Duty Officer.

On October 8th, 1940, a new unit formed at Gravesend, 421 Flight, which was originally a detached flight of 66 Squadron. 421 Flight was equipped with six Spitfire Mk IIs, and commanded by Flight Lieutenant CP Green, an Auxiliary pilot. Another 10 pilots comprised 421 Flight's flying personnel, including Pilot Officer Keith Lawrence, who now remembers:-

'It was in October 1940, that, at the instigation of the Prime Minister, No 421 Flight was formed as a reconnaissance unit at Gravesend, known as the "Jim Crow" flight. The Flight's pilots were drawn from squadrons which had fought throughout the Battle of Britain. Their new purpose, flying singly or in pairs, was to report on the movement of ships or the build-up of Luftwaffe formations over the Channel. Conjecture is that here was cover, put in place by Churchill and Dowding, to use the Ultra code secrets to Fighter Command's greatest advantage.

'Operation Sealion, the code name for the planned German invasion of Britain, was called off by Hitler on October 12th, 1940, following the Luftwaffe's failure

A 421 Flight Spitfire
at Gravesend. The
Flight was originally a
detached flight of 66
Squadron, hence the
fuselage codes of LZ.
To differentiate 421
Flight's Spitfires,
however, a square dot
has been painted
between the code
letters.

to gain air superiority over the RAF fighters defending the South-East and Southern England. The Battle of Britain officially ended on October 31st, but the enemy raids and fighter clashes continued throughout November and December, a period since called "the forgotten months of 1940".

'In November 1940, 421 Flight was stationed at RAF Hawkinge on the high ground above the Straits of Dover. The Flight's first task daily was to fly a weather patrol by a single Spitfire along the Kent coast between North Foreland and Dungeness to obtain met "actuals" on the cloud conditions and formations, at the same time listening out for any operational instructions from Fighter Control. The pilot detailed for the weather flight would take-off between first light and sunrise.

'On the morning of November 27th, I get airborne into a cloudy sky and fly uneventfully northeastwards to North Foreland and then turn 180 degrees at about 8,000' in the direction of Dungeness. There being nothing on the R/T to warn or distract, I cannot but be aware of the beauty, loneliness and apparent peacefulness which one experiences when flying between layers of cloud at that height, more so in the half light preceding sunrise. With not a sound in my headphones, but on constant lookout, I head towards Deal still at 8,000' and flying above some 5/10 stratocu and overhead 10/10 cu and stratocu. Suddenly one corner of that scene turns tranquillity to action, in a second. There, slightly on my port side, 500' below, streaking eastwards through a gap in the cloud towards the coast and France are three Me 109s in fairly close formation. At that speed not a second to lose, full throttle, stuff the nose down, switch on reflector sight, draw a bead. I start firing, three maybe four seconds; one instant later I am falling earthwards in my stockinged feet, slightly to my right I glimpse one wing of my aircraft rotating, falling as if a leaf. Come on now, get things in their right order! Parachute, its D-ring is on your left side, so reach across for it with your right hand; right hand won't move; try assisting right hand with left hand..... I am still falling (presumably by this time at 120 mph) so must get a move on. I scrabble around with my left hand trying to get at the left-sided release handle which will open my chute.

'Success. The proverbial sigh of relief, instantly cut short as I realise I am fast drifting in a westerly wind over the coast and out to a sea capped with white waves. Minutes later I am plunged into the cold, cold sea of late November, about a mile from land. With my right arm useless I must, left-handed, find the tube with which to inflate my life-jacket, unbuckle my parachute harness and somehow keep my head above water. Within minutes I am coughing, spluttering, choking, swallowing much sea water; the parachute shroud-lines are everywhere, like a web. The Mae West does not inflate, its rubber evidently split by the ejection force on my Sutton-harness, which supposedly holds the pilot so firmly in the cockpit. With but one arm and one leg, seemingly I am losing, engulfed in the cold wateriness I cannot rise above.

'Then suddenly it seems looming over me is a high dark wall from which extends an arm of great strength to haul me bodily onto the deck of a boat manned by RN sailors. Most of the next 24 hours are but grey memories. I am in Ramsgate Hospital with fractured right leg, lacerated left leg and dislocated right shoulder. After one week I am considered sufficiently fit to be transferred 90 miles, most painfully, by ambulance with solid-tyred wheels (I am convinced) to RAF Hospital Halton. Here, in due course, I have the broken leg bones replaced in their correct position and fixed with metal screws. This operation is performed by none less than one of the King's personal orthopaedic surgeons who, for the duration of the war, had been appointed Consultant to the RAF Medical Service.

'Thus began, in the company of scores of other aircrew in similar plight, the long return to fitness and flying (for me one year) in the hands of dedicated doctors, nurses and physios whose efforts have so often gone unrecognised.

'This simple recounting of an experience which befell many a pilot or other aircrew shot down in wartime, tells but part of the story behind the announcement in the newspapers or on the radio, "one of our aircraft was lost", and its background and its consequences; one or two I now add as a footnote.

'On the morning of this episode, my arrival at the airfield dispersal hut, being slightly less than punctual (as is the wont of some), I just grabbed the first life-jacket to hand; at a time when only some of the Flight's Mae Wests had been modified by the addition of a fluorescein dye packet. I had it from my naval rescuers that they steered to the still inflated parachute blowing across the surface, but on reaching it, found no body. Only then, some distance away, did they sight my life-saving patch of fluorescent green sea water.

'Many years later when this had become just an event in the distant past, I became aware of a group of young enthusiasts from another generation delving into aviation archaeology and history. One such society was busy trying to locate the engine of my aircraft which had buried itself in soft ground near the village of Finglesham two miles north-west of Deal. This lead enabled me to ascertain for myself, by talking to Finglesham's older inhabitants, that the crashing aircraft had caused no injury. Further enquiries brought about a meeting with a former young farm worker, who, that morning had heard the sound of gunfire above cloud and later the same morning found the wing of my Spitfire in a field.

'Curiosity mounting, I decided to look for information which might tell me more about this sortie flown by four German fighters on the morning of November 27th, 1940. The nearest I would get was from the Dover Post of the Royal Observer Corps' archive covering November 22nd to December 4th, 1940, which recorded each morning within a few minutes of 0700 hours GMT (beginning of first light), "hostile heard". Was my assailant one of a regular dawn patrol flown by a German Schwarm over Kent? The answer to this question may well lie in the archives of the Y Service, the intelligence service which intercepted all German R/T transmissions, but the transcripts of these are closed to public access. However that may be, the historical researchers had access to German records of combat reports and were able to inform me that I was a victim of Oberleutnant Gustav "Mickey" Sprick, Staffelkapitän of 8/JG26. He had been amongst the first German fighter

Oberleutnant Gustav 'Mickey' Sprick, Staffelkapitän of 8/JG26 who shot down Plt Off Keith Lawrence on November 27th, 1940. Sprick was killed in action the following year when the wing of his Me 109F collapsed during a dogfight.

pilots with 20 victories, and had received his Knight's Cross on October 1st, 1940. He was credited with 31 victories. On June 28th, 1941, Sprick was shot down and killed over France.

'It was a little over one year, after recovery in hospital and a refresher course at a Spitfire OTU, that I was again to make close acquaintance with JG26 when posted to a fighter squadron in Malta. Based in Sicily, Luftwaffe bombers attacked the island of Malta three times a day, their fighter escort being provided by 7/JG26.

'What I would have wished to make a final postscript to my adventure was the discovery of the names of my Royal Navy rescuers and their ship. Though this is not yet possible, I give thanks, as must many other of my fellow pilots of those days'.

Flying Hurricanes with 185 Squadron over Malta during the bitter fighting of spring 1942, Flight Lieutenant Lawrence made several more combat claims. The squadron received Spitfires during the early summer, and Keith became CO, but he was posted home in August and became a Spitfire instructor. In September he was awarded the DFC. After other training appointments, he returned to operational flying in February 1945, as a supernumerary Flight Lieutenant on 124 Squadron, flying Spitfires carrying 1,000lb bomb-loads to make dive-bombing attacks on the German V2 rocket launching sites on the coast of Holland. After the war Keith Lawrence returned to his native New Zealand where he served as a Flying Officer and Air Traffic Controller in the Territorial Air Force. He later returned to England and a new life in Sussex, but is now retired and living in Devon.

As is now widely known, the Malvern Spitfire Team's policy is to undertake research as professionally and thoroughly as possible, and it was in this vein that 22-year-old team-member Antony Whitehead peered 'through the looking glass' at the history of Spitfire X4036. During the Battle of Britain this aircraft was on charge with 234 Squadron as AZ-D, and was the regular mount of Flying Officer Bob Doe, one of Fighter Command's top scoring pilots during 1940. In fact, X4036 and Bob Doe have been immortalised on canvas by Frank Wootton in his painting 'Down on the Farm' which shows the Spitfire flying over a downed German aircraft. During the bombing of Exeter airfield in 1941 (see Bob Morris' story), X4036 was on charge with 66 Squadron and was amongst the aircraft damaged in the raid. Finally, X4036 crashed, killing the pilot, at Cambridge in Gloucestershire whilst with 52 OTU at Aston Down. Antony's preliminary research identified the Spitfire's flights with 234 Squadron, and contact was made with Wing Commander Bob Doe DSO DFC, and other pilots, including Flight Lieutenant Keith Lawrence DFC, who had not personally flown X4036 but had been with 234 Squadron at the same time. Although nothing was found at the crash site, a real bonus came from the album of Flight Lieutenant Mike Bush DFC, whose story is also told in this book, which showed a damaged X4036 at Exeter; Mike was also stationed there at the time, with 504 Squadron, and had taken the photograph himself.

Following various correspondence and telephone calls, Keith Lawrence was kind enough to join us at Westland Helicopters for the launch of 'Angriff Westland' in September 1994. It was there that an excited Antony Whitehead related to me the story of November 27th, 1940, as told to him by Keith, and a mental note was made there and then to seek his co-operation in respect of this book, which I already had in mind. As with many of those included in this volume, that co-operation was not at first an easy matter due to the dreaded 'line shooting' syndrome and the pilot's sincere modesty and genuine desire to remain anonymous; Keith Lawrence was persuaded, however, and kindly made his contribution to this book for which I thank him.

Keith Lawrence pictured in 1994.

Chapter Nine

Wing Commander Roger Boulding

Pilot Officer Roger Boulding pictured in 1940 with his dog, Sam.

As an embryonic wartime aviation researcher and author, amongst the first projects I undertook were the histories of several presentation Spitfires from my local area. P8045 and '46 were both Mk IIAs built at Castle Bromwich, and were paid for by donations from the citizens of Worcester. The Spitfires were known as 'City of Worcester I' and 'II' respectively. My project entailed plotting the 'biography' of each aircraft, which of course involved tracing the pilots who once flew to battle in them. One tentative letter of inquiry was sent to Wing Commander RJE Boulding, who, so the Operations Record Book recorded, had flown 'City of Worcester II' with 74 'Tiger' Squadron. The Wing Commander's response was both prompt and positive. Thereafter commenced a long period of friendship during which Roger and I corresponded frequently and met on a number of occasions, and he appropriately became a patron of the Malvern Spitfire Team.

Roger Boulding was a career officer and received his commission in 1938, learning to fly at 6 EFTS Sywell alongside a young Irishman destined to become one of the war's greatest fighter pilots and leaders - Brendan 'Paddy' Finucane. The outbreak of war found Pilot Officer Boulding flying Fairey Battle light-bombers with the Advanced Air Striking Force (AASF) in France. During the *blitzkrieg* of May 1940, Roger flew several sorties, but, 'when things turned a bit sour over there', he managed to escape the disaster of France and flew from Dieppe to Hawkinge in a Tiger Moth. In August he was posted to fly Spitfires with 74 Squadron at Wittering. Previously the 'Tigers' had been heavily engaged in Operation Dynamo and the Battle of Britain from bases in 11 Group, their CO being the legendary South African fighter pilot and leader, Squadron Leader 'Sailor' Malan DFC & Bar. On September 14th Roger damaged a Ju 88 north of Ipswich, and a Do 17 near Sheringham on September 24th. Over Harwich on October 5th he destroyed a Do 215, and an Me 109 over Dover on December 12th. On May 7th, 1941, he destroyed an Me 109 and damaged another in a dogfight over Margate. However, in that engagement his Spitfire was damaged in the petrol tank and coolant system which necessitated a forced landing at Manston.

Roger Boulding's next victory was scored under interesting circumstances.

It was the night of Saturday 10th May, 1941. Flying Officer Roger Boulding flew Supermarine Spitfire Mk II, P8380, ZP-Q, on patrol above London. The capital was ablaze. The German bomber force had commenced an attack at 2315 hrs; during the night over 500 aircraft dropped more than 700 tonnes of high explosives. In the streets of London the firemen fought desperately to control in excess of 2,000 fires - a losing battle as the raid had coincided with a full-moon spring low tide, which severely restricted the fire fighters' water supply. By the end of the raid over 1,000 Londoners were dead and another 2,000 injured. This raid, reflected the night blitz at its zenith.

Night-fighting was, at this early stage of the war, in its infancy. The development of Airborne Interception (AI) radar at the Telecommunications Research Establishment, and its Telecommunications Flying Unit, later to be located at Malvern and Defford respectively, was still in its initial stages. Eventually, AI equipped Bristol Beaufighters and de Havilland Mosquitos would take their toll of the raiders to the extent that the German bomber force was no longer free to roam over the British Isles by night. The night blitz against English cities commenced with the Luftwaffe's defeat in the Battle of Britain, their bombers unable to operate further over England during the day due to the heavy losses already suffered and which it was unable to sustain any longer. Fighter Command faced the enemy with Boulton Paul Defiants and Bristol Blenheims as standard night-fighting aircraft. Supermarine Spitfire and Hawker Hurricane day fighters were used in an attempt to fill the night sky with RAF fighters in the hope that one of them would stumble into a German bomber. The Spitfire was not a good night flying aircraft; visibility was poor, as the two rows of exhausts in front of the pilot glowed brightly and ruined his night vision, and the attitude during the approach to land meant that the pilot's view of the airfield below was virtually non-existent. So desperate was the situation after dark, however, that many Spitfire squadrons were used for nocturnal defensive operations. Co-ordinated efforts of large numbers of fighters were known as 'Fighter Nights'. On such a sortie was Flying Officer Boulding engaged on the night in question, and flying with him were other 74 Squadron stalwarts, including Squadron Leader John Mungo-Park DFC, Flight Lieutenant John Freeborn DFC, Pilot Officer Bob Poulton, and Sergeant Tony Mould.

As he patrolled at 18,000' above the blazing capital, Flying Officer Boulding, or 'Knockout 17' as he was known to the fighter controller below, experienced problems with his airscrew pitch control. Although 74 Squadron was then based at Gravesend, that night it was operating from West Malling. Due to the mechanical defect, 'Knockout 17' turned for home. Having descended to 17,000', on a south-easterly course, Flying Officer Boulding saw a twin-engined machine at the same height, travelling in the same direction and about 200 yards on his starboard side. Cautiously he approached the machine, from behind and below, and identified it as a hostile aircraft. Lining up the squat Heinkel 111 in his gunsight he squeezed the gun button, firing from 50 - 100 yards behind the Heinkel. A hail of .303 machine-gun bullets tore into the bomber in a steady burst. The Spitfire pilot could see De Wilde incendiary ammunition striking the fuselage and a mass of very large, bright sparks. The Heinkel lost height, pursued by 'Knockout 17', who fired further short bursts, but this time experiencing some problems in lining up his target due to ice on his Spitfire's bulletproof windscreen. The German pilot decided that his best tactics were to fly as close to the ground as possible, thus presenting a target that was difficult to see, and which meant that the Spitfire was silhouetted against the moonlit sky to the advantage of the Heinkel's gunners, who fired several accurate bursts at their tormentor. Flying Officer Boulding was able to give a few more short bursts before losing sight of his target, which he last saw still travelling south-east at about midnight, about 10 miles from Maidstone. 'Knockout 17' landed at West Malling at 0010 hrs.

The raider was an He 111H-5 of 5/KG 53, coded A1 + JN. When it reached Ashford the crippled bomber was down to rooftop height, losing altitude in a steady, controlled descent. It eventually alighted in a field behind Church Road, Kennington, Ashford. Within a matter of minutes a detachment of soldiers were on the scene from a nearby guardroom, and captured the crew, Hauptmann Hufenreuther, Feldwebel Führthmann, Unteroffiziers Gerhardt and Berzbach, and Gefreiter Weber.

In 1988 Roger Boulding gave me his recollections of the combat:-

'We were operating from West Malling and the general idea was that, over the full moon period, the AA guns were restricted to 12,000' over Central London. Over Outer London they could fire up to maximum, and outside the barrage the night-fighters were operating under close control. We day fighters were sent up to the central area at 500' intervals to patrol individually. The theory was that you got through the barrage into the patrol area via a "gate" marked by two green searchlights fixed in a vertical position. In practice I don't think this bit ever worked too well!

Views of the 5/KG53 He 111 A1+JN shot down by Plt Off Roger Boulding at Ashford, Kent, on the night of May 10th/11th, 1941. Note the matt black distemper hurriedly applied to the aircraft, indicating the bomber's previous role as a daylight raider during the Battle of Britain.

'I had been on patrol for quite a while, during which time Central London seemed to be at the base of a huge pyramid of flame. Hadn't seen a thing, except the flames, shell bursts and the odd aircraft in flames over the outskirts. Didn't really expect to see anything much with two great rows of glowing exhaust ports right in front ruining my night vision! So when I began to have a bit of a problem controlling the revs, I headed for base and called control. Almost immediately I saw this large twin-engined thing right in front of me going the same way. I only had to line up on him and press the button - it obviously wasn't one of ours! I hit him underneath and the effect was of an enormous burst of sparks, which I flew through. The Heinkel stuck its nose down and headed for the deck, which meant that it was difficult to see against the dark background of the earth, but, of course, his rear gunner could now see me easily against the light, moonlit sky, so he opened up on me every time I tried to get in position to give him another burst - very adjacent he was too!

'We carried on like this until he was indulging in some quite fancy low flying across Kent. I don't think that I hit him again. Eventually I lost sight of him so I circled the area and obtained a radio fix from base, which established where I was, and returned to West Malling. There we found signs of minor damage to my Spitfire, such as to the oil cooler debris guard, indicating that I had flown into small pieces of wreckage. When the position of the radio fix coincided with the discovery of the Heinkel on the ground it was credited to me. The rest of the squadron had droned around all night and seen absolutely nothing!'

In 1978, the Heinkel's captain, Albert Hufenruether, then a teacher in Hamburg, returned to the scene of the crash. There he met several eye-witnesses including a Mr Field, behind whose house the bomber had come to rest. Nothing now remains at the crash site to indicate the wartime drama, but the radio set and radio mast from the Kennington Heinkel are on display in the Kent Battle of Britain Museum at Hawkinge.

German prisoners of war pictured at Darlington, late 1942. Fourth from left, sitting, is the captain of He 111 A1+JN, Hauptmann Albert Hufenreuther. Others are, sitting from left: Leutnant Peyinghaus and Oberleutnant Wolf Münchmeyer (1/ZG26, PoWs 13.08.40), Hauptmann Butzinger, Hufenruether, Hauptmann Alfred Kindler (6/KG2, PoW 31.07.42), Oberleutnant Hans Walter Wolff (6/KG2, PoW 23.08.42). Standing: Leutnant Dieter von Glasow (8/KG53, PoW 05.08.42), Leutnant Siegfried Baden (7/KG26, PoW July '41), Oberleutnant Rudolf Hohenstein (7/KG2, PoW 08.08.42), Leutnant Grasshoff.

Chris Goss

On April 10th, 1941, Flight Lieutenant Tony Bartley DFC of 74 Squadron recorded in his log book: 'Ear drums packed up while diving to intercept Me 109s'. Roger Boulding became Acting Flight Commander in place of Bartley, who was hospitalised. However, the Kennington Heinkel was destined to be his last combat claim; one month later Flying Officer Boulding fell victim to the guns of the Luftwaffe:-

'On June 17th, 1941, I was on a sweep over France, flying Spitfire VB, W3251, leading a section of four 74 Squadron Spitfires, with "Sailor" Malan leading the squadron as wing leader, we were flying as top cover. Having dived down on some Me 109s, and in accordance with the standard drill of that time, we didn't follow them all the way down but attempted to reform, climbing towards the sun and weaving. I was following "Sailor" and another Spitfire was following me. After a while "Sailor" came on the radio telling someone to "look out behind!" I took a quick look and saw the chap still behind me, and was screwing my head round for the trouble when I saw a Spitfire below me violently rocking its wings, which was obviously "Sailor". Suddenly there was an almighty bang on the armour plate behind my seat and it became rather obvious that the chap behind me had been replaced by someone slightly less friendly! With controls gone I had to jump out and floated down from about 12-15,000' in broad daylight, so found a reception committee waiting. And that was that, as they kept on saying "For you the war is over!" '

Above: Flg Off Roger Boulding and Sam pictured at Gravesend shortly before Roger was shot down and captured. This Spitfire is another presentation machine, 'Gibraltar'.
Below: Wg Cdr Roger Boulding, left, and Flt Lt Kazik Budzik, pictured at the opening of the Malvern Spitfire Team's first major exhibition, 'SPITFIRE!', at Tudor House Museum, Worcester, in 1988. Sadly, Roger passed away suddenly in 1993.

After the war and repatriation, Roger remained in the post-war RAF. Swapping Spitfires for Lancasters, he became CO of 35 Squadron, and later of 249, flying Vampire jets in Egypt. After various administrative commands and staff jobs he retired from the RAF as a Wing Commander in 1966, and went into business as an hotelier.

Wing Commander Roger Boulding was a valued personal friend, as indeed are all in this book, and gave me much encouragement and support during the early days of my writing career. It was with great sadness, therefore, that I learned of Roger's death on March 2nd, 1993.

Chapter Ten

Corporal Fred Roberts

Corporal Fred Roberts, June 1941.

On September 21st, 1940, official photographers descended on Fowlmere airfield and recorded on Velox the pilots, ground staff and Spitfires of 19 Squadron. These photographs are now held by the Imperial War Museum, and are therefore easily accessible to researchers. Consequently many have been used as representative illustrations in numerous Battle of Britain books. Invariably however, unless the author is informed, the photographs are given general captions, such as 'Spitfire pilots at rest', without identifying either the squadron or pilots concerned.

   One of the most famous of these photographs is superb, and personifies the harmony that existed between the ground and air crews. Sergeant Pilot Bernard 'Jimmy' Jennings DFM took Spitfire X4474, 'QV-I' aloft and executed aerobatics above Fowlmere for the photographers' benefit. Many photographs were therefore taken of this aircraft.

   The print in question shows Sergeant Jennings in the 'office', door open and apparently about to disembark, with a member of 19 Squadron's groundcrew, probably a Flight Mechanic, standing on the wing adjacent. In the foreground of the photograph is an armourer, removing the Spitfire's underwing panels to gain access to the machine-guns and ammunition boxes. The scene is perfectly described by those lines from Shakespeare's Henry Vth:-

> 'The armourers, accomplishing the knights,
> With busy hammers closing rivets up,
> Give dreadful note of preparation'.

The famous photograph: Sgt Bernard Jennings in the 'office' of X4474, QV-I, at Fowlmere in September 1940. Until publication of the author's first book, 'Spitfire Squadron', in 1990, the armourer had remained anonymous - we now know that he is Fred Roberts.

Imperial War Museum

Anyone prepared to undertake a little background reading would find it fairly easy to identify, from other uses of this photograph, Sergeant Jennings, but of course the flight mechanic and armourer always remained anonymous, their names never having been recorded. When studying the photograph, even as a child, for it is surely amongst the most frequently used Battle of Britain illustrations of all time, I often wondered just who this armourer was, 'accomplishing' his aerial knight.

When I put together my first book, 'Spitfire Squadron', it was frustrating as the publisher severely limited the number of photographs that I was able to use.

This was a great pity as during the course of my research I had accumulated several hundred of 19 Squadron during the pre-war to 1941 period, the majority from the private collections of the pilots themselves. However, amongst the 48 illustrations I had to choose were inevitably some of the official Fowlmere photographs - amongst them the Jennings picture. After the book's release I was delighted to be contacted by the armourer himself - Fred Roberts - and even more surprised to learn that not only had he not previously seen the photograph, but also that he had lived in Worcester - my home town - for 30 years after the war!

Since our first contact, Fred and I have met many times. I was delighted to reunite him with other members of the Squadron. Ironically whilst researching the book I was unable to trace any 19 Squadron groundcrew, but after its release I was contacted by two more, John Milne and Ernest French, and soon all three were back in touch with each other. The now late Wing Commander Frank Brinsden, a New Zealander and 19 Squadron stalwart, visited me during 1990 whilst in the UK for the 50th anniversary of the Battle of Britain celebrations. This also brought Fred and John together with both Frank, a Flying Officer in 1940, and Ken Wilkinson, whose story is also told in this book.

In September 1992, Ramrod Publications launched my second book, 'The Invisible Thread: A Spitfire's Tale', at the Abbey Hotel, Malvern, and on show was a Spitfire Mk XVI which was painted to represent 'QV-I'. Present were both Wing Commander Bernard Jennings DFM AFC RAF Retd, and Fred Roberts. It was quite a moment to reunite them with a Spitfire so painted almost 52 years to the day since the famous photograph was taken. It had been hoped to actually recreate the photograph, but unfortunately the cockpit could not be opened so a unique opportunity was to some extent lost.

Fred always looked after Spitfire 'H' whilst with 19 Squadron, and usually this machine was flown by Flight Sergeant George 'Grumpy' Unwin DFM, 19 Squadron's top scoring pilot and 14th in Fighter Command's list of leading aces by the Battle's end. I was also able to reunite Fred with 'Grumpy', or perhaps more correctly Wing Commander GC Unwin DSO DFM RAF Retd. Indeed, at the launch of 'Through Peril to the Stars' in September 1993, Wing Commanders Unwin and Jennings, and Fred Roberts were all reunited with 'their' QV-I Spitfire.

As a result of 'Spitfire Squadron' opening the door of Fred's Battle of Britain past, he was inspired to record his memories. The following is extracted from them:-

'Myself and another airman, Jimmy Belton, joined 19 Squadron in July 1939 as rooky armourers direct from our six month course at Manby. Full of enthusiasm and expecting to see aircraft everywhere, we arrived at Duxford to find everything quiet and partly closed for the weekend. Of course this was still the "strawberries and cream and fruit cake for tea" period enjoyed by the pre-war air force.

'On Sunday, 3rd September, 1939, several 19 and 66 Squadron armament personnel, including myself, spent the day transporting .303 ammunition from railway wagons in Whittlesford Yard to the Duxford ammunition store. None of the aircraft were yet armed, however. After the Prime Minister's speech the sirens sounded and the Squadron was scrambled. We all thought "they won't shoot much down with empty ammo boxes!" Whilst we worked in the yard, evacuee trains passed by. The landlord of the nearby pub called us in to listen to Mr Chamberlain's speech, he took us into the back room with a free pint as it was not yet 12 noon.

Spitfire Mk Is of 19 Squadron at Duxford in 1938. Note the pre-war codes of WZ (later changed to QV), and the original two-bladed, fixed-pitch mahogany propeller.

'From thereafter the Armament Section was kept very busy as we had to re-sight the new Browning guns and reflector gunsights - when I had arrived some of the Spitfires still had the old ring and bead sights. We also practised re-arming repeatedly until two armourers and assistants could change all eight ammo tanks, cock all guns and replace all panels in around three minutes.

It was early in January 1940, that one of 66 Squadron's Spitfires, N3036, was hit by return fire whilst attacking a Luftwaffe raider off the Norfolk coast. The Spitfire made a wheels-up landing on the cliff tops near Cromer. I and my colleagues went out there to unload the eight guns. We couldn't take out the ammo tanks because of the wings being on the ground, but we had to stay and guard the plane until it was removed late that night.

'At Duxford it was routine work, daily inspections etc. It was early in February 1940, that Douglas Bader resumed his RAF career and joined 19 Squadron. His first flight was in the Squadron Magister and was memorable. He beat up the aerodrome in every way. He will also be remembered for taking the roof off the old peacetime cricket pavilion on landing a Spitfire, removing his tail-wheel in the process.

'On February 29th, 1940, some of the armourers, including myself, along with flight fitters and riggers were detailed to travel by lorry to Whittlesford Village where one of our Spitfires, flown by Pilot Officer Trenchard, had crashed during a night flight. The plane was in a thousand pieces. I remember one oleo leg and wheel a quarter of a mile away with a belt of ammo around it. The engine lay in a crater about five feet deep, the cockpit in bits around it. I have the tip of one of this Spitfire's de Havilland propeller blades made into a picture frame. The prop tip was recovered from the Duxford aircraft graveyard a few days after the crash.

'On May 25th, 1940, 19 Squadron moved to Hornchurch to provide air cover with other squadrons for the Dunkirk evacuation. It was a very hard 10 days that we spent at Hornchurch, up and on readiness at 5 or 5.30 am, remaining on duty until nightfall when the last gun had been cleaned and the last panel buttoned back on the aircraft. Waiting was the worst. It was all strange to us knowing that the Spitfires were actually going into action, so the question in our minds was "who will return?" At Hornchurch we did have the opportunity to meet up with our old 222 Squadron friends, with whom we had previously shared Duxford, who were dispersed close to us.

'Throughout the entire war the most badly shot up aircraft I ever saw was whilst we were at Hornchurch. It was Eric Ball's, and I remember Douglas Bader and his wife coming over from the 222 Squadron dispersal, as Bader was by then a Flight Commander with that unit, and he and Eric Ball counted the bullet holes. They were good friends having already flown together in 19 Squadron's 'B' Flight.

'At Duxford, where the old Watch Tower had stood, there had been erected on the Station Flight and Cambridge University Air Squadron hangar a sandbag-protected machine-gun post. On one particular morning it was manned by "Ginger" Hunt, one of 19 Squadron's Armourers' Assistants. In 19 Squadron's hangar stood a fully armed Spitfire, guns all loaded and cocked, hangar doors open and by coincidence the Spitfire's gunsight was roughly aligned on the gun-post. Pickles, one of our Maintenance Flight armourers, who actually did the office work, was detailed to instruct a new member of the section, a recent boy entrant, on the Spitfire's layout and maintenance procedures. Whilst giving this instruction, Pickles sat in the cockpit whilst the trainee stood on the wing root. I can just imagine the conversation, "To fire the guns young lad, you turn this ring and press this button." Pickles turned the ring and indeed pressed the button. The eight guns sounded terrific as they fired inside the hangar - fortunately the gunner on the Station Flight Hangar roof wasn't physically hurt, but there were a few punctured and leaking sandbags!

'On June 25th, 1940, we moved three miles down the Royston Road and one mile up the country road to Fowlmere. The original Great War airfield at

Fowlmere stood on the Royston to Duxford Road, but our airfield was on a hilltop about half a mile up a farm track from the village and through a farmyard. The location was code-named G.1 and was Duxford's satellite. When we arrived the farmers were still harvesting their May crop, so some of the squadron's personnel were detailed to help and speed the process up. The rest of us were employed erecting Mess tents, bell tents, ablutions, toilets, etc. It was much later that each flight had just a blister hangar. Living conditions were rough and primitive but fortunately the weather was kind, which helped.

'It was between 8 - 8.30 am on August 31st, 1940, that the first bombs dropped on Fowlmere. We, the ground staff, were queuing for breakfast. Our Spitfires were airborne. We heard the noise of what turned out to be a formation of Do 17s approaching. I dived into the nearest slit-trench and looking up from there could see the sun shining on the dots high in the sky. We could also see the first stick of bombs falling. Fortunately they were released late and only two fell on the airfield, one amongst the bell tents making a crater about four feet deep and five feet across. The earth blown out of the crater collapsed one of the tents. There were two lads asleep inside who were partially buried, but neither was harmed. The second bomb exploded near the boundary fence, but the rest of that stick fell in the orchards and watercress beds beyond the airfield. We had permission to collect as many bombed apples as we wanted. Looking back on that event makes me smile, because myself and a few others sat in that trench holding enamel plates over our heads, having dived into the trench from the breakfast queue with plate, knife, fork, spoon and mug in hand.

'One afternoon in September we had Flight Sergeant Unwin's Spitfire up on trestles in the 'A' Flight blister hangar when there was a scramble call. Along with the other pilots came Flight Sergeant Unwin, yelling and swearing for his plane. Of course the plane was having a minor overhaul of some kind, gun panels and engine cowlings were removed, ammo tank panels hanging down, guns unloaded and work being carried out on both engine and airframe. I am sure we held the record for bringing a plane to serviceability after that! He was airborne in less than 10 minutes after the others, with a straight take-off from the hangar across wind and with no engine warm-up. I don't know if George Unwin caught the rest of the squadron up, or took on the Luftwaffe alone, but it certainly showed the courage of the man and the confidence he placed in his ground crew.

'During my time with 19 Squadron, July 1939 - October 1940, there were many changes to the Spitfires. Rotol airscrews replaced the de Havilland examples, rear-view mirrors and armour plating were installed, camera guns were replaced with cine gun cameras, and there were probably others that I cannot remember. Our Spitfire Mk IAs were also replaced with the Mk IIs with Coffmann starters. There were also changes in harmonising guns and gunsights to reflect the changes in Air Ministry specifications. Some pilots insisted in having their own specifications, such as the guns harmonised with the sight on a bullseye target at about 300 yards. There were also at least two changes in the composition of ammunition belts. During the Battle of Britain we used four ball, two armour piercing, one incendiary, one tracer round, then repeated that order.

'it is now widely known, the full facts having been made available from Public Record Office sources in Dilip's first book, "Spitfire Squadron", that for some of the Battle of Britain 19 Squadron was equipped with the experimental cannon-armed Spitfire Mk IB. During this period an armourer, Corporal Paddy O'Brennan, tried to defuse a 20mm high explosive shell by filing off the nose cap, and holding the shell in a bucket of water to release the fulminate of mercury pellet. Not surprisingly the shell exploded and Paddy lost half his hand. Those HE shells were coloured with enamel rings and I suppose would have made good ornaments now. The stoppages with the cannons were numerous, and unsolvable by us on the Squadron. We armourers suffered from these stoppages, however, not only from the work they created, but also the criticism we had to take by all. Fortunately the Mk IBs were replaced by standard, eight machine-gun armed MKIAs. These were largely second-hand and well-worn Spitfires from OTUs. They were flown to Fowlmere by the first female pilots I had seen - members of the ATA (Air Transport Auxiliary).

'The trestles or litters on which 19 Squadron armourers carried their ammunition tanks were designed by one of our officers. They were constructed so that one litter could be fitted on top of another thus holding a complete re-arm for one aircraft. 66 Squadron might also have had these, being with us at Duxford, but I know of no other unit using them. The same officer also designed the re-arming strap we used to pull the cartridge through the fuse chutes and guns during re-arming. Prior to this we used lengths of stiff wire or Bowden cable outer covering or any old thing that was flexible.

'To harmonise the Spitfire's eight .303 Browning machine-guns, the aircraft was raised clear of the ground on nose and tail trestles, levelled fore and aft, then levelled across the cockpit using wing trestles. The guns and gunsights were set on the sighting board and locked with locknuts. The pilot checked the sighting for accuracy before acceptance, then the locknuts were wired together. To sight the guns we used a small periscope which was inserted in the breech of the barrel.

'There were always excellent relations between 19 Squadron's ground staff and aircrew. The pre-war regular officers were real gentlemen in their dealing with us and acknowledged the fact that we looked up to them as responsible people. The NCO pilots were much closer to us, having been through the ranks of course, and were excellent people to work with, men like George Unwin, Harry Steere and Jack Potter. Many others followed on and were also good, especially the Czechs, but they were sometimes a little impatient. Some of the young commissioned pilots that joined the squadron during 1940 did not appear to have the same personality as the older officers and seemed to be stand-offish. Reflecting on this in my old age, I think that really they were shy of us, we being the old hands.

'I felt that all aircrew fully appreciated our efforts to keep the squadron at as high a pitch of efficiency as possible at all times, often under difficult circumstances. We on the ground certainly had our favourites amongst the pilots, mine I suppose being Squadron Leader Brian Lane DFC and Flight Sergeant George Unwin DFM, despite the latter's nickname being "Grumpy George"! I suppose that as I looked after their armament they became personal to me.

'In October 1940, it was with great regret that I was posted from 19 to 151 Squadron at Digby to maintain an experimental cannon. 151 was a good squadron, but the camaraderie that I had so enjoyed in 19 Squadron was missing. Upon the loss of 151 Squadron's cannon Hurricane, I requested a posting back to 19 Squadron, but it was made to deaf ears.

'On my yearly visit to the RAF Museum at Hendon I always stand and look at the Spitfires with a tear of nostalgia'.

Fred Roberts' story again provides us with a unique view of squadron life during 1940 on the ground. What so impresses me is the commitment displayed by these men who were employed in a far less exciting or glamourous role than the aircrews they supported, and as has been seen from both Bob Morris' and Fred Roberts' stories, the groundcrew were often also in the front line by virtue of the Luftwaffe raiding the airfields from which the British fighters operated. The pride with which these men now quite rightly reflect upon their RAF service is similarly touching. We were fortunate indeed that we had men of this quality to attend to those vital matters on the ground, and 50 years later, their input in recording the history of those now far off, but nonetheless dramatic, times is both essential and appreciated.

Wg Cdr Bernard Jennings and Fred Roberts reunited at the launch of 'The Invisible Thread: A Spitfire's Tale', Great Malvern, September 1992. By coincidence, the Spitfire, although a Mk XVI, was actually painted to represent their original QV-I, of 1940!

Chapter Eleven

Wing Commander David Cox DFC

Wing Commander David Cox DFC & Bar.

David Cox's war record is remarkable, made even more so as he failed his initial RAF medical! Another young man whose route to a Spitfire cockpit started by joining the RAF Volunteer Reserve before the war, Sergeant Cox was 19 Squadron's first RAFVR pilot, identifiable by the letters 'VR' above his Sergeant's stripes, when he joined the squadron on May 23rd, 1940. He remained non-operational at the time of Operation Dynamo, but, at the age of just 20 years, flew with distinction during the Battle of Britain until being shot down and wounded on September 27th, 1940. He rejoined the squadron in time for the Nonstop Offensive and was commissioned in July 1941. In September, he was rested and posted to flying instructor duties. In May 1942, Pilot Officer Cox joined 72 Squadron at Biggin Hill. 52 years later he remembers the Offensive:-

'1941 saw the start of Fighter Command's offensive operations over the continent. It was mainly over France for the first part of the year, then Belgium and later Holland. At first it was just a Wing of Spitfires and Hurricanes, either two or three squadrons. When only fighters appeared the Luftwaffe was content to stay on the ground and let Fighter Command waste fuel. To provoke the Luftwaffe, Blenheim bombers joined in the offensive, and later four-engined Stirlings. This resulted in quite a sharp reaction from the German fighters.

'The RAF operations with bombers were called Circuses, which was an apt name as several Wings would escort half a dozen Blenheims. There would be a Target Cover Wing which was supposed to clear the area of enemy fighters before the arrival of the bombers. Some hope!!! There would be a Close Escort Wing, a Top Cover Wing, and a Withdrawal Cover Wing. Sometimes there would be a Wing to meet the bombers when they were back over the Channel. Often there would be a Diversionary Wing well away from the main target to try and deceive the enemy fighters as to the real target.

'Was all this offensive activity by the RAF worthwhile? This question has often been asked. The Luftwaffe certainly had the tactical advantage as these Wings took time to form up and showed up on the German radar. This gave the German fighters time to get well above the incoming RAF formations. Thus their tactics were high-speed attacking dives through the RAF fighters, known as "Dirty Darts", and would carry on down and sometimes even destroy the odd bomber.

'Quite a number of experienced Battle of Britain pilots were lost, like John Mungo-Park and Eric Lock, and of course even Bader and Stanford-Tuck were taken prisoner. By comparison, the number of German fighters destroyed, which was after all the object of the exercise, was quite small.

'But of course Fighter Command had to be given something to do and kept up to scratch as there were only the odd hit and run raids by the Luftwaffe. However, the most important achievement was that it was Britain's Second Front, which was considered most important by Churchill after Russia was invaded. It was said at the time that he was not worried about the RAF losses as we just had to show Stalin that we were doing something to ease the pressure on Russia. There is no doubt, however, that our efforts tied up some important German Jagdgeschwader.

'I was still in 19 Squadron at Fowlmere when the Offensive started. We used to operate from West Malling in Kent where the squadron would be joined by several others from 12 Group to form the 12 Group Wing. This Wing never did such deep penetrations as the 11 Group Wings as we only had Spitfire Mk IIs against their Mk Vs. The Spitfire Mk II was inferior to the Me 109F, the German fighter in use at that time, above 20,000'.

'I have listed below some of the operations on which I flew:-

June 25th, 1941.
Sweep St Ingelvert-St Omer-Gravelines @ 28,000'. Attacks from above by Me 109s. Wing Leader's No 2, a Hurricane, shot down - blew up, just pieces floating down everywhere, not a good sight.

June 27th, 1941.

Daytime Sweep Boulogne-St Omer-Dunkirk. Pilot Officer Andrews shot down.

Late evening sweep Boulogne-St Omer. About 10 miles in from Boulogne and at 30,000' we were attacked from above by Me 109s. For a change the 109s decided to stick around. I got behind and below one at 200 yards. Fired about an 8 second burst. E/A immediately dived away with smoke and flames spewing forth. I made the mistake of keeping my eyes on him too long. Suddenly my Spitfire shuddered and smoke and flames came from the front of the engine. I immediately opened my hood, undid my straps and was about to bale out when the fire went out. It appeared that I had been hit in the coolant tank which in those days was pure glycol. I switched off the engine as the temperature gauge was nearly in the red. I thought that perhaps I could glide as far as the Channel, then bale out and perhaps be picked up in my dinghy. I started to glide at a speed of about 110 mph. After a few minutes I noticed that the engine temperature had dropped. The propeller was milling around so I switched the engine on. This enabled me to maintain level flight for about 7 to 8 seconds before the engine temperature reached danger

level again. I did this several times and later was pleased to find myself over the Channel. I intended to bale out at about 3,000'. When I was down to 6,000', suddenly out of the evening mist I saw Dungeness projecting out into the Channel. By now it was about 10 pm, we were on Double Summer Time. I then decided to try and make landfall. With the aid of a few more bursts of engine I crossed the coast at about 500' and made a wheels-up crash-landing just beyond the beach. As I had undone my straps I was bumped about in the cockpit and my face suffered. My Spitfire came to rest against a bank near a road. Shortly afterwards two Army Officers appeared in a transport. They

Spitfire in trouble. This frame is from the cine-gun camera of Major Gerhard Schoepfel, Gruppenkommandeur of III/JG26 and shows his combat with a Spitfire on June 27th, 1941. Having been inspired by the photograph when included in the Malvern Spitfire Team's exhibition, 'SPITFIRE!', further research by Chris Goss indicates that the Spitfire pilot concerned may actually have been David Cox. Schoepfel via Dr Alfred Price.

said that they had seen me appear out of the mist with a lot of smoke coming from my aircraft and then I disappeared behind some trees. They took me to the Officers' Mess in an old country mansion, despite my only being a Sergeant. I was given some generous swigs of whisky. Later transport came from Hawkinge where I got to at about 1 am. I was taken to Sick Quarters, patched up, and before being put to bed given the best eggs and bacon I've ever tasted! The next morning 91 Squadron flew me back to Fowlmere in their Avro Tutor. I was greeted warmly by the 19 Squadron boys who had thought I was a "goner". The CO, Squadron Leader Lawson DFC, took one look at me and gave me a couple of days off.

Above left: Oberleutnant Gerhard Schoepfel in his III/JG26 Me 109E during the Battle of Britain. Schoepfel later became JG26's Kommodore and survived the war decorated with the Knights Cross, with a total of 40 victories.

Above right: Herr Gerhard Schoepfel (2nd right), aged 83, pictured with historian Michael Meyer at an exhibition in Germany during 1989. The other two pilots are, left, Adolf Glunz of 6/JG26, a holder of both the Knight's Cross and Oak Leaves with 71 victories, and right, Otto Stammberger, a Staffelkapitän of 4/JG26.

Ottomar Kruse

July 5th, 1941.

Top cover to ONE Stirling bombing St Omer. Quite a sight looking down - one Stirling surrounded by about 200 fighters!!

July 12th, 1941.

Patrol Le Touquet-Hardlot. Led again by Squadron Leader Lane DFC of our Battle of Britain days who was on a visit from 12 Group HQ at Hucknall. Great joy in the squadron!

August 7th, 1941.

Sweep Mardyck-St Omer. Many attacks by Me 109s. Flight Sergeant Plzak, one of our Czech Battle of Britain stalwarts, was shot down and killed. I felt this loss deeply.

August 12th, 1941.

After staying overnight at Martlesham Heath, 19 Squadron patrolled Schouwen-Walcheren (Holland) to await return of Blenheims returning from low-level raid on power station at Cologne. We were at 2,000' with broken cloud. Me 109s kept appearing in and out of cloud. I attacked one which started to smoke and then went into cloud. Unfortunately I lost my No 2. I think that he was picked off by an Me 109 which suddenly appeared out of cloud.

'On August 19th, 1941, I was posted to 57 OTU at Hawarden for instructing duties on Spitfires and Masters. On May 29th, 1942, I returned to operational flying and joined 72 Squadron at Biggin Hill. 72 were one of the top squadrons in 11 Group and commanded by Brian Kingcome of 92 Squadron Battle of Britain fame and who ended the war as a Group Captain in Italy. The 'A' Flight Commander was Hugo Armstrong, an Australian who was killed over the Channel in 1943 when CO of 611 Squadron. The 'B' Flight Commander was "Timber" Woods who was lost over the Adriatic in 1943. 72 had been the close escort to the Swordfish during the Channel Dash. Like other 11 Group squadrons, however, they were finding themselves outclassed in their Spitfire Mk Vs against the FW 190. Because of the 190 menace there were no longer deep penetrations into the continent such as to Lille in 1941. It was a case of a quick dash in of a few miles then out again.

'The Wing Leader at Biggin Hill devised the scheme of the Wing sweeping below 100' until the French coast was in sight and then "Climb like Hell" and hope to catch the 190s below, the Spitfires having the height advantage. Once the 190s were level then the advantage was theirs. Then came Jamie Rankin's famous call, "Everybody Out!", a call which years later was used by "Red Robbo" to bring the British Leyland car workers out on strike! On hearing the call everybody dived out low over the Channel as fast as possible. The idea of keeping low approaching France, incidentally, was to keep below the German radar. I have detailed below some of the operations on which I flew with 72 Squadron:-

May 31st, 1942.

Sweep Dieppe. Many FW 190s both above and below. Was able to confirm a 190 in flames after attack by Pilot Officer Rutter.

June 1st, 1942.

High Cover Escort to Hurricane bombers, Bruges, Belgium.

June 2nd, 1942.

Diversion Wing for six Boston bombers attacking Dieppe. A brush with Me 109s but not close enough to open fire.

June 5th, 1942.

Sweep Abbeville area. About to attack FW 190s below us, then attacked by FW 190s from above. Quick exit!

June 20th, 1942.

Four of 72 led by Hugo Armstrong on low-level recce off Boulogne to look for and report any shipping. I was on the right near the French coast and looking out to sea. I reported to Hugo that there was a large ship at 10 o'clock (the clock code was used for reporting direction), and that there were a lot of gulls flying around it. Hugo said to me, "You stupid ***!!, they're not seagulls they are 190s!" We quickly turned for home without having been seen. There were at least a dozen 190s! The explanation for my wonderful report was that it was 5 am and I had had a good evening at the Bromley Country Club!

July 13th, 1942.

Sweep St Omer. 72 Squadron was now commanded by Bobby Oxspring of 66 Squadron Battle of Britain fame. He was later to lead us with great distinction in Tunisia. I was No 2 to Hugo Armstrong. We were attacked by 20 FW 190s. Our section of four got separated from the rest of the squadron, so Bobby Oxspring turned back to help us. There was a running fight nearly all the way to the English coast. We only lost one, Squadron Leader Tidd who was training with us. I damaged a 190 and someone else got another. We landed at Hawkinge very short of fuel.

Butcher Bird. Close-ups of the cockpit area of an FW 190, the fighter which firmly tipped the balance of air power over north-west Europe in the Luftwaffe's favour. This example belonged to the Stabschwarm of III/JG2 'Richthofen' and was the first example captured intact and evaluated by the RAF. Its pilot, Oberleutnant Armin Faber, landed at Pembrey airfield in South Wales following combat with the Exeter Spitfires. These two snapshots are from an extensive series taken at Pembrey by 234 Squadron's Flt Lt Tommy Drinkwater.

July 31st, 1942.

Close escort to 12 Bostons attacking Abbeville aerodrome. Good bombing, NE dispersal well and truly plastered. Attacked by 190s but all got back safely, including the Bostons and despite heavy flak.

August 1st, 1942.

Sweep Bruges-Flushing. Chased back by a gaggle of 190s.

'By this time we were looking forward to receiving our Spitfire Mk IXs, but on August 2nd, 1942, we were posted to Ayr, Scotland, where we did exercises in the lowlands with the Army. This, unknown to us, was in preparation for Tunisia. From July onwards, however, the 11 Group squadrons were re-equipped with the Spitfire Mk IX and so the FW 190 menace at last disappeared'.

In November 1942, 72 Squadron commenced operational flying over the Tunisian desert. David Cox had been promoted to Flying Officer, and continues his commentary:-

November 18th, 1942.

Sweep Béja-Mateur led by Wing Commander Petrus "Dutch" Hugo who shot down a Ju 88 soon after take-off. The Ju 88 split from nose to tail. It was unlucky as it came out of cloud right in front of 12 Spitfires. What a shock for the crew!

November 22nd, 1942.

Souk-el-Arba strafed three times this afternoon destroying most of our Spitfires.

1st - By some 30 mixed Me 109s and FW 190s with bombs. I was hit in the left hand by bomb splinters but was back flying in two days. 2nd - 20 Stukas. 3rd - Mixed bag of Me 109s and FW 190s.

November 26th, 1942.

Sweep Mejez-el-Bab giving cover to 1st Army, encountered six Ju 88s with escort of some 20 Me 109s. Very low down in a valley. Our flight of six allocated the escort. I got on the tail of an Me 109 at about 50 yards who took no evasive action (do not think he knew that I was there) and after some 8-10 seconds of fire his port wing came off and he hit a hillside. I was attacked by an Me 109 whose fire went over my wings. Quick exit!

November 29th, 1942.

We were all sleeping in one large tent. It was a habit of the Luftwaffe to send a couple of Ju 88s to circle Souk-el-Arba at night and drop a couple of small bombs about every 10 minutes - just to keep us awake - then fly off before dawn. This night they stayed a little too long. The first light was appearing as Flight Lieutenant Khrone and myself got airborne. Khrone shot one down over the airfield but the second had disappeared. I reckoned it would be flying east towards the rising sun, so got right down low and flew east. Sure enough near Béja I saw the Ju 88 very low but shown up by the increasing light. After a long chase I eventually hit it and it crashed into a hill some 20 miles on. II and IV Gruppen of KG54 both recorded the loss of Ju 88s over Souk-el-Arba that day. Not long after this the Beaufighters appeared and we were able to get a full night's sleep!

December 2nd, 1942.

Hollywood drama. In the afternoon our CO, Bobby Oxspring, told me that Air HQ wanted a recce of Tunis airfield (El Aouina) to ascertain whether there were fighters there. Air HQ had instructed him that as it was considered to be a hazardous operation neither he nor the two Flight Commanders were to lead the operation. Very dramatic! Would I be prepared to lead a flight of six Spitfires!! I had no trouble in finding five pilots to go with me, but soon after take-off three had to return with engine trouble (not unusual as we had no proper ground crews at that time). So the three of us pressed on at a few hundred feet. Sergeant Hussey on my left and Flight Sergeant Fowler on my right. As we approached Tunis we could see smoke coming from El Aounia and 12 American Mitchells flying away. This did not please me as now the airfield defences would be alert. However, we climbed to be 3,000' over Tunis and dived down over the lake to the airfield, getting up plenty of speed in a wide 'V'. As we approached I saw between a line of trees an He 111 and so opened up at point-blank range. The He 111 just fell to pieces. Just before I opened fire I remember seeing a mechanic on a ladder doing something to the starboard engine. I wonder what his thoughts were on seeing a Spitfire just 100 yards away! As we flew at zero feet over the airfield I noticed Sergeant Hussey turning to the left. I told him to get back with us. I found out later that he had been firing at a motorbike which was weaving across the airfield! Once we were past we did a sharp left-hand turn for home. As we did so we came over a small lake in which nude Germans were swimming. We were too close to fire, but I bet they got a shock at the sight of three Spitfires over them! We were able to report to Air HQ that there were 20 fighters in an orchard north of the airfield.

January 2nd, 1943.

Escort to Hurricane bombers in Mejez area. Bombed a German HQ well and truly - lots of AA fire. A number of Me 109s appeared. I fired at one in a head-on attack - saw strikes so claimed one damaged.

January 6th, 1943.

Near Mateur, myself and No 2, Warrant Officer Gear, were attacked from above by four Me 109s. There was a lot of milling around between the six of us which lasted a good 10 minutes. Nobody fired and in the end the fight was broken off by more or less mutual agreement. However, it should be mentioned that we were 30-40 miles inside enemy territory!

March 2nd, 1943.

Six of us in our new Spitfire IXs were attacked from above by 30 E/As. Then proceeded to outclimb them to 34,000'. E/As then dived away.

March 4th, 1943.

High cover to 20 Flying Fortresses bombing some docks. Attacked by Me 109s. Went to escort damaged Fortress home who fired at us! We complained to the American CO who replied that he had told his boys to fire at any single-engined aircraft!

March 26th, 1943.

Squadron went to Thelepte in South Tunisia to help the Americans. Escorted Airacobras bombing German transport. Attacked by Me 109s who were kept away from the Americans. I climbed after one Me 109 and saw strikes but had to break off with other E/A behind me.

April 3rd, 1943.

On returning from high escort to 16 Mitchells bombing the airfield at St Marie du Zil, the squadron was attacked by a large number of Me 109s near Souk-el-Khemis. My No 2 was shot down and baled out and I was hit in the port wing. I attacked two Me 109s and then attacked the No 1. He was not very good as he just did a slow right hand turn more or less into my fire. He then flicked over and went into the hills east of Béja. One destroyed and one damaged.

April 11th, 1943.

High Cover to Hurricane bombers. Lots of AA fire. Hectic dogfight with Me 109s. Used all my ammo with no result. Squadron got three.

April 12th, 1943.

Sweep Kairouan area. Six Ju 88s escorted by FW 190s and Me 109s attacked by 93 Squadron led by Wing Commander Gilroy who asked for assistance from 72 as the escort was giving him trouble. We came down from 19,000' to about 1,000', firing at the escort as we charged. I blew the hood off a 190 but did not see what happened to it. One probable.

April 18th, 1943.

Self and Warrant Officer Gear had a long dogfight with several Me 109s with no results, except to land wet and tired. My 23rd birthday!

April 21st, 1943.

Sweep Tebourba area. I was hit in engine by AA fire from 88 mm gun. Managed to get back to base with main fuel pipe partly crushed and two holes in port wing. Six Bostons then went out and bombed the AA position concerned!

'We were often strafed ourselves at Souk-el-Khemis and had dug ourselves slit trenches. One day in April about a dozen Me 109s appeared low from over the hills. There was a rush by six of us to the nearest trench. Then a dead stop for there in the bottom was a puff-adder, a very dangerous snake indeed - we decided that the Me 109s were less of a menace!' David Cox's operational tour expired on April 26th, 1943, and he was posted back to the UK where he became a Tactics Liason Officer instructing American fighter pilots. He recalls that his claim to fame was having his own personal Thunderbolt! Whilst in the desert, however, David had risen to the rank of Flight Lieutenant and in fact had commanded a flight of 72 Squadron's Spitfires since December 15th, 1942. Between November 17th, 1942, and April 25th, 1943, he flew a total of 183 operational hours which equated to 135 sorties. Flight Lieutenant Cox had destroyed four German aircraft over the desert, probably destroyed two others and damaged three more. In addition, he destroyed the He 111 on the ground at Tunis airfield. On January 7th, 1943, he received a very well deserved DFC, which was followed by a Bar on July 9th, 1943.

Left: Sqn Ldr Bobby Oxspring DFC congratulates Flt Lt David Cox upon the award of the latter's DFC in the desert, 1943. Note that both officers are armed with service revolvers.
Above: David Cox with his 72 Squadron Spitfire Mk VB, RN-B, 'Pat'. Pat is David's wife and the couple married in 1940.

In January 1944, Flight Lieutenant DGSR Cox DFC & Bar was posted as a Flight Commander to 504 Squadron and returned to Biggin Hill. Later he was given command of his first squadron, 222, and on June 8th, 1944, D-Day + 2, he damaged an FW 190 which brought his final score to nine German aircraft destroyed, two probables and four damaged. After a spell at 84 Group Support Unit, Aston Down, he returned to operations with 1 Squadron at Detling, taking command of the squadron on January 1st, 1945. By that time the Luftwaffe had been ground down to the extent that Allied fighters were virtually free to roam at will above Europe. However, the dangers were not over. One day in March 1945, Squadron Leader Cox was coming in to land at Manston in Spitfire Mk IX MH644 when things went awfully wrong:-

'Suddenly all hell broke loose as I touched down and I went cartwheeling over, wing-tip to wing-tip. The aircraft was in hell of a mess and I was trapped in my cockpit upside down. Fortunately it did not catch fire. What had caused the accident was that when I touched down the tail-wheel was locked at a 45 degree angle and this flipped me over'.

Lucky escape. In March 1945, Sqn Ldr David Cox suffered a landing accident at Manston in Spitfire Mk IX, MH644, JX-M. The aircraft was wrecked, but fortunately David escaped unhurt.

On April 21st, 1945, David Cox was sent to Burma and given command of a Spitfire Wing. By the war's end, therefore, this RAFVR former NCO pilot had been commissioned, risen to the rank of Wing Commander, become a fighter ace and received a DFC & Bar. As I have said, David Cox was a remarkable airman. But it does not stop there, although he did leave the RAF in 1946 having also been decorated with the French Croix de Guerre.

Having approached the Ministry of Defence and the RAF, this stalwart member of Churchill's Few was granted permission to fly as 2nd pilot in a Lightning jet interceptor on September 15th, 1980, the 40th anniversary of Battle of Britain Day. 40 years previously David Cox had been in action over London with 19 Squadron and had destroyed an Me 109. In 1988, David Cox participated in a 'Jim'll Fix It' television programme, during which he flew in the late Nick Grace's two-seater Spitfire, ML407. It came as no surprise to hear that David Cox had taken ML407's controls, but how could we, those of us who never flew to battle in a Spitfire, begin to appreciate the myriad of emotions that this remarkable man must have felt in that intensely nostalgic moment ?

Wg Cdr David Cox DFC & Bar, RAF Retd, pictured at home during late 1994.

Alan Bray

Chapter Twelve

Wing Commander Peter Howard-Williams DFC

Flight Lieutenant Peter Howard-Williams
DFC pictured in 1941.

Peter Ian Howard-Williams was born at Cowes on December 27th, 1919. In April 1939 he entered the RAF College, Cranwell, as a flight cadet. He was commissioned in March 1940 and posted to 19 Squadron at Duxford in May. Although non-operational during Operation Dynamo, Pilot Officer Howard-Williams served throughout the Battle of Britain. It was later, during the Nonstop Offensive, however, that he rose to prominence:-

'I made my first flight on April 30th, 1933, in a de Havilland Moth. The pilot was my father, Wing Commander EL Howard-Williams, and the flight lasted 20 minutes. It is recorded in one of the old style small RAF log books which my father obtained for my brother, Jeremy, and I. In the remarks column, father has written "The first juggle", as he always referred to flying as "juggling with death". He was a Great War pilot and won the Military Cross with the Royal Flying Corps. He eventually retired as an Air Commodore. Towards the end of the war he became Air Correspondent on the Daily Telegraph. Both Jeremy and I followed in his footsteps and joined the RAF. My brother became a successful night-fighter pilot and also won a DFC. This same log book also indicates that on September 6th, 1936, I flew in a Heston Pheonix and in the remarks column wrote "Record speed: 145 mph". Later that year my father flew my mother, my brother and myself to Baghdad in a de Havilland Dragonfly. We had no radio and map read all the way - and weather forecasting was almost non-existent. Quite a trip!

'The problems of a new pilot joining a squadron like 19 were many. Firstly we usually took off as a squadron across the grass. A new pilot was either positioned at the extreme right or left of the formation, which consisted of four tight vics of three aircraft. This made it very difficult to keep up and meant a lot more throttle was required than used by the leaders. Secondly, after Dunkirk, a few new aircraft arrived which were fitted with automatic undercarriages. These aircraft were naturally flown by the leaders, so their u/c came up quickly whilst us poor new boys were hand-pumping like mad and at the same time trying to keep up with the leaders who already had their u/c up. More throttle, thus more fuel used up. When airborne we finally got into battle formation, tight vics in line astern, i.e. one vic immediately behind another. The new pilots were given the job of weaving to and fro at the formation's rear, keeping a lookout for trouble, but again almost at full throttle and so burning up more fuel. As we later discovered, it was a crazy formation which was eventually changed to the "finger four". The Germans had already learned this basic lesson in the Spanish Civil War.

'After the Battle of Britain I went to 118 Squadron which had recently formed at Filton. We were then stationed at Ibsley where we became a Wing with two other squadrons.

'On September 3rd, 1941, I flew Spitfire Mk VB AD210 when we beat up a 400 ton ship off Cherbourg. Later the same day, flying AD209, we went to have another look and found a big convoy off the Cherbourg peninsula. We were not allowed to attack a convoy. Flying west we passed through a rainstorm. When west of the peninsula the weather cleared and there was the most magnificent 'E' Boat flying a large swastika flag. I remember that John Robson was with us and we must have been six or eight Spitfires. I led the attack on the 'E' Boat, and it was soon stopped in the water. We all made two attacks and it was soon a right mess with smoke pouring from it when we all set course for home. We were shot at from the convoy and from the Channel Islands, so someone was on the ball. Now for the odd bit. Later the Germans announced that the Commander-in-Chief of all the western defences had been killed at sea. We put in for one German Field Marshal destroyed! Later we got a message from the Air Ministry saying that there was no proof, and in any case a Hampden squadron had successfully attacked a convoy that night off the Frisian Islands. I can see that 'E' Boat now. It was a really super looking ship, and a mess when we had finished with it. I am still surprised that it had no fighter cover as Maupertus, near Cherbourg, was only a few minutes flying time away. Despite what the Air Ministry said, I remain convinced that the General was on our 'E' Boat. I cannot think what he would have been doing off the Frisian Islands at night, more likely he was on an inspection of AA defences on the Channel Islands. The AA guns on Alderney and elsewhere were very quick to open fire. Against my argument is that there was no fighter cover when Maupertus was so close, and of course the Germans knew that we regularly flew around the area.

'On September 30th, 1941, I did a shipping recce in clear weather flying Spitfire Mk VB AD209. The flight lasted 50 minutes. I spotted two flak ships well to the north of France. An attack was laid on with Hurricane Mk IICs, each armed with four 20 mm cannon. I led four aircraft from 'A' Flight and John Robson led four of 'B'.

Flt Lts Peter Howard-Williams and John Robson of 118 Squadron at Ibsley, 1941.

We were to act as escort to the Hurricanes. The ships were 15 miles north of Cherbourg, much to our surprise, stationary and stopped together to form an 'L' shape. I thought that the Hurricane attack was pathetic - as they came in low their shells fell across the ships in one line. So they got very few hits. They then turned for home. I called up Robbie on the R/T and climbed to 500', so that in a dive I could be sure of every shell hitting the ships. I broke off just over the masts. Robbie and his section did the same. My No 2, Geoffrey Painting, was shot down. He was only 17, which of course we didn't know at the time. There was a lot of publicity in the press about it. I also remember that Robbie was pretty shot up when he got back. We were later informed that one of the ships (600 tons) sank.

'On November 9th, 1941, I flew twice to beat up tanks on Salisbury Plain as a demonstration for munitions workers. By coincidence one of the tank commanders was an old friend, Major Johnnie Aird. He later became secretary of the MCC at Lords. He told me a few days after the exercise that we had actually taken off several of the tank aerials!

'Distilleries were another of our targets whilst flying Rhubarbs. On November 15th, 1941, flying W3943, 118 Squadron attacked four distilleries. I attacked that at La Meuffe and the target furthest south was at St Lô which was attacked by David Fulford's section. There were three Spitfires in each attack. It was a Fighter Command organised attack and many other squadrons were involved. A few weeks later I received a report from the French "Underground" movement that our attack had been successful. In the late 1950s I went to La Meuffe and could still see where our cannon shells had hit. Apparently the attack had been co-ordinated for when all of the distilleries were full of alcohol.

'On January 17th, 1942, we patrolled Swanage as Winston Churchill was there, or at least that is what we were told. I was airborne for one hour and 20 minutes.

'There is an interesting story about when "Widge" Gleed took over our Wing. He had commanded 87 Squadron for much of the Battle of Britain and was an ace. However, after the Battle of Britain 87 Squadron had been re-equipped with Turbinlite Havocs and Hurricanes for night-fighting, so he was a bit out of practice at day operations. However, he insisted on leading the Wing on our first sweep over Cherbourg since his arrival. It was a pure fighter sweep as I remember it. Apparently the Germans had got a little fed up with the way we almost considered the peninsula as home territory, and this day lay in wait. They used the Maupertus Wing and called in the Wings from St Omer and Abbeville. The idea was to clobber us good and proper. "Widge", however, made an error somewhere so instead of hitting the coast just east of Cherbourg to make a sweep inland and out west of Cherbourg, we ended up west of Alderney near the Casquets lighthouse. To divert a moment, the lighthouse keeper always gave us a friendly wave and we often made a low pass around the light. "Widge" decided on this particular trip that there was no point going east to Cherbourg as fuel would soon get critical, so he wheeled the Wing round and we set off for home. It was an interesting journey back as when we had gone about 20 miles, ground control came on saying that there were 20 plus bandits 15 miles astern of us, then 30 plus and then even a third group of Me 109s. We sped up a little and I think that Tangmere were scrambled in support. We didn't see any Me 109s as after 10 minutes they turned for home. Great relief all round. We always said that "Widge" Gleed's cock-up had saved us as someone reckoned that there were 100 Me 109s waiting to pounce from above'.

In November 1941, Peter had been awarded the DFC and the same year also appeared briefly with the other Ibsley Wing pilots in the film 'The First of the Few'. During that time he also flew escort to the He 111 bomber that the film company had used as an air-to-air camera ship. Fortunately Peter was a keen photographer and took many snapshots of the Spitfires and the stars during the making of the film.

On February 2nd, 1942, Flight Lieutenant Howard-

Another of Peter's snapshots taken with his own camera during the making of 'The First of the Few' at Ibsley. This picture shows John Robson, left, and Peter in conversation with actor Leslie Howard. Note the gun-port detail behind Robson.

Peter Howard-Williams with Leslie Howard. The Spitfires are Mk IIAs fitted with the Dowty Rotol Constant Speed propeller; using a control situated next to the throttle lever, the pilot could adjust the pitch of the propeller throughout the entire spectrum of settings and thus enjoyed an enormous advantage over earlier two-pitch propellers. The author was recently given a spinner cap fron such an airscrew in which the previous owner had been happily growing mint since acquiring the item during the 1970s!

Williams DFC flew Spitfire AA964 on 'Rhubarb 87', an attack on the alcohol distillery at Éroudeville. His No 2 was Pilot Officer Ted Ames. Red Section took off from Ibsley at 1120 hrs and set course for France. When 20 miles NE of Pointe de Barfleur, with cloud 8/10ths at 1,000', at just 100' over the slate-grey sea Red One turned slightly west. The Spitfires bobbed along in line abreast formation just 25 yards apart. Five miles further on, at 1150 hrs, the Spitfires were bounced by four Me 109Fs of III/JG2 that 'swept out of the cloud taking our aircraft completely by surprise'. Red Two took evasive action by climbing to 800'. 300 yards ahead an Me 109 overshot and passed across Red One's nose from east to west. Peter immediately snapped off a quick burst at the fleeting target but without result. He then dodged into cloud seeking sanctuary, but upon emerging was immediately attacked from behind by two Me 109s. Turning tightly to the right, he managed to get on the tail of one of his assailants, firing a five second burst of both cannon and machine-gun fire from 200 yards range. Descending, the Spitfire pilot saw an aircraft crash into the sea and believed that it was the 109 which he had attacked. Suddenly, however, Peter was hit from behind, a 20 mm Oerlikon cannon shell entering the fuselage and smashing the wireless set and cutting some of the machine's control wires. A 7.9 mm machine-gun bullet also struck the Spitfire adjacent to the pilot's throttle hand, but fortunately did not penetrate the cockpit and harmlessly ricochetted off. Peter again managed to reach the protective envelope of some 7/10ths cloud, but was again attacked upon emerging. He then had a 'general dogfight' with four Me 109s, during which he hit two of them. By this time the wind had carried the combatants far to the south. Being out of ammunition, and with a seriously damaged aeroplane, Red One found protective cloud and set course for base.

Research indicates, however, that JG2 did not lose any Me 109s in the combat, a fact perhaps confirmed by Peter himself when stating that he again fought four, the total number which originally attacked, when he emerged from cloud the second time. Oberleutnant Bottcher and Unteroffizier Münche each claimed a 'P36' destroyed WNW of Cherbourg, but these claims undoubtedly tally with Peter Howard-Williams and Ted Ames, the latter pilot being lost over the sea. It seems, however, to be yet another example of the speed and confusion of combat deceiving the human eye, as Peter must have surely seen his No 2 crash into the sea and not an Me 109 as he thought.

Peter's return journey was somewhat eventful:-

'It is always difficult to recall the details of so long ago, but I always remember the trip back. I have written some notes but in fact the actual experience was probably more hairy and frightening than I have been able to convey! Certainly the weather was bad across the UK and over the French coast. I think that it was marginal for a Rhubarb.

'I started off in cloud, climbing after a while and found that I was actually flying between two layers of cloud. My radio had been shot up so I was unable to obtain a homing bearing. I continued to steer due north over 10/10ths cloud with no idea where I was. Suddenly I nearly hit a barrage balloon, not the wire but the balloon itself which suddenly loomed up out of the haze. Visibility was very poor even between the cloud layers. I thought that it was either from a coastal convoy or part of the Portsmouth barrage. I turned on to a course due west, and after a while descended to try and ascertain my position. After getting down below 1,000' I decided that this was getting dangerous and climbed again until I was clear of cloud.

'I flew north for about five minutes before finally making the decision to bale out. I opened the hood and side door and undid my straps. I decided to climb out onto the wing.

'Looking out I suddenly saw a small gap in the cloud and a green field! I quickly resumed my seat, did up my straps and started to circle, descending into the hole. At about 500' or less, I found myself below cloud in poor visibility. I flew around for a few minutes and saw a golf course. Just the place for a wheels up landing, I thought, and selected one of the fairways. I made a couple of low passes hoping to clear the golfers away, but they just stood and waved! I returned to cloud base and suddenly saw that Bournemouth was nearby. It was then a simple matter to fly along the coast, turn left to Christchurch and follow the River Avon to Ringwood and Ibsley. Cloud base was still low so I waggled my wings in a low pass past the control tower and prepared to land.

'I knew that my rudder and elevator trim wires had been shot away, so had to be especially careful when landing. The wheels and flaps came down, and in spite of the lack of trim controls I made an ordinary landing. I taxied in, but in view of the time that I had been airborne, people were getting a little worried, especially as control had been calling me on the R/T but receiving no response.

'I went into my Flight Commander's dispersal hut, but in spite of sitting in front of a fiercely blazing log fire I could not stop shaking. There was only one cure. That evening we all went to Christchurch, to the Kings Arms, where I consumed more than my fair share of beer. Mary and Sidney Barker, who ran the famous inn, let me have a room for the night, even supplying pyjamas and a toothbrush. Next morning I drove back to the airfield and resumed normal flying.

'I only ever shot up one airfield on the Cherbourg peninsula, which happened on another Rhubarb. After one pass with all guns blazing, one of the other Spitfire pilots called me up: "Red One, take another look at the aircraft." I turned and

A snapshot of the damage to the fuselage of Peter's Spitfire, Mk VB AD209, sustained on Rhubarb 87.

realised that it was a dummy airfield with dummy aircraft! It was about 20 miles inland from Cherbourg. I never went to Maupertus which was heavily defended.

'In 1943 I was with 610 Squadron flying Spitfires again after an eight month rest job commanding No 2 Delivery Flight at Colerne near Bath. A super job! 610 were at Westhampnett as part of the Tangmere Wing when I joined them, later moving west to Bolt Head near Salcombe, and afterwards to Perranporth in Cornwall for a month. There we did all the usual jobs flying with the Exeter Wing, but we also had some odd jobs too.

'A fishing boat would come out of the Helford River in Cornwall and we would escort it south until it was dark, flying very low the whole time. A day would go by, and the following morning we would try and pick it up in mid-Channel, again keeping low. On landing we would say a code word down the telephone, and immediately be connected to someone in London who wanted

Flt Lt Howard-Williams DFC and Spitfire Mk II at Ibsley, 1941. Note the recently applied day fighter identification band around the rear fuselage. Generally this 'sky' band was painted vertically, but this one appears at a slight angle. Note the pilot's parachute positioned on the wing, straps hanging down, ready for the next scramble.

to know how many were on board and various other questions. The fishing boat had joined the Brest fishing fleet and gone into harbour either with or to pick up agents. We were always the squadron who did this job so far as I know. I have vivid recollections of the fishing boat.

'We would also do the same thing with Navy MTBs. Two would leave Dartmouth, towing small landing craft. We would take them until last light, and be up next morning to pick them up again. Sometimes they would be without one of the landing craft, presumably having beached it and the tide gone out. I presume that they were small Commando raids. Anyway, it was interesting for us to do something different.

'It may interest you to know that I did 294 operational trips lasting 306.55 hours, so the average trip was an hour about. Often though one would be scrambled and after being airborne for 15 minutes would be recalled as the bandits had returned home'.

Peter Howard-Williams remained in the post-war RAF until 1958 when he retired as a Wing Commander. I traced him during 1988 whilst I was researching 19 Squadron during the Battle of Britain, the subject of my first book, 'Spitfire Squadron'. Peter was from the outset extremely helpful and offered great encouragement. I had the enormous pleasure of meeting both Peter and his wife Pamela at the RAF Museum on May 13th, 1990, when 'Spitfire Squadron' was launched, and on which occasion we were privileged to have present every surviving 19 Squadron Battle of Britain pilot resident in the UK. Sadly, however, Peter was a cancer sufferer and eventually succumbed to his illness in 1993, at the age of 73. In the final weeks of his life, Peter, a colourful character full of fun, wrote many letters to me and the foregoing has been largely extracted from that correspondence. He also discussed his treatment and operations but always appeared both cheerful and optimistic. As he said, 'I used to gamble as I had no shoes, until I met a man without feet...' I believe that my friend knew that he was dying and wished to record his memories before it was be too late. My only regret is that he did not live to see this book published with which I know he would have been thrilled. This section of 'A Few of the Many' is my personal tribute to Peter Howard-Williams.

Wg Cdr Peter Howard-Williams DFC RAF Retd pictured shortly before his death after a long illness in 1993. He wrote the experiences recounted in this book during the last weeks of his life.

Chapter Thirteen

Flight Lieutenant Wallace Cunningham DFC

Pilot Officer Wallace 'Jock' Cunningham of 19 Squadron at Fowlmere, September 1940.

My first book, 'Spitfire Squadron', which told the story of 19 Squadron at war 1939-41, illuminated the life, service and death in action of Squadron Leader Brian Lane DFC, the exceptional 23-year-old leader and fighter pilot who commanded the squadron between September 5th, 1940, and June 15th, 1941. The book's thread departed from 19 Squadron on that latter date to follow Squadron Lane's career elsewhere. This was something that, after the book was published and further information came to light, I later came to regret. After the Battle of Britain, and certainly before June 1941, many fighter pilots who had survived the summer of 1940 were posted away on rest to various non-operational duties. At this time Fighter Command's Nonstop Offensive also commenced, but its operations were costly. Many experienced fighter pilots, veterans of the Battle of Britain, were lost over France, either killed or captured. This experience Fighter Command could ill afford to lose. By summer 1941, therefore, due to postings and casualties, the membership of Fighter Command's squadrons was virtually totally changed from that of the previous summer. It is at that juncture that I now wish I had concluded 'Spitfire Squadron', i.e. when the association with the squadron was largely ended by those who had flown during the Battle of Britain.

I arrived at the RAF Museum on May 13th, 1990, for the launch of 'Spitfire Squadron', and rushed around getting things organised, meeting up with Simon Parry of Air Research Publications, my publisher at that time, and John Foreman and Syd Harvey who were at the Museum together with Oberst Hermann Büchner, holder of the Knights Cross, launching 'Me 262 Combat Diary'. I was due to meet at the museum all of the surviving 19 Squadron pilots resident in the UK, all of whom had contributed to my research. Upon my arrival I noticed a man standing alone in a quiet corner. I did not recognise him, but noticed immediately that he was wearing the tie of the Battle of Britain Fighter Association. We introduced ourselves, and I found myself in the presence of a stalwart member of 19 Squadron during 1940 and '41: Flight Lieutenant Wallace 'Jock' Cunningham DFC.

Wallace Cunningham came from Glasgow and was an RAFVR pilot. He joined 19 Squadron at Duxford in June 1940 as a Pilot Officer. His first success came on August 16th, when he destroyed an Me 110, which was followed by an He 111 on September 7th, and Me 109s on both the 9th and 15th. Three days later he shared a Ju 88, and on October 8th received the DFC. On November 15th, 19 and 242 Squadrons were detailed to patrol a convoy off Harwich, but in the event the pilots were unable to locate their charge. Instead 19 Squadron was vectored to intercept bandits approaching England in a north-westerly direction at 25,000'. Two condensation trails were spotted at 35,000', 15 - 20 miles apart, and the squadron separated into flights to give chase. Red Section, comprising Squadron Leader Lane, and Pilot Officers Cunningham and Vokes, chased the leading German and climbed south to get between the enemy and the sun. After a 20 minute chase up the Thames Estuary, the bandits were close enough to be identified as Me 110s. Simultaneously spotting the 'Indians', the 110s turned east and dived. Lane ordered Red Section into line astern and attacked. Subsequently the enemy machine crashed into the Thames Estuary near Southend. Unteroffizier Boschen was killed, but the pilot, Leutnant Heinz von Jakob, was captured. 'B' Flight's target was also sent plunging into the estuary and its crew were both posted missing. Both aircraft were from a reconnaissance unit, 1(F)/22. During the action, Cunningham's Spitfire had been damaged:-

'I was tucked in behind Brian Lane and diving after the fleeting Me 110. Because of our high speed Brian was struggling to get his sights on the target - I was almost jostling him off to get a chance. Before we eventually destroyed the enemy aircraft, after letting the pilot bale out, I had my armoured glass windscreen shattered. Not, we worked out later, by the enemy, but by Brian's empty cartridge cases!' The Thames Estuary was the scene of 19 Squadron's next but final combat of 1940 which occurred on November 28th when the Spitfires clashed with Me

109s of I/JG26 'Schlageter'. With the onset of winter weather, 19 Squadron was not to make another combat claim until June 27th, 1941, during the Fighter Command Offensive over France. On that day another 19 Squadron stalwart and Flight Commander, Flight Lieutenant 'Farmer' Lawson DFC, destroyed an Me 109 over Lille, as did Sergeant David Cox who was himself shot up. On July 21st, Sergeant Charnock destroyed an Me 109, followed by another on August 7th, 1941. In July, Lawson had been promoted to Squadron Leader and took command of 19 Squadron. Cunningham was promoted to Flight Lieutenant and became commander of 'B' Flight. In 1994, Wallace Cunningham remembered those days:-

'I recall the high level sweeps over France, escorting a few Stirling bombers, so mildly offensive that the Germans did not put up any fighters for us to tangle with. I remember also a fair number of low level trips to attack shipping off the Dutch coast. These were extravagant on Blenheim losses. There was one daylight raid on Cologne, I recall it positively because I had an abscess on my backside and a stye in my eye - very warlike I felt!

Jock Cunningham writing home in a Fowlmere Nissen hut.

'During this period we had German night raids on London and Coventry. We were up on some of these but the blinding effect of the glowing Spitfire exhausts right before the pilot's eyes made it both unpleasant and futile. Altogether these raids were very depressing - we could see the explosions of bombs, the ignition of incendiaries, but could not see the bombers. The technique approved was to sit below the AA flashes and hope to see the enemy aircraft silhouetted against them.

'Of course we routinely flew up and down coastal convoys in the North Sea. The graveyard of Dogger Bank showed up the

19 Squadron's Spitfires on patrol, 1941, snapped by Plt Off Scott.

dangerous task of these underpaid, little appreciated merchant seamen. Hopefully our presence frightened off the odd raid. We sat at low level east of the convoys, looking into the setting sun. Any sign of an attacker and we made a great show, chasing off the poacher. Sometimes when it was judged too dark for the bombers we would be instructed to "pancake" - a mile or two west of the convoy and we would see AA flashes. The bomber would have watched us against the setting sun and noted our departure.

'I recall one thick, misty day over the North Sea trying to find a convoy. I would be vectored onto the convoy's position but at a height of several thousand feet which was necessary for radio contact with base. When I descended through the murk to try and find the convoy, trying to guess where fog stopped and sea started, no contact was made. This occupied me for a time but I guess that the controller decided that if I had so much difficulty, having the benefit of his assistance, then the convoy was safe from attack!

Pigeon shooting, Fowlmere style 1941. Flt Lt Walter Lawson DFC picks up the bird despatched by Flt Lt Cunningham DFC, and watched by Sgt David Cox.

Fowlmere, the way it was: 19 Squadron's pilots relax, Flt Lts Cunningham (fourth left) and Lawson (third right) discuss the day's events.

Above: Jock playing shove ha'penny at Fowlmere, 1941. The previous day the pilots had played against the Queen of England!

Left: Jock with his car in the Dutch barn at Fowlmere.

An oft photographed 19 Squadron Spitfire at Fowlmere during 1941 was a presentation aircraft, 'Armagh', another fighter presented by the Belfast Telegraph Spitfire Fund. This aircraft, P7849, was flown by many of the squadron's pilots, but in particular Sqn Ldr Walter Lawson DFC, seen here about to take-off.

A rare air-to-air of a Spitfire Mk IIA, the pilot is Sqn Ldr Lawson DFC and the aircraft 'Armagh'.

One can only guess! Jock Cunningham with 'Armagh'.

'The squadron moved to Matlask, a satellite of Coltishall, about the beginning of August 1941. We were billeted at Itteringham Mill, a beautiful house situated over a mill stream filled with trout. To Farmer Lawson and I this had all the appearance of a rest cure. The ante-room had a large open fireplace with inglenooks. I had a large and comfortable room with my own batman. I even had my dog there. Then we were sent on that stupid trip to Rotterdam'.

On August 21st, 1941, 19 Squadron re-equipped with Long Range Spitfire Mk IIAs, which were received from 234 Squadron. These new aircraft extended the squadron's operational range, so on August 26th, 19 Squadron escorted Blenheims across the North Sea to attack a convoy off the Dutch coast. The operation to Rotterdam docks on August 28th, however, was to prove extremely costly. 19 Squadron Operations Record Book:-

'1800 hrs: Squadron took off from Matlask together with 12 long range Spitfires of 152 Squadron before rendezvousing with 17 Blenheims from 21, 89 and 110 Squadrons. Course was set to cross the Dutch coast south of Oostveine, the bombers being in three boxes of five, six and six at 2,000' with 19 Squadron in sections of four on their port side and 152 on the starboard side at 2,000'. The Dutch coast was crossed at 1900 hrs and the formation then turned to port so that the bombers could cross the target area, the Rotterdam docks, in line abreast. Whilst the bombers went in to bomb their target, 19 Squadron kept to the west to pick up the bombers as they came out. Very heavy flak was encountered over Holland between Rotterdam and the coast both from the ground and ships in the river south of Rotterdam, particularly from a ship which appeared to be an armed merchantman. Some of the flak had a low trajectory of about 100' and range of about a mile. Pilot Officer Marsh reported seeing flak coming from a church tower. The result of the bombing was not observed as the squadron was not over the target area, but one bomber was seen to go down in flames'. The Blenheims certainly had it rough. 110 Squadron Operations Record Book:-

'Low-level attack made from 20', and each aircraft dropped two 500 lb SAP and four dropped 24 incendiaries. Aircraft 'H', flown by Sergeant Jenkinson, scored a direct hit on a red painted ship of 8,000 tons just off dock 14. Flame and bright red smoke was observed. During these operations, Wing Commander Cree reported seeing a Blenheim crash into a warehouse on the north-west corner of Maashaven, which started a large fire. The same pilot also reported seeing a Spitfire going down in flames. Aircraft 'H' reported a further Blenheim seen to crash into the river from low-level shortly afterwards. Considerable AA fire encountered and aircraft 'K' hit several times although damage not serious'.

The Spitfire down was Sergeant Savidge of 152 Squadron. Whilst all of 110 Squadron's Blenheims returned safely, 21 Squadron was not so lucky:-

'Four of our aircraft did not return'.

19 Squadron:-

'Whilst over Holland, Pilot Officers Marsh, Stuart and Strihavka shot up a ship in the river south of Rotterdam. Sergeant Charnock and Pilot Officer Edmunds shot up a machine-gun post each and Sergeant Sokol a factory. When the bombers came out from the target area they were escorted home. Pilot Officer Marsh landed 25 minutes after the rest of the squadron to report Squadron Leader Lawson DFC missing. Both pilots had apparently become separated from the rest of the squadron and were coming home on the starboard side of the bombers. When 15 miles off the Dutch coast, Pilot Officer Marsh saw his leader on the tail of an aircraft which he thought was a Spitfire. Squadron Leader Lawson did not appear to go into action and had no aircraft on his tail. Likewise there was no flak, but Squadron Leader Lawson broke away and Pilot Officer Marsh did not see his leader again, so joined up with 152 Squadron and returned to base'.

Squadron Leader Lawson was missing over the cold and inhospitable North Sea in Spitfire P7995. 6/JG53's Me 109s had been scrambled, and Feldwebels Krantz and Göthe each subsequently claimed Spitfires destroyed. One is believed to have been Lawson, the other a 41 Squadron aircraft off Yarmouth. Jock Cunningham, however, disputes this:-

'I am interested to know that Marsh claims that Farmer went down 15 miles off the Dutch coast. It would be interesting to know at what altitude as I did not see any enemy fighters at mast-height - the altitude at which we were flying. I missed Farmer about 6-8 miles inland on the way in'.

From records, Pilot Officer Marsh was certainly the last person to see Squadron Leader Lawson alive, which was after leaving the Dutch coast. By that time it is assumed that the Spitfires had climbed to a more appropriate altitude, which is when the Me 109s attacked, having a more suitable opportunity for an ambush than amongst the maelstrom of aircraft at zero feet over Rotterdam docks which was in any case a hotbed of flak which knew neither friend from foe. Or was it just a question of yet again the speed of combat deceiving the human eye - and if so whose? Whatever happened, Squadron Leader Lawson DFC remains missing to this day.

Jock Cunningham recalls his own experiences of that day:-

'During the 100 mile North Sea crossing we flew so low that the Blenheim airscrews made a furrow on the sea's surface. Our height was held down so that we did not show up on the German radar. 19 Squadron with Squadron Leader Lawson leading crossed the coast south of Rotterdam and continued flying east for a few miles. The Blenheims turned more sharply after crossing the coast and went for their targets in the harbour. By this time we had turned 180 degrees and flew down the estuary just above the Blenheims' height. There was no sign of any German aircraft and in any case we were too low to be useful in that respect. We continued drawing fire, however, from the naval vessels in the harbour. I was hit by a multiple pom pom and started streaming glycol. My No 2 called "Jock, you're on fire, better climb." I started to do so but the engine began labouring. I could not gain enough height to bale out so I made for the beaches south of Amsterdam. I crash-landed on the sand - in front of a gun post. A machine-gun there from fired a few warning shots and two soldiers came over and took possession. My efforts to start a fire were unsuccessful. As I had descended, my No 2, Peter Stuart, a fine Canadian, said "Cheerio Jock - good luck." Sadly he was killed the next day, shot down off the Dutch coast.

Flt Lt Cunningham was captured on August 28th, 1941; the loss of yet another experienced pilot and leader which Fighter Command could ill afford. Here Jock is pictured with his flight shortly before he was shot down. From left to right: Plt Off Johnson, Sgt Boswell, Flt Lt Cunningham DFC, Flg Off Michael Lyne, Plt Off Burke (on wing), Plt Off Andrews and Plt Off Stevens.

Flight Lieutenant Cunningham DFC's war had come to an end, shot down not in aerial combat but by anti-aircraft fire. The German machine-gunners of Küstenposten 3 der 9 Kompanie III Battalion, Infantrie Regiment 723, were credited with having shot Jock down. That claim, however, Jock now disputes:-

'That is horsecock! I was absolutely positive, beyond question, that the hits which knocked me down came from multiple pom-poms on a ship in the estuary.

The hits ruined my engine, I became a streamer and after comment by Peter Stuart, my number two, instead of heading out to sea, I tried to gain height. As I got back to the coast (going west), my engine seized and so I turned south to make a wheels-up landing on the sand. At this stage Küstenposten 3 der 9 Kompanie III Battalion, Infantrie Regiment 723, fired a few machine-gun bullets at me from a post in the dunes. Then a platoon of "goons" took over'.

Now a prisoner of war, Flight Lieutenant Cunningham was taken to their Officers' Mess:-

'After a glass of champagne and some tomato sandwiches it started to penetrate that I was a prisoner of war, that I had survived and had a future! Such a thought had actually been excluded from my mind since the start of the war. In the Mess they had a three-piece orchestra playing "J'attendrai" and "Sur le pont d'Avignon", all very emotional for a shot-down airman.

'After a night in a cell at Amsterdam gaol I travelled with the crews of two Blenheims to Dulag Luft at Doasch near Frankfurt. This was an interrogation centre through which aircrew passed en route to less pleasant conditions. I then had nearly four years in a PoW camp. Waiting for me at the gates of Dulag Luft was Dennis Cowley, also of 19 Squadron, who greeted me with "Your ____ dog!" My dog had bitten Oxlin's thumb, so he couldn't fly. Cowley was going on a 48 hour leave but took Oxlin's place. Cowley was then shot down - another little drama.

'I suppose that the episode of our trip to Rotterdam at least provided a paragraph in the "Daily Mirror" , "Yesterday our aircraft bombed ____".' The loss of both its Commanding Officer and a Flight Commander hit 19 Squadron hard. Arthur Vokes found himself promoted to Acting Flight Lieutenant and assumed temporary command of the squadron. The following morning, he led 11 of 19 Squadron's Spitfires on a search for Squadron Leader Lawson, as the Operations Record Book relates:-

'East coast was crossed at 12,000' and the squadron proceeded on a vector of 130 degrees from base in order to arrive in the area where our missing pilot was last seen, about 10 - 15 miles off the Dutch coast from the Hague. Our aircraft swept the area but without success and were just about to return home when they encountered a formation of about 10 Me 110s at about 500'. The enemy aircraft were in line astern and apparently engaged in bombing practice as there were smoke floats in the sea'.

Martin Drewes was amongst the Me 110 pilots of 6/ZG76 engaged by 19 Squadron over the North Sea on August 29th, 1941. Leutnant Drewes shot one of the Spitfires down into the sea. He is pictured here later in the war whilst a Major and having received the Knight's Cross as a night-fighter pilot.

The Me 110s belonged to 6/ZG76 which was employed on coastal defence. The combat that followed was ferocious. Although the Me 110s were outnumbered by one aircraft, this combat must represent one of the rare occasions when the twin-engined Me 110 came off significantly best against the Spitfire: 19 Squadron lost four Spitfires. Pilot Officers Stuart and Edmunds, and Sergeants Davies and Parkin, were all killed. One of the successful enemy pilots was Leutnant Martin Drewes, himself a veteran of the 1940 air battles over England and who was to become an ace during the forthcoming nocturnal defence of his Fatherland. 19 Squadron claimed the destruction of two Me 110s and two more damaged. In reality, however, only one Me 110 suffered '15%' damage. For 19 Squadron the sortie was clearly an absolute disaster. No trace of Lawson was found.

A week later, Acting Flight Lieutenant Arthur Vokes was also dead. On September 5th, 1941, the Temporary Commanding Officer of 19 Squadron took off on a ferry flight from Coltishall to Matlask in Spitfire P8166. Visibility was poor and the cloudbase descended dangerously low. As the pilot emerged from the cloud he realised just how low he was, desperately attempted to flatten out but crashed into a field near Langham aerodrome. Undoubtedly the loss of his two close friends, Farmer Lawson and Jock Cunningham, had played on his mind. On February 2nd, 1942, Flight Lieutenant Cunningham wrote to Arthur Vokes' mother from Oflag XC:-

'Pilot Officers Andrews, Cowley and myself, all of the same squadron, send our very deepest sympathies to you and Mr Vokes. Arthur and I were together for a very long time. We were on duty together and spent our leisure hours together. I don't know how I should have felt if I had been left with both he and Farmer gone. Arthur was always happy in what he was doing and most certainly fulfilled the greatest duty asked of him by his country'.

Jock Cunningham now adds:-

'With Farmer's death and accompanying losses, a period of stable operation ended and the squadron, I understand, was withdrawn from active service for a period. Farmer Lawson had been a good friend to me for what was, in those days, a long time. Like Brian Lane, who was also killed in action and similarly reported missing over the North Sea, he was another very competent and respected leader. I always regretted, however, that my departure from the scene had not been on a more worthwhile project'.

Caged fighters. From left: Plt Offs Andrews and Cowley with Flt Lt Cunningham, all of 19 Squadron, with an unidentified pilot, whilst prisoners of war.

Left: Margaret Balfour pictured whilst in the WAAF and serving at Duxford in 1940.
Right: Walter 'Farmer' Lawson pictured whilst a Flight Commander with 19 Squadron at Fowlmere during 1941. Sqn Ldr Lawson DFC was shot down over the North Sea by an Me 109 of JG53 on August 28th, 1941, and remains missing to this day.

Apart from his comrades in 19 Squadron, Squadron Leader Walter 'Farmer' Lawson DFC was also mourned by his sweetheart, Margaret 'Peggy' Balfour, a pretty young member of the Women's Auxiliary Air Force. In 1994, Margaret recalled Farmer Lawson:-

'A week or two after we had arrived at Digby, I remember going to a Camp dance held in the Sergeants' Mess. I had never before been to a dance unescorted, and without really knowing who would be there or what it would be like. However, I was standing in the hall doorway, in the shadows, taking stock of my surroundings before venturing in. It all looked great fun. The music was playing merrily and everyone seemed to be dancing happily. I remained where I was. Then someone came over and asked me to dance with him. What joy - he was tall and danced beautifully. I loved dancing. We danced and chatted, and then he called across to one of his friends, "Tubby, guess what, I'm dancing with a WAAF who is asking about centrifugal force!" I had asked him. I wanted to know. I had been reading an article, which I did not understand, about it in my "Times" that morning in Ops. I learnt that my dancing partner's name was Jack Lawson and that he was a Sergeant Pilot in 46 Squadron flying Hurricanes, like many of the other pilots present. Before 46 Squadron left Digby I got to know Jack "Farmer" Lawson well. He never fussed me, and danced beautifully, completely to my liking. And above all he was great fun and made me laugh.

'I always liked the Guard Room at Digby. The guards were friendly and always helpful. When Jack was free he used to send notes to the Guard Room asking when he could meet me. It was all fun. Jack had a car, so we were able to leave the camp. We used to visit local pubs, or buy fish and chips and eat them out of newspaper. The weather always seemed fine and sunny. We laughed a lot, and were always talking, we talked about everything, putting the world to rights, and we argued as we certainly did not agree all the time. I remember that he always teased me about my ideas, and I think he thought me a little mad. But we enjoyed our jaunts into the countryside and had lots of fun.

'By this time we WAAFs had all met lots of people on camp and were finding our way around. We started playing tennis, although Jack and I never managed one game together, duty always intervened. Once we did manage to get our racquets out of their presses, and were actually out on the court, when the siren sounded and Jack had to fly. That is the only time that I ever saw him angry, but he was then. We had tried so hard to get a game together, but it was not to be, it seemed. We did enjoy life. There were dances attended by the whole camp, and I usually danced the last dance with Jack.

'Jack was commissioned from Digby and was posted to 19 Squadron at Duxford in April 1940. He wrote often, his letters always cheerful, telling me about his activities, or at least as many as he was allowed to relate. The sweeps over the south coast seemed never ending, the poor old White Cliffs - Dunkirk, and the Thames. And the endless night-flying, there seemed so little respite from it all. At Digby we were out of it, but I would sometimes sit and worry about what went on down south.

'June and July 1940 were busy months in Ops. I received letters from Jack Lawson, scribbled in haste, telling me how the squadrons moved around, how once his aircraft had been shot up and how lucky he had been. And how, on an airfield they had visited, they were able to make use of the swimming pool there, lovely during the hot weather, but only once - the next day it was blasted to rubble and they were off again. He always made light of the activity taking place on the south coast, teasing me about my "holiday camp" in the north. In a letter to Jack around that time, complaining about red tape and discipline, I must have sounded gloomy. He wrote back telling me off, said it made him gloomy and sad. I never did that again. In no way would I ever be a burden to him as I knew that flying required 100%. Life was difficult enough just staying alive from day to day. In one letter written from Coltishall, Jack had to break off to "mount aloft" as he put it. Back again, he told me that he had "caught nothing, better luck next time". I used to worry and his letters made me think, there was no respite, and life was so fragile. However, nothing was gained by being miserable. And so the summer passed.

'In June 1940 I passed a Commission Board at the Air Ministry. By that time Jack was a Flight Lieutenant and commanding 19 Squadron's 'A' Flight. They were always flying, all sorts of horrible things had happened to 19 Squadron. It was wretched being so far away, not really knowing what was going on from day to day. I see from one of Jack's letters that early in September he had a 48 hour leave and flew up to Digby. It was the only leave that we ever had at the same time. The weather was lovely, the sun shone, and it was warm and mild. As we now had no car, we walked and visited local pubs, it was great fun and we enjoyed ourselves, it was such a change and of course we actually met so seldom. In the evening we danced on the camp and met friends - all very civilised. The time flew. Although

I had not managed to get across the airfield to see Jack arrive, I did get over to the Watch Office to see him off, or so I thought. The Magister flying up to return him south was late arriving. I was simply furious I remember. I stamped my foot and stomped off. However, we had enjoyed our 48 hours.

'During that visit to Digby Jack spoke a little about flying. He was almost casual about his exploits in the air. I knew little of what went on down south, and little about 19 Squadron. He told me about the night flying, how cold and dark it was. He told me how he enjoyed life - usually -the squadron, and flying. And then he told me that there was just one thing he dreaded, for the hood of his Spitfire to get stuck, preventing him from baling out if necessary. I froze. Suddenly a vivid picture, a blue sky, vapour trails, movements everywhere, racing and diving aircraft, and one aircraft in the midst of them, a blazing inferno, its pilot trapped. I couldn't move or speak. Then Jack turned to me and said, "Remember, whatever happens it is always in God's hands." The spell was broken, the picture faded. I was pleased that he told me of his fear. Standing there I suddenly knew that no-one else would ever take Jack's place. For me that was it, forever. I did not tell him at the time as I did not want him to think about anything else but flying, everything else must wait.

'In October I received a wire from Jack saying that he was flying up for the evening of our Ops dance. I had written inviting him, but never really thought that he would be able. My delight was unbounded. As I was off duty all that evening I walked over to the Watch Office to find out if I could watch Jack's aircraft arriving. Although the airfield was out of bounds for WAAF, the Watch Office staff were so helpful. They found out when the aircraft was due, and let me wait with them in the warm. It was very interesting and the staff explained much to me. It was a cold, clear evening but not quite dark. I watched the aircraft approaching, and one of the landing crew escorted me right to the runway. It was very exciting. The pale sky, the flarepath, only dimly lit, and the twinkling lights from the aircraft as it circled and finally landed. I should not have been there. It was very unofficial. The field looked very calm in the half light. The stationary aircraft, all put to sleep for the night, such peace. To me it was magic that I was there at all, but Jack told me that nothing I ever did surprised him! We walked back across the field, straight into the dance. Everyone was there, from the Station CO to the last Ops plotter. The dance was in full swing when we arrived and everyone was so pleased to see Jack back again. They thought it such an achievement, to get up to Digby just for that Ops dance. We danced and talked and argued as usual. I introduced Jack to the other girls I lived with in "Haywire Shack" and we had a party on the spur of the moment. The band played our favourite tunes. What an evening. Midnight came around so soon, and our 'A' Watch had to go on duty and Jack had to return to Duxford at dawn. All a mad rush, but great fun, and I never, ever forgot it.

'During November Jack's Distinguished Flying Cross was confirmed. I had a 48 hour pass and as the weather was fine thought that I would hitch-hike down to Cambridge, not far from Duxford. Jack was flying in the daytime so could only get to Cambridge late in the evening. But it was fun to meet just for dinner, and walk around the old pubs. I thought that he looked tired, the first time that I had seen him so, but as he said, the squadron was flying all day and on stand-by at night.

'I had booked a room for myself at the Red Lion Hotel in the centre of Cambridge. Jack said that I would be alright there and I found out later that he had spoken to the desk clerk and asked him to look after me. I gave Jack his pullover, which I had so laboriously knitted and actually completed before the cold weather. He told me that it fitted and was doing well in keeping the cold winds at bay when he was flying. I hope it did. In Ops we WAAF must have looked a strange sight, sitting round the table needles clacking'.

On that fateful day, August 28th, 1941, Margaret was off duty. However, she returned the following day to find that a friend had left a note in Ops informing her that Jack Lawson was missing. The following is extracted from Margaret's diary:-

'I must not give in. I must write something in my diary, but what can I say, just that Jack has been shot down. He is missing, there is no hope for him. 19 Squadron is nearly all gone, those left are searching for remnants this morning. I can't think of anything yet, I am just numb, and shattered. I can't feel anything at all. I hope that I'm alright when I come to. I'm not going to think about Jack, I've put all memory away for a time. In a day or so I will be alright, but not now. We are very busy, there is so much talking and 'phoning round to do, finding out more about 19 Squadron. No-one has mentioned it to me, we never talk about anything like this when it happens. But already I have been brought three mugs of tea and it is still only 1030 hrs. They are all such dears. Someone on the top desk even pulled out a chair for me when I came on duty. I thought that no-one knew about Jack and me, it feels as though they have all taken one step closer, but no-one will say a word. I couldn't bear to have sympathy, that would finish me. I must get through the next few days with no fuss'.

True to her word, there was only Jack Lawson for Miss Margaret Balfour.

This story certainly illustrates the uncertain future faced by a fighter pilot during the Second World War. Just take three friends, all of whom had survived the entire Battle of Britain together - Squadron Leader Jack 'Farmer' Lawson DFC: killed in action, Flight Lieutenant Wallace 'Jock' Cunningham DFC: captured by the Germans, and Acting Flight Lieutenant Arthur Vokes: killed in a flying accident - all within the space of just one week.

Jock Cunningham reunited with a Spitfire at Duxford in 1980. By coincidence, in this particular Spitfire, AR501, owned and operated by the Shuttleworth Trust, Andy Sephton performed a stunning display of aerobatics over Yeovil at the launch of the author's fourth book, 'Angriff Westland' in September 1994.

Chapter Fourteen

Flight Lieutenant Cedric Stone DFM

Sergeant Cedric Stone pictured at Biggin Hill, September 1941.

The presentation Spitfire P8045, 'City of Worcester I', initially flew with 72 Squadron. My research into its history during the mid-1980s brought me into contact with several wartime pilots from this squadron, amongst them Cedric Stone. Cedric had some interesting memories to share:-

'I learned to fly before the war, one hour per month. I went solo after 1¹/₂ hours dual. When I joined the RAF it took 11 hours for me to shake off instructors! I was nearly thrown off my advanced training course by three senior instructors. Was it luck or fear of a high casualty rate that persuaded the powers that be to keep me on? Since the war I have been an instructor myself in an honorary capacity.

'As a Sergeant Pilot I flew my first 72 Squadron Spitfire, RN-N, on a patrol of Gravesend, Manston, Maidstone, Tonbridge, etc. Squadron Leader Desmond Sheen DFC was CO. Flight Lieutenant Clark was 'B' Flight Commander. Many of the squadron boys, including myself, went to Squadron Leader Sheen's wedding. Max Aitken DFC, "Sailor" Malan DSO DFC, Al Deere DFC and Brian Kingcome DFC were all pilots amongst us when we became a part of the Biggin Hill Wing. I remember on one occasion Sholto Douglas (Lord Douglas of Kirtleside) and Leigh-Mallory visited Biggin Hill. They later joined an Officers' Mess party where Douglas was debagged!

'Cedric Masterman took over 72 Squadron about October 1941. Bocock was then 'B' Flight Commander with whom I paired frequently. My own 72 Squadron Spitfire was a presentation aircraft paid for by the South Africans of Basutoland. In this aircraft I often flew daylight escorts to Stirling bombers, sometimes as close escort, sometimes we went over France as the bombers were leaving. On one occasion I came out of France in a Spitfire Mk V to the Seven Sisters, the famous white chalk cliffs in Sussex. The radar fixes on me, both sides of the Channel, were said to indicate that I crossed the Channel in ONE MINUTE! This is actually unlikely, but if fixes were taken five miles to sea from each coast, then my ground speed would have been 600 - 700 mph. Thank God for the Spitfire!

'In fact, on that particular sortie, our job was to relieve the squadron who had escorted the bombers to France. We were deep in France and in tight formation when suddenly from 7 o'clock behind us, we were about to be attacked by a German unit of Me 109s. Desmond Sheen was leading us and he turned sharply left. I was his No 2 inside the turn. To avoid collision I had to throttle back to keep station, and tighten my turn. There was nothing for me to do but stall, and in the unexpected stall I lost height quickly, in a spiral spin. By the time I had recovered and sorted out the spinning, I realised that the squadron was too far away for me to catch up. I was in the middle of nowhere, and very vulnerable, 20,000' up or so, with no cloud cover and a long way from home in a very hostile environment and over territory that I did not recognise. My only hope was to return to England as soon as I could. The next question was, where was the French coast and English Channel. My compass was slow to settle down after the spin and recent turmoil. Slowly, however, I could see north and recovered my bearings. Heading north I seemed to be the only aircraft in the sky. It was a moment or two later that I saw a speck on the horizon. I kept an eye on that speck. I weaved to enable me to see the horizon all around me. The speck came nearer and nearer and seemed to divide into two specks. Then I could see, they were each a pair of aircraft heading towards me. I took my time. I prepared my sights and turned my gun button to "fire". I examined those two specks again. They were aircraft. They were 109s. I prepared for action. Fine pitch and a re-check. I was ready for a fight. I must keep firmly seated as otherwise the gunsight, including range finder, would be distorted. The second pair were now positioning themselves. I had one pair on each side of me so that I could be attacked one after the other from two sides. I could not play cat and mouse with them because there were no clouds in which to hide. My only move was to climb to gain the advantages of height. With a half roll and shuddering in a violent tight turn I felt gravity drain the blood from my eyes. I levelled out to a point that I regained full sight of one. Then in another turn I knew that only a superhuman, fitter man than I, could undertake an even tighter turn. Therefore it was unlikely that anybody could tighten his turn to get a "bead" on me. I then suddenly came out of the turn with my gun platform, to pocket my first victim, and immediately rolling in the opposite direction whilst also performing a barrel roll. I felt flushed, sweating, but determined. My engine was purring marvellously, even though it was being overworked. I offered a gentle prayer as I felt two 109s had been put out of action. I did not see the next to leave, I just knew there were only two left in the ring, and I'd not felt a bullet in me yet! As they made another effort, I got one of them on a beam attack. I'd no more ammunition left! As the third went down I turned again for the fourth. He, however, headed for home but I was fully prepared to collide with him rather than be his victim. However he was shy and left me to gather my wits and reconsider where I had got to. I could do no more, I had no more ammunition, so home I must go. As soon as I had sighed my relief, I looked down at my instruments. My goggles were misted, I was wet with perspiration. I could see nothing in the dark floor of the cockpit. It took a moment or two to reorganise myself, to find north, to find a mark on the French landscape to which I could relate on my map. Then with another check for bandits, the sky appeared clear. I put my nose down for home, checked the fuel, pitch of the propeller, and revs of the engine. My speed was too high for a German to catch me up! I reached the French coast, and then the greatest sight of all was the white Seven Sisters of England's coastline. I had survived - four Germans had strategically arranged themselves and attacked, but had now to lick their wounds. I returned safely.

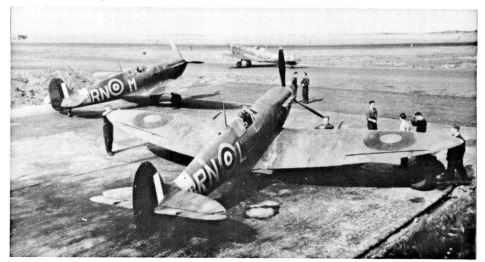

72 Squadron Spitfires at Gravesend, 1941.

Spit-fire! A brand new 72 Squadron Spitfire Mk VB has its guns harmonised in the butts, Biggin Hill 1941. Both cannon and machine-guns are being fired.

'If my memory serves me well, on one occasion we were patrolling at 30,000' over the English Channel in a cloudless, sunny sky. The Spitfire Mk VB cruised at about 250 - 300 mph. Wing Commander Robinson (later to become an Air Vice-Marshal) was our Section Leader, and Jamie Rankin was his No 2. I was "tail-end Charlie" in our section of three aircraft. No other aircraft were visible, although we had been vectored to the patrol area in anticipation. R/T silence had been observed throughout our flight and patrol. Suddenly a message from base informed of 'E' Boats in the Channel. Our instructions were to "seek out and attack!" Wing Commander Robinson answered "Roger" and we went nose down at full throttle. We gained speed rapidly. The Air Speed Indicator needle went beyond the dial figures and ceased to record! The Altimeter showed a very rapid descent. The aircraft vibrated badly and I throttled back to save the engine which was already well over maximum permissible revolutions per minute. I became conscious of our No 2 aircraft having problems holding station. Suddenly his perspex canopy flew off and nearly hit me. The later post-mortem indicated that "Robo" had fired his guns. An empty cartridge case hit Jamie's canopy and damaged a perspex panel which allowed the air to enter. That in turn created a surge of pressure in the empennage, blowing the rivets on the panels so that the canopy broke away completely. I had followed, but fortunately avoided the shower of debris, although it felt like riding a bicycle on corrugated iron sheets. Our speed was probably the speed of sound (*sic*), i.e. almost twice the normal maximum for which the Spitfire was designed.

'We three landed safely, but the flying characteristics seemed different from normal. All three Spitfires were recorded as unserviceable until checked. In fact the wings had been bent to a permanent set of some 8 degrees. Luckily they did not break off, another accolade to the designers and manufacturers of this superb fighter! The three aircraft were all stripped down and re-built, never to fly again in their distorted state. I was not informed whether the 'E' Boats had been hit!

'I was posted overseas at the end of January 1942, and joined 73 Squadron in North Africa during April 1943 flying Hurricanes - an awful comedown!

'Dilip, I would like to say how wonderful is that you, and people like you, can share in the excitement of the Spitfire. To think that after all these years those who flew them are of interest to people like you, a little over a third of their age. Thank you'.

Cedric Stone was to meet Cedric Masterman, one of his former 72 Squadron COs, after the war, during the 1950s, when the latter enrolled Cedric into the Secret Service in the Far East - although perhaps the less we know about those adventures the better! But it does make you realise what incredibly interesting and exciting lives these men - our heroes all - have lived during what were troubled times. The very least that my generation can do is show respect, gratitude and record their memories for posterity.

Cedric Stone is now retired and living in Sussex, not far from the Seven Sisters cliffs towards which he once hurtled in his Spitfire. An enthusiastic member of the Spitfire Society, Aircrew Association and recently formed 72 Squadron Association, he is another whose life has been forever touched by the Spitfire legend, of which he is himself a part.

Cedric Stone pictured in 1993.

Chapter Fifteen

Warrant Officer Peter Fox

Sergeant Peter Fox.

On September 15th, 1940, two 'sprog' pilots arrived at Boscombe Down in Wiltshire to fly Hurricanes with 56 Squadron. Sergeants Peter Fox and Dennis Nichols were both 19 years old and from the RAFVR stable. Their new squadron was a regular air force unit with a great tradition, having been one of the most outstanding fighter squadrons during the First World War. 56 Squadron had received its Hawker Hurricanes in April 1938, and in May 1940 was amongst Fighter Command's squadrons being overwhelmed in France. Withdrawn to Digby at the end of that month, in June the squadron returned to its home base, North Weald. From there it was heavily engaged in the Battle of Britain, where Wing Commander 'Taffy' Higginson OBE DFC DFM RAF Retd, then a senior regular Sergeant Pilot, recalls that 56 'suffered a bit of a beating'. Certainly the squadron had sustained five of its eight Battle of Britain pilot casualties whilst flying from North Weald. By the time of 56 Squadron's withdrawal from 11 Group, Fighter Command had devised the Stabilising Scheme which categorised squadrons 'A', 'B' or 'C'. Category 'A' were those up to strength and in the front line, 'B' were those being rested due to previous losses but which could be called upon if necessary, and 'C' squadrons were those unlikely to be recalled to action due to their heavy casualties but usable as an extension of the OTU process by providing tactical instruction to new pilots prior to passing them on to either 'A' or 'B' units. On September 1st, 1940, 56 Squadron had been downgraded as a 'B' unit and consequently arrived at Boscombe Down where it replaced 249 Squadron, the latter taking 56's place in the front line at North Weald. The day after their arrival, however, the two teenage Sergeants, Fox and Nichols, were introduced to the dangers of squadron life when they were both pall bearers at the funeral of a fellow NCO pilot killed during dogfight practice.

Whilst 56 Squadron received an influx of replacement pilots, as a 'B' unit it still had to remain prepared to do battle. 10 Group, in whose area the squadron now reposed, covered the West Country, wherein were situated a number of targets of interest to the Luftwaffe. On September 25th, 1940, KG55's He 111s had obliterated the Bristol Aeroplane Company at Filton. Two days later an unsuccessful attack was made against the Parnall aircraft factory at Yate. On September 30th, 40 HE 111s of KG55 returned to the West Country, tasked with the destruction of the Westland aircraft factory at Yeovil. Amongst those squadrons intercepting was 56, and Sergeant Peter Fox, with 20 hours flying time logged on the Hurricane, caught his first glimpse of a massed German 'Valhalla'. 'I just couldn't believe it', he later wrote. The Heinkels were approaching the English coastline at Lyme Bay. Peter selected one of the rearmost bombers, 'aimed firstly at one engine, pressed the gun button and sprayed across to the other'. His target suddenly slowed down significantly and peeled off to port. Peter followed, still firing, 'when there was an explosion and I noted that there was little left of my instrument panel'. Fortunately his hood was already half open, otherwise it could have jammed when the enemy round hit the cockpit. 'I broke to starboard, pulling upwards and away, with all controls apparently working correctly. I got over land at about 3,000' and was wondering whether I could make Warmwell when I saw flames coming up between my legs. I don't think that I even thought of my next action but instinctively rolled the kite upside down, released my harness and saw my feet above me and the plane above my feet, presumably stalled. Where was the ripcord? I told myself to calm down, and pulled the 'D' ring straight away! I had never before pulled a ripcord, never seen one pulled, never seen a parachute packed, and never had any instruction. The 'D' ring was flung into the air, followed by some wire. Obviously I had broken it. Then I felt the small tug of the pilot chute followed almost immediately by the full wrench of the main parachute. I was safe! The next second I was aware of an "enemy" which I assumed was going to shoot me. It was, however, my flaming Hurricane which literally missed me by inches. The kite slowly screwed round, going into a steeper and steeper dive until almost vertical, aimed directly at the cross-hedges of four fields to the NE of a wood towards which I was drifting. It hit the cross-hedges spot on, a short pause and then a huge explosion followed by another pause before flames shot up to a great height. I'm glad that I wasn't in it!' Sergeant Fox drifted down, his knee slightly wounded, and was taken to Lyme Regis Police Station. KG55's He 111s had been escorted by the Me 109s of JG2 and 53, and Me 110s of ZG26. All of these units claimed to have destroyed British fighters, so Peter's Hurricane was undoubtedly hit by either an Me 109 or 110. The raid, however, was a complete failure as the West Country had been totally shrouded in cloud; instead of the formation's bombs hitting Westlands, they fell entirely on the nearby, picturesque town of Sherborne.

A week later, Ju 88s of II/KG51, with a fighter escort identical to KG55's raid, attacked Westlands. However, as if by some divine intervention, again no bombs fell on the famous aircraft factory; instead all fell on Yeovil town centre. Amongst the RAF fighter pilots defending the West Country that day was Sergeant Dennis Nichols, himself also being shot down during his first clash with the enemy. Dennis baled out, but was not as fortunate as his friend Peter Fox; his back was broken in a heavy landing and thereafter followed six months in hospital.

In November 1993, the Malvern Spitfire Team returned Dennis Nichols to the crash site of his Hurricane at Alton Pancras. It was his story that inspired me to research and write 'Angriff Westland', telling the full stories of both Westland raids in great detail and from all viewpoints. This research of course led me to Peter Fox, although there was some considerable work involved in respect of his loss on September 30th, 1940, as various incorrect contemporary records had produced a veritable historian's minefield in respect of times, dates and locations concerning several of the West Country casualties, not least Sergeant Fox and his Hurricane, N2434, US-H.

Peter Fox and I enjoyed some lengthy correspondence, and one fascinating story arising therefrom is as follows:-

'It was in August 1940, the Battle of Britain in full swing, when two planes flown by Sergeant Pilots Neil Cameron and Peter Fox dived to attack the enemy. We were actually still smarting, having had our applications for commissions withdrawn by Squadron Leader Verdon-Roe. He told us that pilots who tear away telephone wires from golf clubs with aircraft would never get anywhere in the RAF.

'Intrepid as we were, we went straight into the attack when we saw the enemy whilst having a practice dogfight. "Rat-a-tat" was heard over the R/T. Numerous sweeping attacks were made by each plane in turn, and the German rear gunner's sights locked time and again onto each ...but he did not press the button and fire, neither did either of the British pilots. In fact, none of them really could.

'One could be forgiven for thinking that the pilots were very brave young men, attacking the enemy unarmed, but they were both, in fact, full of fun and love of flying without thought of danger as they flew their yellow Miles Master training planes time and again to within range of the German gunners.

After a while we ceased making machine-gun like noises over the R/T and returned to our base at No 8 FTS, Montrose in Scotland.

'Also based at Montrose was an operational Spitfire squadron, 602 'City of Edinburgh'. Several days after our encounter with the enemy, the Montrose Spitfires were scrambled, engaged the enemy and promptly shot down one Wellington bomber. It crashed into a skating rink in Aberdeen, killing the complete all-GERMAN crew and a number of civilians.

'After the German invasion of Norway and the speedy evacuation by the British, a number of our aircraft were apparently left behind, one a Wellington which the Germans craftily used for reconnaissance up and down the east coast of Scotland. It seems that they had not changed the squadron markings and they were seen by a member of aircrew who had been in Norway and later reported it.

'Myself and Neil Cameron had had our fun with a Wellington crew, watched the guns sweep over us, but had no idea that the crew really WAS the enemy!

'Squadron Leader Verdon-Roe was 50% correct in his assessment of our careers: one became a Lord, Chief of Defence and Chief of Air Staff, and the other remained uncommissioned - I won't say which!' A reference manual regarding the biographies of the Few published in recent years indicates that on November 16th, 1940, Sergeant Fox and Pilot Officer MR Ingle-Finch crashed at Tidworth in a Magister whilst en route to Kidlington. Peter Fox comments:-

'It was November 18th, not 16th, when the Magister was flown into a haystack, NOT by me, possibly neither of us was flying it!'

Pilots of 234 Squadron at Warmwell, summer 1941. Sergeant Peter Fox is third from right, standing.

Pilots of 234 Squadron. Those identified are, top row, second right: Flt Lt Mortimer-Rose, middle row, from left: Sgt Sapsed, Sgt Walker, Sgt Macleod, Plt Off Burchill, unidentified, Sgt Broad. Kneeling, from left: Sgt Fox, Sgt Shepherd and Sgt Nankeville.

On June 28th, 1941, Sergeant Fox joined 234 Squadron at Warmwell to fly Spitfires. Warmwell, located slightly inland of Weymouth and again in the West Country, well positioned the Spitfires for sweeps of the Cherbourg peninsula and to provide protection for convoys. It was on such duties, during the Fighter Command Offensive, that Peter found his new squadron engaged. However, Sergeant Fox soon became yet another casualty of the so-called Nonstop Offensive:-

'It was not long after the CO of 234 Squadron, Squadron Leader HM Stephen, told me that he would hold back his recommendation for my commission by two weeks (because in a fortnight my Flight Sergeant's crown would be due and which meant that if I was commissioned thereafter it would be not as a Pilot Officer but as a Flying Officer) that things started to go wrong. About time! I first missed being commissioned at No 1 ITW, Cambridge, due to a posting; then at No 8 FTS Montrose, a post with telephone wires interfered with the process, and then, in 1940, whilst serving with 56 Squadron at Boscombe Down, I was flown into a haystack. One may think that a haystack would be soft enough, but it was 3½ days later that I woke up again with a broken back. Meanwhile the commission passed by once again!

'However, it was a lovely morning on October 20th, 1941, at Warmwell airfield in Dorset, and everything seemed to be going well - my back had mended, I was 20 years of age, my commission was on the boil again, and I was poised to go home to Oxford on leave.

Presentation Spitfire P8046, 'City of Worcester II', made just one flight with 234 Squadron, a strafing attack on Maupertus airfield (now Cherbourg airport), on August 26th, 1941. Whilst Sgt Fox blew up a petrol bowser, Sgt Clifford Jacka was hit by machine-gun fire over the airfield and ditched 'II' in the Channel. His body was later washed up on the French coast and buried by the Germans at Cherbourg cemetery. Peter Fox had the unenviable task of visiting Sgt Jacka's parents at their Bournemouth guest house and breaking the sad news. This photograph shows 'City of Worcester I', P8045, outside the Castle Bromwich Aircraft Factory. No photographs of 'II' have so far been found.

Courtesy Worcester Evening News.

 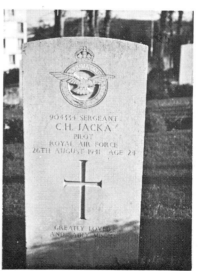

Above left: Sgt Clifford Jacka of 234 Squadron. From Bournemouth, Jacka attended the town's Grammar School and was a keen motor-cycle enthusiast who worked in the local motor-cycle shop.
Above right: The grave of Sergeant Clifford Jacka in Cherbourg cemetery.

Brian Owen

'In one pocket of my best uniform was a signed leave pass, and, in another, a snapshot of some of the pilots, including myself, standing round the squadron transport with "234" painted on the windscreen. My parents would have been interested to see it in a few hours time after I had been flown to Kidlington in the station Magister. I was also intending to show my parents the identity disc with "Rissole" on one side and "234 Squadron. F/Lt Mortimer-Rose" on the reverse. My flight commander, "Morty", had only recently given me the dog. There was also my invention! I had drilled a small hole in the lever of the CO_2 bottle which, when pulled, inflated the Mae West. A piece of cord was then passed through the hole and was tied with a bow to the buoyant cushion which, on top of a parachute, formed a seat for the pilot. This would give automatic inflation of the Mae West, whether or not the pilot was conscious, having baled out over the "drink". It was just necessary to remember to untie the bow before getting out of the plane at base.

'It was lunchtime and the squadron was about to be "stood down". "It won't count off your leave!" was the CO's response to me volunteering for a "nuisance" raid over France. Sergeant Sapsed volunteered as my No 2. The sortie was to locate and blow up an ammunition dump sited just inland and to the east of Cherbourg. Another volunteer pair were to strafe an aerodrome to the west of Cherbourg.

'Wind blowing from west, so a course was calculated from Portland Bill to a bay east of Cherbourg. All four Spitfire Mk VBs, each armed with two 20mm cannons and four machine-guns, were ready to go. Take-off on Warmwell's grass runway, with wind from the west, meant taxying away from dispersal, the full length of the aerodrome and then turning into wind. Peter applied his brakes to turn into wind for take-off and a tyre burst! Undo harness, undo bow to CO_2 bottle and out; run the length of the aerodrome and into another Spitfire, AZ-H, AD203, in place of "C726" which I usually flew and which was now standing empty at the far end of the field with its burst tyre. No revolver or Verey pistol in the pocket of the new Spitfire!

'Over Portland Bill, course set, and no sign of the other pair, just "Sappy" following me, flying just above sea level across the Channel. What appears to be the correctly-shaped bay appears in just under 1/2 hour; cross the coastline and what seems to be a single machine-gun opens up - a thud and the oil pressure gauge drops to zero; I tell Sappy over the R/T "I've had it!", but the R/T doesn't work, probably damaged by the same bullet. No revolver or Verey pistol with which to destroy the Spitfire, so must turn back to sea to dump it, hoping to then swim back to land. Engine now objecting to running without oil, and sounding very rough. I fired a short burst of my guns in anger until I noted the poor cows scattering in the field ahead. Coast in sight, engine stops, speed drops, and I hit a telegraph pole with one wing. The aircraft slews round and gently tips on its nose and then settles back. Quite a gentle crash really. Must try and escape - undo harness, jump up - up blows Mae West, can't get out! Bags of fumbling, a great raspberry as the Mae West pressure drops, out I get, run across a couple of fields and dive under a hedge where the cover is good and thick.

'I was in the hedge quite deep, at the junction of hedgerows, and had time to take off my Mae West, undo my escape kit, take off right shoe and sock and place money, maps and compass under the instep before replacing sock and shoe. Voices come closer, a male French voice shouts "Come out, boy. He see you or he shoot." Two shots ring out, although I do not know whether fired into the hedge or air. After some quick thinking I decide that discretion is the better part of valour, and crawl out hands up to face a small crowd of civilians and a German soldier armed with a rifle on the farther side of a fence to another field. Mae West thrown over fence, two hands on top of fence, a great leap and I am in their field. I well remember the civilians' applause for my athletic prowess! In an endeavour to convey my sadness at not having been able to destroy my plane, and my knowledge of the German language being schoolboyish in the extreme, I point to my Spitfire, klaxon blaring, in the centre of the adjacent field. I placed my hand on the German soldier's rifle. Our conversation in German must have been absorbing as he let go of it! A moment later a couple of German officers appeared - one slapped the soldier's face, snatched the rifle from me and returned it to the soldier. Life returned to "normal". Salutes having been exchanged, we all walked across the field to a road. There a soldier ran out of a building to take my photograph. I will never know why on earth I raised my arm over my face to prevent the photograph being taken, as such a photograph could have been used to show a "Terror-Flieger" - ashamed.

'We then went off to Maupertus aerodrome near Cherbourg where I met some Me 109 pilots of I and II/JG2. Most of the pilots spoke English, but I considered it wise not to tell them that on August 26th my squadron had strafed this airfield - I had blown up a petrol bowser! We enjoyed considerable good humoured banter, but they would not let me fly an Me 109 to formulate a comparison! Whilst playing table tennis with one of the pilots a very different type of uniformed officer abruptly stopped the game and it was a hard bed in a small cell for me for the rest of the night.

'Immediately on arrival at Maupertus I had been searched; my Mae West, photographs, leave pass, English money and dog-tag were stuffed into a bag and parcelled up with no inspection of any item having been made! All was neatly tied up, a label on the parcel's outside duly filled in and an official stamp applied.

'Off next day by car and train, via Paris, to a PoW camp called Dulagluft, near Frankfurt. The Me 109 pilots had kindly pooled their weekly chocolate ration and gave it to me in a small box. It was all British chocolate, presumably captured during the evacuation in 1940. I only had to carry this small box, until my guard decided that the much larger parcel of confiscated items could best be carried by his prisoner.

'Off the train in Paris, into a taxi to a building to the south. Here my guard bade me a temporary good-bye whilst he went off for food, leaving me in a room with three new guards and my parcel. The window was fully open, about 10' off the ground, and I could see planes taking-off and landing at a nearby aerodrome. There was general friendly conversation between us all, plus boredom on the guards' part. To pass the time I opened my parcel and showed the guards my Mae West - making sure that my leave pass, photograph and dog-tag went into my pocket before re-parcelling it!

'Then a forlorn hope, a striped sentry box was at the gateway entrance to the buildings about 30 yards from the window. On the opposite side of the internal roadway was a narrow building running the full distance. I worked out that if I jumped out of the window and ran three paces, the guard would have to run a full 20 yards before he could get a shot at me. At the bottom of the garden was an even shorter distance and woods lay beyond that to the airfield. A nursemaid with a baby in a pram was chatting to the sentry, the light was fading and with it the possibility of the window closing and black-out.

'I tore up the leave pass, replaced it in my pocket, chewed up the photographs in true spy drama style; guards all sitting down, thoroughly bored at having had English money explained to them at length, wander over to the window and OUT! Quick recovery, onto my feet, over the road, down the narrow side of the building - and there is the sentry already, rifle sighted "HÄNDE HOCH!" The sentry had not run towards me, but along the road for four or five paces where he had a full view of the bottom of the garden. I was later aware of complaints from the guards about my double-cross after our friendliness earlier, but fortunately they did not harm me.

'Then off again in a taxi through Paris for the train to Dulagluft. The taxi window was open and somewhere in some Parisian road were thrown a dog's name tag, a leave pass in little pieces and a chewed up photograph. Having bought me grapes en route during the long train journey, the guard left me with my Mae West parcel at Dulagluft after wishing me well on my next escape attempt! Sadly those good wishes were of no avail, as I was to make five more abortive escape attempts - earning a total of six and a half months in solitary confinement with bread and water.

'Five main PoW camps plus three working party camps and 3 1/2 years behind barbed wire had elapsed before I was home again in England and able to read in my log book the entry: "20 OCTOBER SPITFIRE H203 MISSING - SHOT DOWN BY FLAK OVER LA MAZERIE'.

War, in some cases, can be excellent for accelerated promotion; by 1945, Peter's 56 Squadron contemporary, Dennis Nichols, was a Flight Lieutenant, having flown Beaufighters in the Middle East after recovering from his Battle of Britain injuries, but as a prisoner Peter remained uncommissioned, eventually leaving the RAF in 1946 as a Warrant Officer.

Before leaving the air force, Peter met Beryl, a WAAF serving at Cosford, and the couple later married. They live near the sea in the West Country of England which Peter, now a retired surveyor, once fought to defend during the Battle of

Britain. He sees himself merely 'as an also ran who came in very late on'. The Battle of Britain exploits of both Peter Fox and Dennis Nichols were told in 'Angriff Westland', and it was an honour that both should join us for the book's launch at Westland Helicopters on September 24th, 1994. Peter Fox was full of enthusiasm for the whole project and occasion, and was found to be as full of fun and humour as his correspondence suggested. When shown an artifact restored by Dennis Williams from the crash site of his 56 Squadron Hurricane, Peter's eyes lit up as he rushed off to show Beryl this mangled cog, once part of a machine from which he only narrowly escaped violent death at the hands of the Luftwaffe. By the time of this book's publication, we anticipate that our project to eventually return Peter to Wootten Fitzpaine and clear his Hurricane's crash site will have been undertaken. At the time of writing I look forward very much to that occasion because I know that it will be a laugh a minute with Peter Fox around, despite his 74 years! One can only assume that his enthusiasm and great sense of humour were perhaps the main things which sustained him during his period of captivity.

Chapter Sixteen

Flight Lieutenant Ken Wilkinson AE

Flight Lieutenant Ken Wilkinson poses with his 165 Squadron Spitfire Mk IX.

In 1988, I traced and contacted Ken Wilkinson in connection with my research into Spitfire R6644, the subject of my second book, 'The Invisible Thread: A Spitfire's Tale', to ascertain whether he had flown this aircraft whilst with 616 Squadron. The answer was negative, but Ken did send his record of service:-

'I was a pupil at Cheltenham Grammar School and my father worked for the Gloster Aeroplane Company at Gloucester. I joined the RAFVR at Cheltenham and completed my pre-war flying at Staverton. I would have transferred to the RAF but the war started whilst I was still in the VR. Completed flying training between May 1940 and August 1940, then went to 7 OTU at Hawarden to fly Spitfires, thence to 616 Squadron at Kirton-in-Lindsey who were at that time a 'C' squadron taking in and training replacement pilots as an extension of the OTU system. In October 1940 I joined 19 Squadron at Fowlmere. Early in 1941 I became an instructor at a Fighter Gunnery School, but returned to an operational Spitfire squadron, 234, in the Orkneys early in 1943. We then went south to Church Stanton near Taunton, thence to 165 Squadron at Ibsley, Kenley and again Church Stanton. From there to instruct at a fighter OTU, thence to fly Spitfire Mk XIVs at Cranfield, and finally to chase bombers training navigators and air gunners, both day and night, until released in November 1945'.

In 1994, during the research for this book, Ken Wilkinson eagerly volunteered to record his experiences in greater depth. During the years since first we made contact, Ken and I had come to know each other well, and he had always enthusiastically supported the Malvern Spitfire Team's various projects. I think that this friendship is reflected in the extent to which Ken has allowed his memory to be 'unlocked', as per the following:-

'In January 1943 I was at Martlesham Heath where we had a visit from the AOC, during the course of which he came to 1488 Gunnery Flight and in the dispersal came to me and said, "How long have you been here?", to which I replied "Too bloody long, Sir!" Now this is not the way for a Warrant Officer to talk to an Air Marshal, but nevertheless, within a fortnight I was back on a Spitfire refresher course at 61 OTU, Rednal. The RAF being what it is, I did a refresher course and became an instructor as well.

'I was soon posted to 234 Squadron at Skaebrae in the Orkneys. They were flying Spitfire Mk VIs which had a very extended wingtip. This allowed the aircraft to fly much higher than normal and also made sure that the aircraft was very difficult to land. In addition, the pilots were bolted into the pressurised cockpit so that they did not suffer too much from the height. 234 Squadron's job was the defence of Scapa Flow and hopefully to intercept aircraft flying from Norway out to the Atlantic to interfere with our convoys. It involved a great deal of sitting in cockpits at the end of the runway for two hours at a time. Sometimes we were scrambled, but there was very rarely any contact. We also had patrols up to Shetland and back, dusk and dawn. The dusk ones always started in daylight but finished in darkness. On one occasion when I was returning from a dusk patrol as No 2, the duty pilot had put the wrong direction on the runway so the section landing in darkness was landing downwind. The section leader did not quite appreciate his excessive speed and went off the end of the runway and tipped up, which is no joke when you are bolted into the cockpit. I was able to appreciate the excessive ground speed, however, so when I landed it was full left rudder and brake and stick hard back right down the runway until I managed to turn left down the perimeter track, without any damage. I'd saved an aeroplane. I switched off, got out and went to the aircraft which had crashed. That was okay, so I went back to my own aircraft and a senior officer came up to me and said "You were lucky, weren't you?" When you are a Warrant Officer you do not say what you think to senior officers on occasions like that!

'The squadron moved down to Church Stanton in 10 Group during June, and we were there put back on Spitfire Mk Vs. Early in July I was posted to 165

Squadron at Ibsley, where there was an increase in activity such as convoy patrols, recces to the Cherbourg area and the Channel Islands, and a bit better than it would have been at Church Stanton.

'At the end of July I was posted overseas, actually I had been asked to go to North Africa but before I could get onto the boat I was recalled to 165 which had moved in the meanwhile to Kenley. The reason for this was "Exercise Starkey" in which the intention was to entice the Luftwaffe into the sky and inflict upon them as much damage as possible. In fact the night before Exercise Starkey we were addressed by no less a personality than "Boom" Trenchard in RAF uniform, and it was really something to see that great man. The preparatory attacks for Starkey were nearly always with 72 Marauders with 165 as escort cover, the targets attacked were spread over northern France, Belgium and Holland. They were fairly regular whilst preparing for Starkey. One such target that 165 went to was Courtraix, and at the briefing we were told that there were other targets being attacked simultaneously. We rendezvoused with our 72 Marauders and went across the Channel, but soon after passing over the French coast we were bounced by the Luftwaffe and there followed a merry mix up all the way to the target. At the briefing we had been told that there was very little flak at Courtraix but when I got over the target where we were mixing it with enemy fighters there seemed to be hell of a lot of flak, far more than the Intelligence Officers warned us about. We were kept busy so the main thing was to make sure that the Marauders could carry on and do their job. When the raid was over and we were returning I was able to settle alongside the other Spitfires only to find that it was not 165 Squadron! However I stayed with them until I got back over England and then returned to Kenley where I was told that I had, in fact, been on the raid to Lille!

'A' Flight of 165 Squadron at Church Stanton, autumn 1943. Ken Wilkinson is standing on the wing at left.

'On the day of Exercise Starkey there were a great deal of landing craft in the Channel and a lot of Canadian soldiers, and 165 Squadron did a lot of standing patrols over Boulogne but the Germans did not take the bait, so what was to be the greatest air battle of all time was actually a damp squib.

'165 Squadron returned to Church Stanton and there we had Spitfire IXs that were an absolutely marvellous aircraft. We did lots and lots of Rodeos around the Cherbourg and Brest peninsulas, and for what ever reason I don't know but I seemed to be constantly given calibration flying, "30,000' Start Point to Guernsey" and the like, perhaps straight and level flying at height was the thing I was best at. One of the other things at a different level was to fly extremely low when approaching the French coast and in particular the Bay of Saint Malo. On one occasion I saw fish flying at the same height as my wings. When I reported this upon my return, I was told to take more water with it! The funny thing about it was that in later years on the television there was a programme which showed flying fish getting 10' high before dropping back into the water. Point made!

'Other things we had to do, boats escaping from France carrying agents and so forth, bomber crews ditched near the French coast, all had to be protected until ASR got there and generally this period of flying was fairly good. But I had to go back to teaching at a Spitfire OTU and then in June 1944, just after D-Day I went down to Redhill to a GSU on Spitfire IXs, and then to Cranfield on Spitfire XIVs, which was the best Spitfire ever, so far as I am concerned, and the adjutant of the unit at Cranfield was Noel MacGregor who had been a Sergeant Pilot with me on 19 Squadron. One day he said to me " how do you fancy flying in the Midlands?" Well, being from the Midlands and being married with a baby on the way, and with the flying on offer being at Honeybourne it seemed reasonable enough. The flying turned out to be a fairly obscure sort of thing, it meant pretending to be a German night-fighter and training bomber crews. The obscurity was such that on December 31st, 1944, I had drawn the short straw and was flying, chasing Wellingtons and the like, and after a while I became aware that there were not any clients. In those days the Hurricanes that we had could only receive but could not transmit and no one had thought sufficiently to tell me that there was no more work to do. They didn't tell me either that the weather had closed in and that the visibility at Honeybourne was remarkably restricted. Now, going into Honeybourne over Fish Hill when you can't see any runway lights is no joke. It was New Year's Eve and there was hell of a party going on in the Mess and I was frustrated. It took me three attempts before I got that aircraft down safely onto the runway; I didn't even get to the party as it had finished by the time I had landed. As you can imagine I had no great need for laxatives after that!'

Ken Wilkinson is now a retired surveyor. A widower, he lives alone in the West Midlands where he has become quite a chef, and is a keen golfer. He remains actively interested in aviation and is a member of both the Battle of Britain

Fighter Association and the Spitfire Society. A 'character', Ken Wilkinson is always a popular personality at our Ramrod Publications and Malvern Spitfire Team enthusiast's afternoons - we look forward to his friendship and support for many years to come.

Ken Wilkinson at the launch of 'The Invisible Thread: A Spitfire's Tale', *Great Malvern, September 1992.*

Dennis Williams.

Chapter Seventeen

Flight Lieutenant Mike Bush DFC

Flight Lieutenant BM 'Mike' Bush DFC.

On August 20th, 1939, Basil Martin Bush joined the RAFVR at Cambridge. From September 1st to October 26th he completed his 'square bashing' at No 1 Initial Training Wing, Cambridge, where he was billeted in St John's College. Thence he proceeded to No 6 EFTS at Sywell to learn to fly the de Havilland Tiger Moth. After flying Masters at Montrose, 'Mike' arrived at Hawarden and 7 OTU to fly 'Hurricanes at last!' Sergeant Bush's operational posting was to 504 'City of Nottingham' Squadron of the Auxiliary Air Force. He joined the squadron at Castletown in Scotland on July 16th, 1940. On September 5th, 504 flew south to Hendon and participated in the Battle of Britain. There, as the pilots awaited the call to scramble, Mike remembers that appropriately their favourite tune was 'Vera Lynn singing "In Room Five Hundred and Four".' Two days later the Luftwaffe bombed London for the first time in daylight, and Sergeant Bush was shot up by an Me 109 over the Thames Estuary. A cannon shell passed through his instrument panel and into the reserve petrol tank beyond: 'I was damned lucky not to catch fire as when hit petrol splashed all over me'. The encounter resulted in a forced landing on the Isle of Sheppey. On September 25th, He 111s of KG55 executed a precision and surprise attack on the Bristol Aeroplane Company at Filton. The following day saw 504 moved from Hendon and 11 Group to Filton in 10 Group as a precautionary measure against further attacks against targets in the West Country. The move was more than justified when the following day 504 and other 10 Group squadrons routed an attack on the Parnall aircraft factory at Yate by Me 110s of Erprobungsgruppe 210 which were escorted by those of ZG26. On September 30th, KG55 was briefed to attack the Westland aircraft factory at Yeovil, but found the West Country shrouded in cloud. In roughly the right place a town similar to Yeovil appeared through a hole in the cloud. The target was bombed but a tragic error had been made; the bombs fell entirely on the quaint Dorset town of Sherborne, which was of no military significance whatsoever. In what was the last truly great daylight battle of summer 1940, 504 pursued the Heinkels to within sight of the Cherbourg peninsula. Sergeant Jones shot two down into the sea and Sergeant Bush damaged another as did several more pilots. The return flight over the sea was long, however, and Mike Bush was unable to make Filton. Low on fuel and in decreasing visibility, he made a wheels-down landing near the village of Priddy in Somerset. The Hurricane involved, P3021, TM-N, was actually the same aircraft he had flown on September 7th when shot up over the Thames Estuary:-

'After the interception I was unable to obtain radio contact with Filton. As it was getting dusk and I was lost somewhere south of Bristol I was fearful of getting caught in balloon cables, so decided to land in a field. I picked what I thought to be a long landing run in a particular field which I had spotted, but on the approach I came in low over a hedge and landed, only to discover that it

504 Squadron Hurricane Mk Is at Castletown, mid-1940, before the unit moved south and participated in the Battle of Britain.

was a much shorter field than the one that I had selected, and ahead saw a brick wall. Having landed I could do nothing but jam on my brakes and switch off the engine. The action of applying the brakes hard resulted in tipping my Hurricane up on its nose. It then flipped over onto its back and I was left hanging by my harness upside down and several feet from the ground. Thankfully I was soon rescued by men of the Observer Corps from nearby Priddy village'.

At that juncture, however, 'Mike' and 'N' parted company for good. P3021 went on to have further adventures with other pilots before finally crashing and being written off over a year later.

On December 17th, 1941, 504 Squadron moved from Filton to Exeter, also in 10 Group, where it was later joined by the Spitfires of 66 Squadron. During that period Sergeant Bush often flew night interceptions:-

'We were sent up to take over from the ack-ack at Plymouth during a raid on February 10th, 1941. The guns were supposed to stop firing and let us have a go. The result, however, was that

Mike Bush's Hurricane Mk II in 1941. Note the 'Saint' painted below the cockpit and exhaust shields for night-flying.

they kept firing. It was apparent that they didn't care who got hit, so we got fed up and returned to base!'

Mike was commissioned on July 7th, 1941. Three weeks later No 81 Squadron formed at Leconfield, its personnel having formerly been members of 504's 'A' Flight, the CO being Squadron Leader Tony Rook and one of the Flight Commanders being his brother, Flight Lieutenant Michael Rook. On August 16th, Pilot Officer Bush left 504 to join 81 Squadron on HMS Argus, bound for Russia. 134 Squadron had formed on August 12th and for the same purpose, so the aircrew of that unit also embarked with 81. The purpose of the expedition was for the squadrons' Hurricanes to defend the North Cape convoys which shipped war materials to Russia. On September 1st, the pilots landed at Vayhenga, near Murmansk. Hundreds of Hurricanes were subsequently delivered in crates and the RAF squadrons had to provide an adequate air defence in addition to training the Russians to fly the Hurricane. Both squadrons became operational on September 12th. On that day 81 Squadron was in action over Russia, five Hurricanes intercepting five Finnish Me 109s which were escorting an He 126. Three of the Me 109s were claimed destroyed but Sergeant Smith was killed. Later that day Pilot Officer Bush damaged an Me 110, and in a further action Pilot Officer Walker and Flight Sergeant 'Wag' Haw destroyed three more Me 109s. That action set the scene for the next few months, during which, on October 6th, the Germans raided Vayhenga. By the end of that month, some 60 Hurricane MkIIs had been assembled. On October 28th, 134 Squadron was ordered to hand over its aircraft to the Soviet Air Force, and 81 did likewise in November and also returned to England. Although the Russian expedition was of a fairly short duration, 81 Squadron must surely have been an inspiration for the Russians, who at the time were suffering extremely heavy losses, in destroying over a dozen enemy aircraft during the first two weeks of their stay at Vayhenga. Mike Bush has some extraordinary memories of Russia:-

'Our Flight Commander, Mickey Rook, got separated from us during an interception and seeing "our" formation above him climbed up, saying on the R/T "Coming up to re-join you." When nearly there he realised with a start that "we" were actually six Me 109s! He beat a hasty retreat, but later on the blackboard in the Readiness Room someone drew a picture of some Me 109s with their pilots' heads peering out of their cockpits with question marks indicating astonishment! Mickey took some "flak" from us when he returned safely, which was actually much to our relief.

'The "bogs" or "loos" in that part of the world consisted of a deep hole dug in the ground and a five-sided hut placed over the hole. Although there were five compartments inside, there was no seated accommodation, so one had to "hover" with bent knees to accomplish anything, and, as the wind and cold were blowing like nobody's business, to use the very rough paper that was supplied one had to go in armed with stones to make sure that it dropped safely in the hole and was not blown back at you - a most interesting performance I can assure you!

'There were two parties given before we left Russia, one hosted by the Russians with ample supplies of vodka to make us merry, and another by ourselves with whisky and jugs of "water" to dilute if required. It was required and the Russians helped themselves to the "water", which, unknown to them, was actually neat gin. The result was excellent!'

81 Squadron Pilots making their way around the airfield at Vayhenga and adding a new meaning to the term 'Squadron Transport!' Mike Bush is at extreme right.

Perhaps such a scene could only be recorded in Russia. The old and the new at Vayhenga.

81 Squadron Hurricanes at Vayhenga, Z5227 in the foreground.

An incredible photograph. These contrails represent a high-altitude dogfight between Vayhenga's Hurricanes and Me 109s over the airfield.

81 Squadron arrived back in England on December 17th, 1941, and became stationed at Turnhouse. There the squadron exchanged its Hurricanes for Spitfire Mk VAs, and Pilot Officer Bush celebrated New Year's Day 1942 by making his first flight in the new type. On March 4th he was posted away as an instructor, on which duties Mike remained engaged during most of that and the following year. On June 10th, 1943, he arrived at Shobdon, near Leominster in

Herefordshire, to instruct army Hotspur glider pilots in preparation for D-Day. On July 29th, Mike's old 504 and 81 Squadron friend, Charlton 'Wag' Haw, himself now a Flight Lieutenant with the DFM to his credit, flew a Spitfire to visit him at Shobdon. Mike recalls that 'He "lent" me the Spitfire for 20 minutes, during which time I went aerobatics mad - smashing time!'

On April 20th, 1943, Flying Officer Bush was posted to Kidlington where he flew twin-engined Airspeed Oxfords as a prelude to converting to the de Havilland Mosquito, the legendary 'Wooden Wonder', with 1655 Mosquito Training Unit at Warboys. The experience required to fly a Mosquito at night over Germany also comprised a course at 1521 Beam Approach Training Flight at Wymeswold where pilots learned 'blind flying' techniques:-

'Whilst there the WAAF that used to wake us in the morning with a "cuppa" told us that she was posted, and that another girl would do the honours the following morning and that it might be a surprise! Well, it certainly was! She told us that she had instructed the newcomer what to do! I was awoken with a cuppa and a kiss, and a "Good morning, Sir!" To my astonishment she went round all the others with the same treatment and there was I thinking that I had been the only one singled out for such affection - no such luck! So much for the merry month of May, 1944!'

The de Havilland Mosquito had been conceived in 1938 as a private venture which the Air Ministry considered to be unorthodox. Its all-wood airframe lacked defensive armament, the designers believing that the 'Mozzie' could rely upon its superior speed and height for evasion. The prototype flew in November 1940, and by mid-1941 the new aircraft's incredible performance had earned it full-scale production orders. One of the earliest Mosquito bombers in fact, outpaced a Spitfire Mk V which was using emergency boost! Between entering service and 1945, the Mosquito undertook numerous roles, including reconnaissance, bomber, night-fighter, anti-shipping scourge and submarine hunter. The incredible thing was that, whatever the role, the Mosquito retained the performance of a fighter.

139 Squadron Mosquitos head into the dusk for a raid on Germany.

On August 2nd, 1944, Flight Lieutenant Bush joined 139 Squadron to fly Mosquito bombers at Upwood in Huntingdonshire:-

'There I flew a total of 54 night bombing raids, 18 of which were to Berlin, the "Big City" itself. The last trip of my war to Berlin was in good old "S" for Sugar on March 27th, 1945'.

To put that into perspective, the period summarised in a sentence by Mike Bush, the normal straight tour of operations was 30, and the chances of surviving that number was slim (although statistics indicate that Mosquito crews flew four times the number of sorties per aircraft loss than Lancasters), but 54, and straight off! What Mike does not mention is that for that sustained period of flying he won a much deserved Distinguished Flying Cross.

A 139 Squadron Mosquito is 'bombed up' at Upwood.

Nearly at the war's end, Flight Lieutenant BM Bush DFC was rested from operations once more and sent on April 17th, 1945, to be OC Flying at 1696 BD Flight at Bourn. There Mike flew Spitfires, training bomber crews against fighter attacks, and concluded his air force service in September 1945 with a total of 2053 flying hours.

After the war Mike returned to banking, from which he is now

Flt Lt Mike Bush DFC, right, with his navigator at Upwood.

retired and enjoying life with his wife in a tranquil spot in Lincolnshire. Although a member of the Battle of Britain Fighter Association, Flight Lieutenant BM 'Mike' Bush DFC has all but faded into obscurity. One of the Few, Mike undoubtedly has the credentials of a true war hero, but, typifies the modesty of such men who only recall for the inquisitive the amusing side of their flying days, omitting mention of either danger or decorations. He is yet another accomplished wartime pilot who saw himself as merely doing his job and personally as nothing special. However, Flight Lieutenant Mike Bush DFC, you are certainly special to us!

Basil Martin 'Mike' Bush, now retired from a career in banking, pictured at home, late 1994.

Mark Postlethwaite.

Chapter Eighteen

Flight Lieutenant Hugh Chalmers AE

Flight Lieutenant Hugh Chalmers, October 1942.

Hugh Chalmers enlisted in the RAF Volunteer Reserve on March 15th, 1939, at Glasgow. His weekend flying training was subsequently conducted at Prestwick on Tiger Moths. Between March 19th, and August 5th, Sergeant 745344 Chalmers recorded 25 flying hours in his log book. He has an amusing memory from this period:-

'Having gone solo, the adjutant collected five shillings from me for a licence for cross-country flights. It was never issued, but after the war, and having completed some 1100 hrs and still fit, I applied for the licence but it was refused. It was necessary to have a medical and there was so much red tape that I rebelled. I thought that if I wanted my money back then authority would reconsider, but no! I later received a postal order for five shillings!'

Hugh was mobilised on September 1st, 1939, and thereafter had to first report daily, then twice weekly, and then just weekly to Glasgow Town Hall. Finally the RAF said 'don't call us, we'll call you'. Eventually, on December 2nd, Hugh was posted to No 3 Initial Training Wing at Hastings. Elementary flying training was then undertaken at Burnaston, Derby. The threat of invasion, however, was constantly in mind:-

'Old cars were pushed, sometimes driven, all over the airfield after each day's flying as an anti parachute landing measure. Each of us was issued with a rifle and five rounds of .303 ammunition. It was at the time of Dunkirk and although I never experienced any violence, there was expressed a feeling of anger by returning soldiers at the apparent absence of the RAF over the beaches'.

At Burnaston, Hugh had learned to fly the Miles Magister monoplane, but then took a step backwards to fly Tiger Moths again, although this time at night (dual), on his Pre-Fighter Course. The Harvard was used as a fairly high performance monoplane trainer as a prelude to Spitfire or Hurricane flight, and Hugh flew Harvards at 15 Service Flying Training School at South Cerney. There he was able to practice solo night landings in that type. Eventually he arrived at 7 OTU, Hawarden, where he was passed in the dual environment of the Miles Master, before at last reaching his goal - to fly a Spitfire:-

'The undercarriage of the Mk Is that we were flying had to be pumped up by hand, and the fore and aft movement of the aircraft controlled on take off by the other. I can vividly recall therefore my first solos! I only managed about 7 hours on the Spitfire as the weather was poor'.

On October 28th, 1940, Sergeant Chalmers reported to fly Spitfires with 65 'East India' Squadron at Turnhouse in Scotland. Previously the squadron had been heavily engaged during both Operation Dynamo and the Battle of Britain. The Battle of Britain officially ended, according to the Air Ministry, on October 31st, 1940. To be eligible to wear the coveted Battle of Britain Bar to the 1939-45 Star, and therefore be considered one of the Few, the pilot concerned had to have flown at least one operational patrol between July 10th and October 31st, 1940, with one of the units accredited as having taken part. Hugh's first flight was beyond those parameters, but he accepts that the squadron had been withdrawn north as a 'C' unit in the process of rebuilding to strength and training replacement pilots away from the 'sharp end'.

On December 8th, 1940, 65 Squadron moved south, to Tangmere in Sussex, and Sergeant Chalmers flew with them:-

'It was a relatively quiet period with more or less uneventful patrols and the odd offensive sweep with little opposition. My Flight Commander was Gordon Olive and he noticed just how little flying time I actually had on Spitfires and so pushed me on, especially on dusk patrols and night flying. This opportunity of gaining extra experience undoubtedly enhanced my chances of survival later on'.

On February 26th, 1941, 65 Squadron were relieved at Tangmere by 616 Squadron. They swapped over aircraft, and 65 flew to Kirton-in-Lindsey, recently vacated by 616, in the latter squadron's former Spitfire Mk Is. Hugh remembers:-

'My new 'A' Flight Commander was Stanley B Grant. Although again not in the front line, 65 flew a lot more from Kirton. It was at the time of Fighter Command's Offensive and 65 would sometimes stand by at Duxford or Fowlmere or join a practice sweep. More often it was to West Malling - sweep - then refuel and return to Kirton well after dark (more night flying practice!). "Sam" Saunders was our CO, the other Flight Commander was Tommy Smart. I was still an NCO pilot along with MacPherson, Oldnall, Stillwell, Mitchell, Hewlett, Baxter and Rose.

'I shall never forget one scramble as Stan Grant's No 2. An intruder over Hull. Cloud was at 1,000' and I had to close in. We climbed to 19,000' and were still in thick rain cloud. No 1 suggested to the controller that as he could see nothing then neither would the intruder. We were recalled but I had to stick with him all the way back as I figured that it would be safer two together than alone. We got back to the circuit and Stan landed on the flarepath which was two poles with red, orange and green lights and a string of lights into wind. The strain on my eyes must have upset my judgement because I smacked the left-hand post with my port wing and trailed a whole string of lights up the grass. The interesting and comforting thing was that although the wooden post was snapped like a matchstick, not a mark could be found on the leading edge'.

Left: Sgt Hugh Chalmers climbing out of his Spitfire after a sortie from Kirton. Note the non-regulation sheepskin gloves!

Below: Sgt Hugh Chalmers (seated at top of bonnet), with, from left: Sgt Ron Stillwell, Sgt Vic Lowson and Sgt Chris Oldnall at 65 Squadron's dispersal, Kirton-in-Lindsey 1941.

On October 9th, 1941, 65 Squadron moved to Westhampnett:-

'Being closer to the continent, shipping patrols and offensive sweeps were the order of the day. After one low flying squadron sweep and return, Squadron Leader Saunders' aircraft was found to have a small calibre bullet passed right through the fuselage, about a foot behind the cockpit, luckily for Sam. I was given the task of ferrying the Spitfire to Hamble for repair. I was so concerned with the barrage balloons round Southampton that I landed with the wheels up. I remember it as one of the softest landings I ever made, but I felt a proper fool! Thankfully the Supermarine rep there was very considerate and put it down to enemy action. I heard no more about it'.

65 Squadron pilots at Tangmere, February 1941. The weather had closed in, flying had been postponed and the pilots, in best blue, were off to Brighton on a different kind of sweep! However, as they were about to leave, official photographers arrived and the pilots became models! From left: Sgt Hugh Chalmers, Sgt Peter Mitchell (killed on active service 1942), Sgt Rose (on wing, killed on active service, 1941), Intelligence Officer, Flg Off 'Paddy' Finucane DFC (killed in action 1942), Flg Off Ron Wigg, Sgt Orchard (killed in action the next day).

By December 23rd, 1941, 65 Squadron was based at both Debden and Castle Camps:-

'We were training almost exclusively for night flying and to co-operate with the searchlights now that the German day offensive had dwindled. How strange it was to fly to Castle Camps in the afternoon then sit in dispersal wearing dark glasses (CO's idea) and long seamen's woollen stockings (pilots' idea as it was dashed cold in the December night air in our unheated cockpits). The Spitfire was definitely not suited to night take-offs. When the throttle was opened, flames, sparks, etc., shot past at eye level blinding the pilot who had to "eyes down" quickly and use instruments. Latterly we found we could safely get off with zero or even negative boost. The Hurricane's configuration, however, made it a better bet for night flying as I later found out. In January our CO, Humphrey Gilbert, who had taken over from Sam Saunders, killed himself in a Spitfire and Tony Bartley then took over.

'My last flight with 65 Squadron was with the late Ron Stillwell. With snow on the ground we took the squadron Magister and followed the railway line up to Kirton and returned with as many eggs as the farmer could spare. He had been as kind when we had previously been stationed there.

'On February 25th, 1942, myself and five other pilots left Mount Batten in a Sunderland flying boat (L5798, KG-B), stopping at Gib before carrying on to Malta, arriving at Kalafrana at 0700 hrs. The captain was very keen to get rid of us and get on his way. Later on I realised why! Even as we travelled in the pick-up to Hal Far we saw two Me 109s in formation just offshore going round the island. That was the morning patrol, we were told. No wonder the Sunderland pilot was keen to get en route for Cairo!

'Because I had been night flying on Spitfires I was sent on to Takali to join 1435 Flight MNFU with Hurricane Mk IICs. Only a few nocturnal patrols were undertaken, however, as aircraft were drained away to the day boys at Hal Far. Squadron Leader Westmacott was the CO, but latterly a Pilot Officer Oaks was left in charge.

'Eventually only one Hurricane was left and after the toss of a coin Sergeant "Timber" Wood went on an intruder flight. In that aircraft, BE347, he was shot down and killed over Sicily on April 26th, 1942. Night-fighter Beaufighters started to arrive on the island and I was duly appointed ground control pilot at Luqa. Wing Commander "Jumbo" Gracie was in charge at Takali. He allowed airmen to draw rifles and ammunition to shoot at E/A attacking our returning fighters. By this time batches of Spitfires were coming out from Gibraltar. The last line of one of Gracie's memos was "Don't shoot wildly, don't panic, don't shoot at a Spitfire!"

'On July 10th, 1942, I arrived back in the UK and on July 30th reported for instructor duties at 56 OTU, Kinnell, Dundee. There I instructed on Masters and Hurricanes. I was commissioned on October 5th, and after the usual OTU tour of six months was posted to 501 Squadron flying Spitfires in Northern Ireland. Only one exercise stands out in my mind, a Fighter Night over Belfast. The whole squadron was deployed with gaps of 1,000' between each aircraft. It was not funny when a Spitfire slid right across my canopy with only feet between us. Thank goodness that we suffered no casualties but the exercise was never repeated. Shortly afterwards the squadron moved back to England and Westhampnett.

'On May 10th, 1943, I was suddenly posted to 277 Air Sea Rescue Squadron, 'C' Flight, at Shoreham, Sussex. My Flight Commander was an Australian, Dicky

Vere, and CO was a Squadron Leader Brown. My 10 month or so stay with 277 was extremely pleasant - much like the camaraderie I had found in 65 Squadron. The only real worry was the long over-sea trips with just one "fan". I flew three trips on D-Day but had no customers. There were so many ships in the Channel that no-one could have landed in the sea anyway!

'On January 14th, 1945, I left 277 ASR and went to 55 OTU, Aston Down to learn to fly Typhoons, which were a completely different proposition from the sleek Spitfires and even Hurricanes - more like driving a bus than a racing car!

The Chief Flying Instructor was Ron Stillwell DFM DFC, my old NCO mate from 65 Squadron days. After converting to Typhoons, the idea was that I was to join a 2nd TAF squadron in Holland, but for some reason I was posted to Karachi, India. Whether this was due to my efforts, Ron's influence or my inaccurate attempts at releasing rockets and bombs in the Bristol Channel I don't know, but there I was in a Sunderland once more, this time flying from Poole.

Flt Lt RL Stillwell DFM, commander of 'B' Flight, pictured with his 65 Squadron Spitfire Mk IX, YT-X, MH908, in 1943. Sqn Ldr Ron Stillwell DFM DFC AE RAF Retd died suddenly in 1993.

Hugh joined a drogue towing unit in India on May 6th, 1945:-

'Hurricanes, Vengeances and Defiants were in use. The Defiant had the gun turret removed and a winch installed (No, Dilip, a winch, not a wench!). Later I moved to take over the flight at Poona. Although things in Europe were still dicey for our aircrew, we knew that the horror was coming to a close. We just had to press on, but not as regardless as before. For us, however, both VE and VJ Days were most depressing. Authority had thought that there would be a break out of celebratory violence and all sidearms were withdrawn - even the rotors of motor transports were removed. However, I think that we all felt then so far from home and family, that even the celebrations on the steam radio deepened the depression.

'My total war flying hours were 1100, including 600 on Spitfires and 160 on Hurricanes'.

Hugh Chalmers left the RAF as a Flight Lieutenant. His story is a perfect example of the pilot who was there, ready and prepared to play his part whenever and wherever that call came, the very inspiration that stimulated this book. Hugh could just have easily flown a Typhoon over war-torn Europe during the closing months of the war but for the chance stroke of a pen which sent him to India on more mundane and safer flying duties. For others the pen stroked in the opposite direction, flinging them into the crucible of combat which they would perhaps not survive. For all of these men, however, nearly six long years saw them have no control over their destinies.

Hugh is now a retired Physical Training Instructor and as such remains as fit as a fiddle - I always find it hard to come to terms with how senior he is in years! His enthusiasm for the Spitfire and 65 Squadron remains unbounded, and both Hugh and his wife, Elizabeth, are frequent guests to Malvern Spitfire Team and Ramrod Publications functions. They are both now retired and living in their native Scotland. Keen caravan enthusiasts who often journey south, completely out of the blue I will get a call at work, 'There's a Mr Chalmers at the front desk to see you' - I look forward very much to the next surprise occasion!

Reunited. Early in 1941, Sgt Chalmers of 65 Squadron soared aloft in Spitfire Mk IIA P7350, YT-F. That Spitfire is still flying today, with the RAF's Battle of Britain Memorial Flight. Here Hugh is reunited with P7350 at RAF Coningsby in June 1991.

Chapter Nineteen

Squadron Leader Buck Casson DFC AFC

Pilot Officer 'Buck' Casson, 616 Squadron, 1940.

On May 11th, 1941, two Spitfires of 308 'City of Krakow' Squadron scrambled from Baginton (now Coventry airport), to intercept a 'Bogey' reported in the Kidderminster area of Worcestershire. The plot was later identified as friendly, however, but the two Polish Spitfires continued their patrol high over Worcestershire. Over Malvern, the section leader, Pilot Officer Franek Surma, was forced to bale out of R6644 when its engine suddenly burst into flames. The pilotless fighter then plunged vertically, impacting into a meadow at Madresfield and exploding into a thousand pieces. Pilot Officer Surma, already a veteran of the Battle of Britain, survived the experience but sadly was killed in action just six months later, probably a victim of Hauptmann Johannes Seifert, Gruppenkommandeur of I/JG26. I first learned of R6644's crash in 1985, and subsequently resolved to research as complete a history as possible concerning both Spitfire R6644's 'life' and that of Franek Surma. Identifying the pilots who once soared aloft in this aircraft with some units was a surprisingly easy task, those flights being listed in the Operations Record Books of the squadrons concerned, but in respect of others not so well documented it was necessary to trace pilots who were with the unit at the same time as R6644. One such unit was 616 Squadron, with whom R6644 flew between October 7th, 1940, and February 26th, 1941. Between those dates, 616 was a 'C' squadron, based at Kirton-in-Lindsey in 12 Group, recuperating after its mauling during the Battle of Britain and training replacement pilots. The squadron was rebuilt around some of its few Battle of Britain survivors, men like Flying Officer Hugh 'Cocky' Dundas and Pilot Officer Lionel 'Buck' Casson. A letter despatched to Group Captain Sir Hugh Dundas quickly confirmed that he had indeed flown R6644 on several occasions. The similarly positive response from Squadron Leader Casson was appropriately received on the very day that the Malvern Spitfire Team recovered R6644's remains from the Madresfield crash site in September 1987.

The story of R6644 and Flying Officer Franek Surma VM KW was eventually published in my second book, 'The Invisible Thread: A Spitfire's Tale'. The book-launch which took place at the Abbey Hotel, Great Malvern, on September 5th, 1992, was spectacular, with a Spitfire on show, over 20 of the Few in attendance, and a superb flying display by David Pennell in his Spitfire Mk IX. The occasion also saw the launch of the 'Surma Memorial Trust for Youth', now a registered charity, the aim of which is to 'educate and assist young people in Malvern'. Squadron Leader Casson and his wife, 'Dorfy', had kindly joined us for the weekend, and it gave us great pleasure to present Buck with a mounted piece of R6644 restored by Malvern Spitfire Team expert Dr Dennis Williams. Since that time, the Cassons have been keen supporters of our projects and welcome guests at our events. Although I wrote briefly about Buck in 'The Invisible Thread', our closer association in the meantime has herewith enabled publication of a far more detailed firsthand account.

'On July 23rd, 1939, I was commissioned as an Acting Pilot Officer in 616 South Yorkshire Squadron of the Auxiliary Air Force. Our annual summer camp at Manston commenced on August 24th, and there I flew the Avro 504N and Tiger Moth. Between October 7th, 1939, and March 23rd, 1940, I undertook my service flying training at No 2 FTS at Brize Norton. There we flew the Harvard and Oxford aircraft and I passed second on course, being assessed as 'above average' overall. On April 6th, 1940, I reported back to 616 Squadron at Leconfield. There I served as Duty Pilot, Orderly Officer, and Operations Officer. On April 29th, however, I was posted to No 6 OTU at Sutton Bridge. First we had dual testing and instrument flying on Harvards before going solo on Hurricanes. Then we practised Fighter Command attacks, 1 & 2 then 3 & 4.

'At this time some Hurricane squadrons had already been sent to France, and when the shooting started in May 1940, they soon began suffering losses. We had been trained as replacements, so on May 15th, I was posted to Arras to join the British Expeditionary Force's Advanced Air Striking Force. I set off at 3.00 pm and left my car at Peterborough. Got train to London by 7.00 pm. No transport so train to Uxbridge by 11.30 pm. Reported, signed forms and collected equipment. I then kept a diary of those chaotic times:-

May 16th, 1940.

Got to bed 3.30 pm. Up at 6.00 am. Paraded 7.30 am and left Uxbridge 9.00 am. Boarded steamship with kit at Southampton and departed at 2.30 pm but had to wait off Portsmouth for tide.

May 17th.

Docked at Le Havre 6.00 am. Changed money and enjoyed seeing the town. 10.30 pm entrained for Arras.

May 18th.

Train left 3.00 am and arrived Amiens 2.15 pm. Bridge and line ahead blown up. More air raids. Night at YMCA.

May 19th.

Left kit behind and caught a train leaving south. Reached St Roche marshalling yards and heavily bombed for 1 hour 20 mins by Ju 87 and Ju 88. Engine and first carriage OK, but rest of train smashed up. After being terrified by the bombing, managed to return across the lines and scramble up the bank onto the road. Walked by roads to Aumale and Gournay with little sleep or rest. Got mixed up with lots of refugees, some dead and some wounded, dead horses, etc. Finally got to Rouen and given meal by Scottish Highland Division. Departed early and luckily was able to halt a long low-loader with two aero-engines on board from Glisy airfield.

May 22nd.

Climbed aboard and relaxed 'en-route' all the way to Cherbourg. Next morning in 'Duke of Argyle', escorted by two destroyers, left in a hurry and arrived Southampton 3.30 pm. Then posted to 79 Squadron at Biggin Hill. Took train and taxi to Uxbridge but no room available, so I joined Tom Murray and we booked a room at the Charing Cross Hotel and went without cash to the Paradise Restaurant where we were very well looked after.

May 23rd.

Reported Uxbridge 10.45 am. Changed French money and bought toilet requisites, socks, shirt, underwear, etc. Had first bath since May 14th. Left Charing Cross Hotel without payment requested!

May 24th.

Drove in Tom's 5S to Biggin Hill and CO (Squadron Leader Joslyn) of 79 Squadron gave us 48 hours leave. Got new uniform etc. at Moss Bros. Caught train home and arrived 6.40 pm.

May 26th.

Drove South in my car (my sister had collected it from Peterborough) and arrived Biggin Hill 6.25 pm.

June 5th.

My first operational sortie with 79 Squadron as bomber escort. Attacked by some Me 109s and the squadron split up. I was alone and luckily a single Me 109 passed about 1,000' below me and I opened fire on it; it turned over and dived towards Cherbourg leaving a stream of black smoke. I must have hit it, but how badly damaged it was I could not tell so I did not make a combat report. I returned escorting the Blenheim bombers and found our squadron at Biggin Hill all refuelled.

June 6th/7th.

Escort and patrol Abbeville/Amiens from Manston.

June 8th.

On offensive patrol Le Tréport/Aumale and again our squadron split up when attacked by more Me 109 aircraft. I was alone and seeing a flight of He 111s made two quarter attacks on the leading aircraft then being short of fuel I broke off. I was able to locate a small grass airfield at St André de l'Eure and landed there. Fortunately a French officer was on the scene; he took me quite some distance in his car to breakfast, having instructed the groundcrew to refuel my aircraft. He drove me back and we exchanged the top button of our uniforms! He left me assuming everything was OK for take-off, but there were no ground staff about. I found it impossible to start the engine and had to call over a labourer who was digging a trench round the airfield.

I got out the starter handle from under the fuselage and inserted it on the starboard side of the engine. I showed the labourer what I wanted him to do and climbed back into the cockpit. Then I gave 'thumbs up' and pressed the starter while he wound the handle, and luckily the engine fired OK. I replaced the handle, taxied to the end of the field then opened up at full bore. I was not airborne before reaching the boundary trench, but striking the mound of earth was just sufficient to enable me to keep the plane up and then climb away. I flew to Dreux where the squadron had been instructed to go originally, but I found only three of 79 Squadron there. The Engineering Officer told me that my plane had been refuelled with 90 Octane and would have to be altered. Finally, because the rest of the unit had returned to Biggin Hill, we four were released eventually and luckily got back to base without mishap.

June 9th.

At dusk I was a pilot at 'readiness' in 'A' Flight of 79 Squadron when we were scrambled from Biggin Hill to intercept a plotted X Raid over the English Channel. This was most unexpected for as day fighters we were on the point of being released, and in fact our dispersed Hurricanes were undergoing their Daily Inspections, one-by-one, ready for the morrow.

As luck would have it I found my aircraft being serviced when I reached it and so was directed to another. Parachutes had not been moved and I was happy to use the one in situ, but there was no helmet and the ground staff couldn't find mine which I had left in my own aircraft.

The CO and the other four pilots were by now at the end of the airfield ready for take-off and in my eagerness not to let the side down I raced up to join them but without a helmet. This mad, misguided enthusiasm which could have had disastrous consequences taught me a lesson I shall not easily forget.

We took-off and climbed up over the sea into the last rays of the setting sun; I without oxygen and no RT. Without radio reception and relying on observation only, my reactions to changes of formation, direction, etc. were necessarily slow and the CO after several efforts to contact me by RT realised the situation and waved me to break away.

I turned homeward and descending found myself over London in darkness. I could pick out the Thames but could not find Biggin Hill. Eventually I stumbled upon Kenley although I didn't recognise it at the time and it was only as I made a low run across the area that a floodlight, briefly turned on then off again, gave me a clue and I was just able to discern the hooded runway lights. I prepared to land and as I made my final approach with the aircraft landing lights on the ground floodlight was turned on again and I touched down.

Quite unaware that Kenley was a bit like an inverted saucer, I found myself rapidly reaching the end of the runway and had to swing to starboard to avoid overshooting. This resulted in a burst port-tyre and I was admonished by the Station CO for the incident. Shortly afterwards, however, after getting in touch with my unit and learning that not only was I an AAF pilot but that my night flying experience was limited to only two hours dual and 2.10 hours solo on Harvards at FTS, he was kind enough to tell me, over a drink, I had put up a good show whilst naturally enough warning me against such a foolhardy exploit in the future.

According to my log book, that flight lasted 1.10 hours and brought my grand total on the Hurricane to a mere 18.50 hours, plus 12 hours carried out at Sutton Bridge OTU.

June 10th - July 3rd.

Patrols Hawkinge, Dungeness. Escort and patrol Calais/Merville.

July 4th.

Able to drive north as at last posted back to 616 Squadron at Leconfield, and to fly Spitfire Mk Is. CO was Marcus Robinson.

July 7th - 31st.

Formation and cloud flying. Air drill. No 3 fighter attacks. Gun co-operation - Saxton. Air to air firing at Acklington. Aerobatics, X Raids. Dusk and night flying.

August 1st - 11th.

Dusk and night flying. X Raids 25,000' and 27,000'. On 11th crashed on take-off but survived - some story!!

August 15th.

Two X Raids to east coast - Ju 88 aircraft from Norway attacked Driffield but many got shot down.

August 19th.

The squadron with 15 aircraft moved to Kenley and I followed with a replacement on the 24th.

August 25th - 26th.

Went on loan to No 615 Squadron as Tom Murray and I were the only Hurricane pilots with experience. Our own 616 Squadron was so badly mauled that we had to return. There was no activity for us on the 27th.

August 28th.

We had five hours flying on X Raids at 20,000' over Thames estuary and Manston and Hawkinge.

August 29th - 31st.

I flew on nine X raids and claimed He 111 bombers - 1 probable and 1 damaged.

September 1st.

I flew five sorties and claimed one Me 109 probable and one Do 17 confirmed. Hole blown in my port wing.

September 2nd.

Airborne four times patrolling base - no action because raiders retreated.

September 3rd.

Got my kit packed by 9.00 am. About 11.00 am scrambled to 15,000' - no action. 2.15 pm flew to Coltishall as squadron withdrawn from 11 Group due to heavy losses. Billy Burton was promoted as our CO. I went with him and Wing Commander Beisigle to Wroxham for evening.

September 4th.

Given 48 hours leave from mid-day. 9.30 am my car arrived so I drove home taking Dick Hellyer to Doncaster.

September 6th.

Arrived at Coltishall and flew sector recce. Only Holden, Brewster, two NCOs and myself left to fly.

September 7th - 8th.

Airborne for X raids and practice formation attacks. Colin Macfie joined us as Flight Lieutenant.

September 9th.

Moved up to Kirton-in-Lindsey.

September 10th - 30th.

X raids. Training new pilots (including Johnnie Johnson and 'Nip' Hepple). Repeated trips to Duxford G1 (Fowlmere). To Ringway.

October 1st - 4th.

At Ringway as air support for troops embarking at Liverpool, but too foggy to give air cover.

October 5th.

Bought my fox terrier 'Mac'. Flew sector recce then returned to Kirton.

October 6th - 31st.

X raids. Air drill.

November 1st - 11th.

X raids. Flight formation. Army co-op. LFP and aerobatics.

November 13th - 20th.

To and from Ringway - X raids and sector recces.

November 21st - 30th.

X raids. Formation practice. Attacks 1, 3 beam. Tom Murray left to go as test pilot.

December 16th - 24th.

After German air raids on Sheffield, I had flights at 21,000' over the city on the 16th, and followed with a 'goodwill' formation over Doncaster, Sheffield, Wortley etc. on the 24th. On other days practised attacks 1 and 3, cloud and formation, battle climb to 31,000'.

January 1st - 12th, 1941.

Battle climb to 32,000'. Cloud flying. Beam attacks.

January 13th - 16th.

I had bad cold - danger of sinus.

January 17th - 18th.

Beam attacks. X raid and flew to 25,000' after a Ju 88 but lost it in cloud - landed back in a snowstorm.

January 19th - 31st.

Fog, mist and deep snow. I had seven days leave. Operated on Link trainer. Did compass checks.

February 1st - 16th.

Air drill. Cloud flying. 1, 3 and beam attacks. Battle climb 28000'. Night flying twice. Convoy patrol.

February 17th - 21st.

Fog and very low cloud. More snow and sleet. Lecture on RDF, IFF, CHL, GCI, AI etc., guns.

February 22nd - 25th.

X raids 20,000'. To Wittering, then with 266 Squadron on sweep over French coast at 29,000'. Landed Duxford then to base.

February 26th.

To Tangmere. Changed our aircraft with Spitfire IIs of 65 Squadron. Did a sector recce (Branscombe)'.

By this time, 616 Squadron had worked back up to strength and was recategorised an 'A' unit. As covered in detail elsewhere in this book, 1941 saw Fighter Command go on the offensive. Douglas Bader was to find that his controversial 'Big Wing' tactics of the Battle of Britain were to have a natural place in offensive operations over France, commencing that year, and in March 1941 he was promoted to Wing Commander and posted to Tangmere as Wing Leader. The association of the Bader Wing and Tangmere airfield, near Chichester in Sussex, has since become legendary. When Bader arrived, the Wing comprised three Spitfire squadrons: 145, 610 and 616. Buck Casson remembers Bader from those days:-

'I had first met him at Coltishall on September 3rd, 1940, and he tried to tick some of us off for having our top buttons undone in true fighter pilots' style. I came to know him briefly during early 1941 when we occasionally joined up as a 12 Group Wing flying from Duxford or Wittering. I came to know him better at Tangmere, from March 1941 onwards. We enjoyed playing golf with him at Goodwood, and at the house where he was billeted we carried him to the pool where he swam extremely well. He always wanted company so we often went to his digs for a drink and chat'.

Above left: The legendary Tangmere Wing Leader, Wg Cdr Douglas Bader DSO DFC, pictured at that station during the 'season' of 1941.

Above right: Wg Cdr Bader demonstrates the fighter pilot's headgear of 1941.

Left: High tea, Tangmere style. Douglas and Thelma Bader lived at the Bay House in Aldwick, near Bognor Regis, and there the Wing's pilots would gather to socialise and discuss tactics. I wonder what the joke was about on this occasion? From left: Flg Off Hugh 'Cocky' Dundas, Sqn Ldr Billy Burton (CO of 616 Squadron), Douglas and Thelma Bader.

Buck's diary continues:-

February 7th - 28th 1941.

Billeted in Rushman's house by Oving Village. Very low cloud and heavy rain - no flying, my Spitfire I (X4184) changed to Spitfire II (P7753).

March 1941.

Wing Commander Douglas Bader, 'Dogs Body', always flying from 616 Squadron dispersal. He and 616 Squadron would lead the Wing. We also flew Channel sweeps 35,000', patrols of Dungeness, Selsey Bill, St Catherine's Point and Boulogne/Calais at 15,000'/35,000'. We also practised air drill, cloud flying, dusk and night patrols. Tangmere was bombed by Ju 88s on 12th/13th and buildings and vehicles hit. Played golf at Goodwood with Douglas Bader and Ken Holden.

April 1941.

I flew into Gatwick to give an army General and others details and demonstration with Spitfire. Six other aircraft types there also. More patrols from I.O.W. and Dungeness. Slept at dispersal for night flying. Cloud flying. Escorting 18 Blenheims to Cherbourg and return. There escorting 17 Blenheims to Le Havre and return - lost Sergeant Sellars. Formation and line astern aerobatics. At 5.50 am, more Ju 88 bombing - six killed and 15 injured.

May 1941.

Often up for readiness at 4.25 am for dawn patrols. Also on night flying duty. Air drill. Channel patrol. Moved to Westhampnett airfield. Tangmere badly bombed, but Hampden and Whitley bombers landed on return from raids. On 5th I intercepted a reconnaissance Ju 88 at 15,000' over Portsmouth; it dived south to 100' over the sea - I shot the rear gunner, but got hit and my glycol leaked. I had to return, and just crossing the coast at 950' with cockpit full of smoke turned the aircraft over and baled out near Littlehampton. On 30th played golf with Douglas Bader and Ken Holden, then I collected Douglas Bader's wife, Thelma, and sister Jill. We all went to Brighton for evening.

June 1941.

Formation aerobatics. Flick rolls and spins. Escorted 18 Blenheims to Le Havre. Sweeps - Straits of Dover, Boulogne, Dunkirk. Wing Circus, Straits, 20000'. Wing Circus Dungeness, Boulogne, Gravelines. Wing to Hastings, Berck, St. Omer, Gravelines. Wing to Dungeness, Berck, Hazebrouck, Dunkirk. Other wing sorties to Mardyck, Lille, St. Omer - Le Touquet, Hucoueliers, Desvres, Gris Nez, etc.

July 1941.

On July 3rd, I borrowed Douglas Bader's black night-flying Hurricane II and flew via Kirton-in-Lindsey to Doncaster, then got bus to Sheffield and home at 10.00 pm. On 6th, the family saw me off from Doncaster and I arrived Tangmere 8.00 pm. Escorting Stirling bombers on several raids over France. Other Wing sweeps over France. Tested Spitfire VB cannons on height test. Air drill. Convoy patrols. Colin Macfie confirmed as POW. Orde made good sketch of me and some others. 145 Squadron left for Catterick and replaced by 41.

Photographs of 616 Squadron Spitfires are rare. Identification is also difficult on occasions as both 92 and 616 Squadrons used the code letters 'QJ' for an overlapping period. This example does belong to 616 Squadron, however, and was taken during the summer of 1941 when the squadron formed a part of the Tangmere Wing. Sadly the pilot posing with this aircraft, Sgt Mabbett from Cheltenham, was killed in action over France on July 21st, 1941. The Germans buried him at St Omer with full military honours.

August 1941 continued in much the same vein for the Tangmere Wing. Douglas Bader drove himself and his pilots hard. In July and August 1941 he led 10 sweeps in seven days. On August 9th, 'Bader's Bus Company' escorted Blenheims on a Circus operation. The RAF formation crossed the French coast south of Le Touquet at 26,000'. Soon battle was joined; Wing Commander Bader and 616 Squadron attacked a climbing enemy formation comprising 20 Me 109Fs. Bader's section dived onto the leading Schwarm, the Wing Leader shouting over the R/T 'Come on boys, there are plenty for all, pick one each!' In the mêlée which followed, Bader either collided with or was shot down by an enemy fighter. Not without some difficulty, he eventually managed to extricate himself from his Spitfire's cockpit and bale out, albeit leaving one of his artificial legs behind. The enemy pilots involved in the action were of JG26 'Schlageter', and for them August 9th, 1941, had started as any other day. When they learned, however, that one of the Allied pilots captured as a result of the combat was the legendary Douglas Bader, the day concluded as anything but routine. Wing Commander Bader was entertained by JG26's Kommodore, Oberst Adolf Galland, at St Omer airfield. The occasion is actually often identified by many of JG26's ground personnel as the most memorable incident throughout their entire war.

In the dangerous sky over France that fateful day, Leutnant Kosse of 5/JG26 had taken careful aim at a Spitfire and, after squeezing the trigger on his control column, was able to claim his eighth victory. Flying Officer Casson also failed to return from this operation, and research indicates that he was probably Kosse's victim on this occasion, the Tangmere Wing Leader having possibly fallen to Oberfeldwebel Max Mayer of 6/JG26 who reported having seen his victim descend by parachute (although Bader always maintained that his Spitfire had suffered a collision and had not been shot down). After the war, Buck wrote to Douglas Bader about his experiences of August 9th, 1941:-

'Now for the day we disgraced the Tangmere Wing, and you say that you want the whole story!

'When we dived to attack the Me 109s that were climbing in formation, I was to starboard and behind you with three other aircraft of 'B' Flight. My No 2 was a Rhodesian Sergeant, whose name I forget, and Roy Marples was on my right with his No 2.

'I watched you attack with 'A' Flight and break to port as I was coming in. I was well throttled back in the dive, as the other three had started to fall behind and I wanted to keep the flight together. I attacked from the rear, and after having a squirt at two 109s flying together, I left them for a single one which was flying inland alone. I finished nearly all of my cannon ammunition up on this boy, who finally baled out at 6,000', having lost most of his tail unit. The other three 'B' Flight machines were in my rear and probably one of the lads saw this.

'I believe that we had crossed the French coast at Hardelot some minutes in advance of the other squadrons from Tangmere, as we were alone when we sighted and attacked the "Goons", but by the time I had finished my little scrap the Wing squadrons had joined and were well above me and on their way out towards Hardelot again.

'I climbed to about 13,000' and fell in with Billy Burton and three other aircraft, all from 'A' Flight. We chased around in a circle for some time, gaining height all the while, and the Me 109s were directly above us. Eventually we formed up in line abreast and set off after the Wing.

'Billy had the other three 'A' Flight machines with him, flying in pairs abreast, and I flew abreast but at about 200 yards to starboard. We were repeatedly attacked by two Me 109s which had followed us and were flying above and behind us. Each time they started to dive I called out and we all turned and re-formed, the Me 109s giving up their attack and climbing each time.

'About 15 miles from the coastline I saw another Spitfire well below us and about ¹/₂ a mile to starboard. This machine was alone and travelling very slowly. I called up Billy on the R/T and suggested that we cross over to surround him and help the pilot back as he looked such a sitting duck. I broke off to starboard and made for the solitary Spitfire, but then, on looking back for Billy and the others, I was amazed to see them diving away hard to the south-west for a low layer of cloud through which they soon disappeared. I realised then that my message had either been misunderstood or had not been received.

'Like a greenhorn I had been intent upon watching Billy's extraordinary disappearance to the left, and the lone Spitfire to my right, and in the process had lost sight of the Me 109s that had been worrying us. I remember looking for them but upon not discovering their position assumed that they had chased Billy instead. I was soon proved wrong, however, when I received three hits in both the fuselage and wing. This occurred just as I was coming alongside the lone Spitfire, which I could not identify as it was not from Tangmere. I broke for some cloud at 5,000', which I found too thin for cover, and was pursued by the Me 109s.

'I then picked out two more Me 109s flying above me so decided to drop to zero feet, fly north and cross the Channel at a narrow point as I was unsure of the damage sustained and the engine was not running smoothly. I pressed the teat and tried to run for it, but the two Me 109s behind had more speed and were rapidly within range, whilst the other two flew 1,500' above and dived from port to starboard and back, delivering quick bursts. Needless to say I was not flying straight and level all this time.

'In the event I received a good one from behind which passed between the stick and my right leg, taking off some of the rudder on its way. It passed into the petrol tank but whether it continued into the engine I do not know. Petrol began leaking into the cockpit, oil pressure was dropping low, and with the radiator wide open I could smell the glycol overheating.

'As the next attack came, I pulled straight up from the deck in a loop and on my way down, as I was changing direction towards the sea, my engine became extremely rough and seized up as white glycol fumes poured forth. There was no option but to crash-land the aircraft.

'I tried to send you a hurried message as I had no idea that you were also in trouble. I then blew up the wireless and made a belly landing in a field about 10 miles south of Calais. The Goons, having seen the glycol, were decent enough not to shoot me up as I was landing, but circled about for a time and gave my position away to a German cavalry unit in a wood at a corner of the field.

'Setting fire to the aircraft was an easy matter as I was carrying a Port fire and the cockpit was full of petrol. I had no sooner done this than a party of shrieking Goons armed with rifles came chasing over and that was the end of me!

'What eventually happened to the lone Spitfire I went to help out I have no idea. As the Me 109s followed me he must have been okay, I certainly hope so. As Billy Burton was killed later in the war I have never discovered who was flying the other three Spitfires in his formation.

'Well DB, that's the story and one which I shall never forget I suppose, for I have gone over that bloody day so often in my daydreams'.

Back at Tangmere on August 9th, 1941, there was a feeling of total desolation with the losses of both Bader and Casson, the latter a longstanding and popular member of 616 Squadron. Of course there was to be some uplifting news eventually as both were not dead, as had naturally been feared, but were prisoners of war.

Buck Casson now faced several years in captivity:-

'I had crash-landed in a field on the edge of a wood near St Omer. Germans with rifles rushed out before I could escape and I was brought before a German General. I then spent the night in a room with two German guards. On August 10th, with guards, motored to Lille then by train via Cologne to Frankfurt. On 11th had day in "cooler", clothes taken and searched. On 21st, Bader arrived and joined me in Dulag Luft at Oberusel but not for long. On 24th, about 10 of us left and went to train at 3.15 pm, arriving at Lübeck late evening on 25th. Marched to Oflag XC. Searched and fingerprints taken'.

Whilst in captivity, Buck Casson kept a 'Kriegie Diary'. Whilst most of the others featured in this book who became prisoners of war conclude their stories when captured, Buck has shared with us his diary which provides a unique insight into life behind the barbed wire:-

September 1941.

Two more parties arrived from Dulag Luft - some army from Crete. We had similar food daily; at mid-day it was thin cow turnip soup and two potatoes, and for tea 1" of loaf (if yellow changed for usual green mouldy one) a nub of speiser fat and sometimes a bit of jam. Much of PoW Reich ration was sold off in Lübeck. Cold at night with only one blanket. Walked round compound. Lost a lot of weight. Inoculated TAB.

October 1941.

First coal issue of $1^1/2$ bricks per room for two days. USA reps visited camp. On 8th entrained 4.00 pm in horse-boxes. On 9th arrived Oflag VIB Warburg 11.00. On 11th issued 1/3 American parcel. PoWs from other camps came and Red Cross reps appalled by squalor. On 22nd first issue of bed linen. RAF separated. Issue of greatcoats.

November 1941.

Received first food parcel. Had wisdom tooth extracted. Visit by American Legation and then by Swiss YMCA.

December 1941.

Camp searched. Ankle deep in mud. Issue of a Red Cross blanket.

January 1942.

On 21st to "cooler", cold - 43 degree frost, released to camp on 26th.

February 1942.

Blizzard and snow drifts. Issued Red Cross trousers. Identity photo taken.

March 1942.

Snow gone and camp flooded.

April 1942.

On 5th Easter - Went to HC. On 8th played my first game of rugby football. On 10th three escapes - appell all morning and searches. On 16th visit by Swiss. On 18th 10 more escapes.

May 1942.

Nothing very special.

June 1942.

On 3rd, King George VI birthday - we held celebration parade.

July 1942.

On 29th inoculated. 30 RAF prisoners left for Sagan. On 31st postal restrictions started. Reprisal measures.

August 1942.

Five tunnels found and filled with excrement from latrines - one was from our room. Older army men left for Oflag 9 A/Z. On 31st escape of 25 by ladders up and across double barbed wire and fused the lights. Most were recaptured later.

September 1942.

On 4th searched at 4.00 am. Entrained 2nd class 9.30 am - had quite good journey and arrived Schubin 5.00 pm. 5th Oflag XXIB had been a girls school and parts of the camp were nice to draw or paint. Two young storks landed in compound.

October/November 1942.

Nothing very outstanding.

December 1942.

On 3rd a photographer came to take private groups and I bought some. On 16th two escaped in bread lorry. On 17th whole camp was searched by SS, Gestapo and police. On 25th received Red Cross Christmas parcel.

More caged fighters, this time all of the Tangmere Wing's 616 Squadron taken at Schubin on December 3rd, 1942. From left: Flt Lt Buck Casson DFC, Flt Lt Colin Macfie DFC, Sgt Philip Wareing, Plt Off Ralph Roberts.

January 1943.

On 1st SBO Wing Commander Day asked for better discipline. On 13th home-made 'Cresta' run completed and on 16th in full swing with higher starting platform. Forbidden to possess over 30 RM!! Gave money to Sergeants and Privates.

February 1943.

On 3rd I paid 130 RM for ¹/₂lb chocolate. Two batches of Americans came from Dulag Luft. More searches.

March 1943.

Fleas gave me trouble at night. On 6th escape of 43 from 'abort' tunnel at night. On 8th locked indoors early and a new Kommandant was put in charge. On 9th Gestapo searched for 8 3/4 hours. On 11th the SS came in and questioned the guards. On 14th most PoWs were captured. On 25th visit by Swiss Legation.

April 1943.

On 11th left by 3rd class train and spent night in Posen sidings. On 12th arrived Sagan; searched and fingerprints taken . On 14th inspection by Luftwaffe General. On 21st I took over as Block Adjutant under Wing Commander Trumble.

May 1943.

At Stalag Luft 3 we were in the East Compound. Extra platforms were erected on guard boxes.

June 1943.

Our 3rd parade for George VI birthday. On 11th escape of 25 from West Compound, then 20 caught and searched by Gestapo.

July 1943.

Had body search on appell. Fly plague. Had tooth stopped. Visit by Swiss. Finished our home-made cemetery.

August 1943.

Finished my 'Kriegie Alphabet' in pictures. Funeral of Lewis who apparently leapt under train. More Americans arrived.

September 1943.

First view of Me 323. Various towns evacuated by Germans. Our radio news good.

October 1943.

Visit from German Foreign Office. Visit by Swiss with German General. On 28th long search of our rooms. On 30th three escaped by tunnel under wooden horse. I helped to vault over it and carry it back to disperse sand.

November 1943.

Visit by Chief of YMCA. I made a pipe of silver birch from cemetery - my only visit out of camp on parole. Block searches on 9th and 13th. On 25th Thorough search and everything thrown out of our hut and we had to move to hut 69. On 29th we moved back in rain and collected our wet-through belongings.

December 1943.

Received Christmas parcels. On 24th went to open bar in hut 65. On 25th snowing. Drinking until midnight. On 27th all stills were confiscated. 'Scharnhorst' sunk.

January 1944.

21 transferred to Belaria PoW camp. Found silver paper 'RT interrupters' from Berlin raid.

February 1944.

35 transferred to North Camp. Dilly and Bear discussion on 'Commercial Art'. Jewish workmen asking for food.

March 1944.

On 14th all tin stores now withdrawn. Noticed great bird migration. On 25th escape of 5 by 150 yard tunnel from North Camp. On 28th/29th more searches of huts 65, 68 and 69. I started 2nd tour as "Duty Pilot" and returned as Block Adjutant.

April 1944.

On 6th SBO announced that 41 of 75 escapees had been shot. On 16th their names published. On 17th Swiss visited.

May 1944.

More PoWs arrive and our rooms become overcrowded. Saw three waves of American bombers unmolested.

June 1944.

Our 4th celebration parade for George VI birthday. On 6th news of invasion landings. On 24th saw three more waves of American bombers. On 26th large force of 50 German fighters seen.

July 1944.

On 20th attempted murder of Hitler. On 25th three more repatriated. Inoculated for TAB.

August 1944.

On 9th, PoW for three years. Allied landings in France. On 21st saw two jet aircraft. Two new purges arrived.

September 1944.

More PoWs arrived and taken to centre compound. Now on $^1/_2$ food parcel ration. On 12th saw three waves US bombers. Old Germans on defensive manoeuvres in the woods. Two PoWs attempted suicide.

October 1944.

Bed bug plague in hut 62. Much bird migration. Constructed 3-tier bed and start of room break up.

November 1944.

Hut fumigated for bed bugs. Visit by Luftwaffe General. Himmler forbade any food reserves and Red Cross Stores were confiscated for German hospitals. On 24th visit by Swiss Red Cross. On 25th weekly parcels forbidden.

December 1944.

On 5th visit by YMCA. On 8th outside all morning as hut searched. On 22nd issue of $^1/_2$ American Christmas parcel. On 24th to evening carol service. On

25th church service. On 31st snowing all day.

January 1945.

On 10th, Hut 62 searched again. On 18th issued 1/3 BRC parcel. On 23rd full parcel. I made a haversack. On 27th Russians getting closer. On 28th left compound 7.30 am in deep snow - to Halbau by 4.00 pm then into church. On 29th moved from church to school. On 30th left 7.10 am to Selingersruh and at 5.00 pm billeted in church. On 1st left 6.10 am to Muskau and at 5.15 pm stopped at glass factory - first chance to eat anything.

February 1945.

On 1st left at 11.00pm - dark, raining and roads very bad. On 2nd arrived Graustein 7.20 am then left again at 11.00 am and reached Spremberg 3.00 pm. At 6.15 pm boarded cattle trucks. On 3rd travelled via Hohenbucka, Plessa and Halle. On 4th through Limmer (Hannover) and Verden to reach Tarmstedt-Ost. Left the train, walked in rain (I bare footed) to Marlag by 6.00 pm and waited in rain for search at 1.30 am. On 9th two long check parades and searches. On 15th camp inspection by Kommandant and 1/2 parcel issued. On 17th at last received first batch of spring beds! Given normal Reich rations. On 20th/21st we had cooked chicken traded for cigarettes. My feet now OK. 1/2 parcel issued. On 24th/25th British and US aircraft in view.

March 1945.

Bed bugs and lice found in hut. Had three calcium injections. Saw V2 launched at sunset. Reich rations cut. Food parcels overdue. Our bombers over day and night.

April 1945.

On 10th left camp 10.00 am then night halt near Zeven. On 11th only did 12 klm - two PoWs killed and seven wounded by Tempest aircraft. On 12th to Harsefeld and camped outside at 2.30 pm. Weather lovely. On 14th only 4 klm to Hedendorf. On 15th walked 20 klm to camp at Cranz. On 16th boarded ferry across the Elbe to camp near Blankeneser. On 17th on to Ellerbeck. On 18th no move - traded cigarettes for a pram. On 19th on to Glashütte. On 20th did 15 klm to Elmenhorst. On 22nd on through Bad Oldesloe to Kleine, Barnitz. 18 klm then into barns. On 23rd to Poggenpohl - into barns. On 24th/27th no move. On 28th went 10 klm south-west to very large farm estate. On 29th/30th permanent camp.

May 1945.

On 2nd, German guards locked up. At 1.05 pm a Lieutenant and Corporal arrived in armoured car to officially release us! On 3rd taken into Lübeck in stolen jeep but soon returned. On 4th at 8.00 pm left in convoy, driven over the Elbe by pontoon bridge to Lauenburg - deloused and slept on floor. On 6th got away by MT to Sulingen - given light meal. On 7th passed Diepholz and on to Borghorst by 4.15 pm. On 8th taken to Rheine airfield and slept in flight office. On 9th left by Lancaster 10.00 am and landed Dunsfold 12.17 pm. After beer at Bramley drove to London and given meal at Endsleigh Hotel. Train Euston to

Wolverhampton then by lorry to Cosford. Given toilet items - bath and bed. On 10th got new identity passes. On 11th to Hednesford for 'demob' clothing and arrived home about 6.00 pm'.

So ended Buck Casson's war. During his time as an operational fighter pilot, Buck had destroyed 3½ enemy aircraft, probably destroyed four, and damaged four more. His DFC was gazetted the week after he was shot down and captured. In May 1947, Buck was re-commissioned into 616 Squadron at Finningley, the unit having become the RAF's first jet fighter unit in 1944, but at that time operating Mosquitos as a bomber squadron of the Auxiliary Air Force. In 1949, the squadron re-equipped with Meteor jet fighters, and thus Buck joined the jet age. In 1950, Squadron Leader Casson became 616 Squadron's CO, serving as such until leaving the service in 1954 with an AFC.

Squadron Leader Buck Casson DFC AFC RAF Retd is now retired from his working life and recently celebrated his 80th birthday.

Sqn Ldr Buck Casson DFC AFC RAF Retd at the launch of 'The Invisible Thread: A Spitfire's Tale', Great Malvern, September 1992.

Dennis Williams.

Chapter Twenty

First Officer Martyn Steynor (ATA)

First Officer Martyn Steynor, immediately identifiable with pipe, amongst ATA pilots flying out from White Waltham to ferry aircraft to and from various locations.

The Air Transport Auxiliary (ATA) often appears to be an organisation which supported the front-line RAF squadrons but has only received due recognition through its former members publishing their autobiographies, including female pilots such as Lettice Curtis and Diano Barnato-Walker.

The ATA was formed in February 1940 at White Waltham, but only became a properly organised body in mid-May with the appointments of Winston Churchill as Prime Minister and Lord Beaverbrook as Minister of Aircraft Production. The role of the ATA was to provide a complete aircraft ferry service and thus relieve RAF pilots of what was an extensive undertaking. New aircraft, of course, had to be ferried from factories to Maintenance Units, damaged ones in squadron service had to be flown to repair units and later back again, not to mention another 101 reasons for aircraft movement throughout the RAF and FAA. The ATA provided the opportunity for women to take an active part in the war, and notable amongst the female pilots, in addition to those previously mentioned, was Monique Agazarian, descended from the French and Armenian aristocracies, who had one brother, Noel, flying Spitfires in 1940 with 609 Squadron, and another brother, Leon, who later flew Thunderbolts in the Far East with the 'Forgotten Air Force'. Monique was to enjoy a lifetime of aviation, which saw her flying range from de Havilland Rapide biplane passenger aircraft to high-tech flight training simulators in the winter of her days. Miss Agazarian sadly died recently and remains sorely missed by many who knew her.

Male ATA pilots tended to be those who were too old for operational flying with the RAF, or in some way unfit for those duties. Consequently few remain alive today, and those that do are most senior in years.

One such man is Martyn Steynor, who now lives in a beautiful country house in Worcestershire, with Leigh brook meandering through his garden in which he still regularly wets a line for trout, despite his 84 years. He was actually the first man I ever met who had flown a Spitfire, an aircraft type which had captivated me since childhood, and his flying stories fascinated me. Early in my research I was able to photocopy Martyn's two flying log books, his own research having already identified that he had flown at least two extant Spitfires and Hurricanes: on August 24th, 1943, he ferried the Birmingham Science Museum's Hurricane Mk IV, KX829, from Silloth to Manston, via Hawarden, and on April 27th, 1945, he similarly flew the Battle of Britain Memorial Flight's Spitfire PRXIX, PS915, from Brize Norton to the Photographic Reconnaissance Establishment at Benson.

On January 7th, 1995, Martyn and I sat in the conservatory of his home enjoying the remaining minutes of a day uncharacteristically beautiful for the

Martyn Steynor prepares to embark upon yet another ferry flight, 1945.

time of year. We spoke of his ATA days, and in particular his route to flying with the service:-

'Before the war I had a Private Pilot's Licence and was a member of the Civilian Flying Club at Hanworth, where we flew Gypsy Moths for fun. In October 1939 we moved to Gatwick and I had a medical to join the RAFVR. However, I was turned down because my eyesight was too poor. By this time I had about 100 hours solo flying time, and as the RAF needed Link Trainer instructors, about 150 of us old and decrepit types were made Sergeants and reported from Cardington to No 3 ITW at Hastings. Whilst we were there, there was a great invasion scare in March 1940. I was posted to the Cambridge University Air Squadron as a Link instructor. By November 1941 I was still dying to fly but failed another medical. I contacted the VR and told them that as I was above call-up age I wished to be released, which I knew would stir them up. They said that if that was the case I would be sent with the LMF people - Lack of Moral Fibre supposedly - but all I wanted to do was fly, not be a Link instructor! One of my fellow instructors was an MP, however, so I told the VR that if I did not get some action soon I would have him raise it in the House - two weeks later I was released without problems!

'In fact, prior to my release I had spoken to my sister-in-law who was a Ferry Pilot in the ATA. She arranged a flight test for me in November 1941 which I passed. By that time the war was in full swing, so when I left Cambridge and the VR I rang the ATA every day. Eventually on New Year's Day 1942 I reported for duty at 9 am with the ATA at White Waltham'.

Martyn successfully completed his Class 1 training, likewise completed the Ferry Flight course and then went back to school to complete his Class 2 training. On December 8th, 1942, his report at Training Pool stated: 'A smart and well-behaved Officer whose Training Pool work has been very satisfactory. He is a competent and enthusiastic pilot and should make a good Ferry Officer'. A week later First Officer MB Steynor joined No 9 Ferry Pool, later joining No 2 Ferry Pool where he was reported as having undertaken 'excellent work'. He then passed Classes 3 and 4 training, but on September 3rd, 1943, was 'severely reprimanded for failing to notice obstruction in front of Fairchild Argus FK341 when taxying'. Two months later his Commanding Officer judged him to be 'an excellent type of Officer. Is steady and reliable as a pilot and is progressing rapidly. Will make a first class Ferry Pilot'. By May 1944 his rating was 'excellent in every way'.

Martyn flew at least, not to mention different marques of the various types, 37 wartime aircraft. In the UK alone he landed on roughly 800 aerodromes, a number which includes not only major airfields but also temporary landing strips and satellites. It can perhaps be appreciated, therefore, that Martyn Steynor's flying adventures were numerous, but he has picked just one to recount for us:-

'As a "junior trainee" in the ATA during September 1942, I flew three hours on the Hurricane Mk I at White Waltham, my base, after which I commenced ferrying Hurricane Mk IIs from the Hawker factory at Slough, where they were made. Destinations were usually Scotland - Prestwick, Silloth, Kirkbride, etc. These obscure and long range destinations were given us, I suspect, to test how we would cope with the murky weather, balloon barrages, the industrial haze of Merseyside, etc. We only had compasses and maps - we had no radios so relied on our basic aids and our watches to get to our destinations!

'Before we left base we consulted the WAAF "Met" officer who in those days gave us a largely guessed state of the weather en route together with locations of balloon barrage areas. It was sometimes a bit terrifying as in that winter, apart from the industrial haze, there seemed to be a lot of "lows" around drifting in from the Irish Sea meaning that we had to keep offshore to avoid the Scottish hills and navigate around Millom where there was a "bolthole" aerodrome at sea level.

'I particularly remember that on one day several of us in the Training Pool were given Hurricanes to fly to Scotland. My destination was Kirkbride. Approaching Millom, following the coast along the seashore with a low moving in from the west, I noticed another of our contingent formating closely on my inside. Concerned that he would hit me, I edged further out to sea and as the Irish mist enveloped me I was startled to notice the other Hurricane edging in even closer to me. I could not shake him off but somehow found the coast again and landed at Kirkbride. I booked into flying control, turned around and there was our Training Officer having landed just after me - he must have ferried an aircraft for a change just to see how his pupils were coping! He didn't often do this, he merely remarked to me "don't let me catch you doing that again." I was, and still am, an inveterate pipe smoker and I must have been smoking furiously as the Officer said "I got close to you as I knew it was one of my trainee pilots but couldn't recognise who since the cockpit was so full of smoke!"

ATA pilots at White Waltham; Martyn Steynor again identifiable by his ever-present pipe!

'I don't think that I smoked again in an aircraft until I was on twins when I was able to light up when my flight engineer or passengers knew my habits. I still maintain pipes are safer than cigarettes - confirmed when a passenger in my Wimpey let his cigarette fall out of his mouth when we hit an upcurrent over the Wrekin - I pushed him smartly out of his seat into the bowels of the Wimpey to extinguish his smouldering stub which could have started a fire since the stomach of these planes seemed to collect all sorts of odds and ends!'

In all the years I have known Martyn Steynor it is fair to say that I have never seen him without his beloved pipe! Former First Officer Martyn Steynor was amongst the Malvern Spitfire Team's first Patrons, and he has enthusiastically attended every function we have ever organised. I hope that inclusion in this book will go a little way toward providing some recognition for the hard work of the likes of Martyn who flew in all weathers to keep the flow of replacement aircraft moving. The ATA of course also suffered casualties, so the job was certainly not a 'cushy number' - as with any flying, especially 50 years ago, dangers were ever-present, perhaps a fact often overlooked?

Reconciliation. Martyn Steynor, right, and former Unteroffizier Paul Moeller, an He 111 torpedo bomber pilot, meet as friends at a Ramrod Publications enthusiast's afternoon at the Abbey Hotel, Great Malvern, February 1994. The Luftwaffe summer issue flying helmet worn by Paul Moeller once belonged to Oberleutnant Zöllner of 9/KG27, an He 111 pilot shot down over Somerset by Sqn Ldr John 'Catseyes' Cunningham DSO DFC on May 3rd, 1941.

Peter Ainsley.

Chapter Twenty-one

Air Vice-Marshal Michael Lyne CB AFC

Pilot Officer Michael Lyne in 1940.

Michael Lyne joined 19 Squadron at Duxford fresh from Cranwell in August 1939. The squadron's first full-scale brush with the enemy was fought over Dunkirk on May 26th, 1940, but in a textbook Fighter Command Attack on a formation of Stukas, the CO, Squadron Leader Geoffrey Stephenson, was shot down and captured. During the afternoon, Flight Lieutenant Brian Lane led the squadron on another patrol over the evacuation beaches. However, on that occasion the squadron was bounced by Me 109s, and Pilot Officer Michael Lyne was shot up in his Spitfire, probably by Oberleutnant Paul Temme of I/JG2. Michael managed to clear the surf and crash-land on Walmer Beach. Wounded, the escapade was to put Pilot Officer Lyne out of action until February 19th, 1941, when he re-joined 19 Squadron at Fowlmere. In 1941, during the Battle of the Atlantic, when the German 'U' Boats and FW Condors in particular menaced our convoy lifelines, a scheme was devised to afford the merchantmen some protection. Thus the Merchant Ship Fighter Unit (MSFU) was born with its headquarters at Speke near Liverpool. The MSFU's function was to supply Catapult Aircraft Merchant Ships, or CAM ships, with aircraft and the personnel required for their operation. CAM ships were 7,000 ton cargo-carrying vessels of the Merchant Navy, sailing on trade routes such as to North America, Russia and Gibraltar. Each CAM ship carried one fighter, a Hurricane, known as a 'Hurri-Cat'.

The Hurricane was loaded on a trolley fitted to a 70' steel runway which was mounted to extend beyond the forecastle. The trolley was propelled by rockets which were fired electrically by the Catapult Directing Officer, and the position he occupied was in a blast shelter situated beside the catapult. Of course, once an aircraft had been so launched, it was unable to return to the ship, and nor could the aircraft itself be replaced until said ship returned to port.

Above left: Flying Officer Michael Lyne, second left, poised to board the SS Empire Tide at Liverpool. Note the Hurricane on the catapult arrangement.
Above right: Flying Officer Michael Lyne and his MSFU 'groundcrew' aboard the SS Empire Tide.

The RAF crew involved per Hurricane consisted of two officer pilots, a fitter, rigger, radio telephone operator, and an armourer. In addition there was also one Naval Fighter Directing Officer and a seaman torpedo man, the latter for the catapult's operation. The FDO controlled the aircraft exactly as a land-based ground controller would do.

The aircraft was only launched operationally and upon visual identification of an hostile aircraft. If the Hurricane pilot was fortunate and he was within range of land, after the interception he would make landfall and return to earth safely. Should he not be so fortunate then the only option was to bale out near to his ship and hope to be rescued quickly from the water by the crew. In practice, it was reckoned to take some 4-7 minutes to pick a pilot up, and the Merchantmen boasted in July 1942 never to have lost a pilot.

This photograph gives some idea of an Atlantic voyage!

Should an interception launch not have been made, when a CAM ship approached port the Hurricane was launched and the pilot then flew to an aerodrome where his machine would be serviced. Barges would then later return the aircraft to its ship.

The pilots, by necessity, were all experienced Fighter Command aircrew. Upon joining the MSFU their training took just two weeks, after which they teamed up with an FDO and other essential members of their crew and joined a ship's company.

A pilot could expect a round trip of between four to eight weeks at sea. The normal tour of duty with the MSFU was four voyages which usually took about a year to complete.

Pilot Officer Michael Lyne volunteered for these rather hazardous duties:-

'The pilots were recruited by a letter backed by Winston Churchill. Squadron commanders were not allowed to hold people back. We tended to be rather wild individualists and, like some of the RNVR FDOs, had already seen battle. My FDO told me what his Mess Deck had looked like after an attack by a German commerce raider.

'One of our earliest pilots had earned his DFC in a daylight raid behind a leader who won the VC. We all liked a glass and a yarn together. In fact, it was a Naval Officer's search for free beer in a "WRENNERY" that led me to my future wife. She too had played her part in the Battle of the Atlantic, sitting out the disastrous bombing of May 1941 in the Liver Building. She operated the last unbroken teleprinter line out of Liverpool. Our wooing on the Aigburth tram is another story, but the foundation it laid led to our recent Golden Wedding!

'The mixture on the MSFU made for a cheerful Officers' Mess at Speke. The food was poor at first. With Liverpool smouldering we were on emergency rations of hard biscuit and Bully Beef. But we were no sooner booked in than we were off on a one shot catapult course before going off to sea.

'My colleagues must have also felt the weight of responsibility at having the only aircraft in a convoy of 110 ships. The least academic amongst us could calculate that some 5,000 pairs of eyes would note our performance.

'There could be no excuse for failing to take off if a Condor showed up. Certainly in storms, and on one occasion in a full hurricane, I would ponder on the fact as I watched the spume being torn off the top of giant waves. "No place to be on a parachute," I would say to myself quietly! The alert against Condors only lasted to mid-Atlantic. The expectation of torpedoes was perpetual. An unexpected hardship was living always in heavy clothes. It would have been selfish to turn up in a lifeboat in pyjamas and expect a whipround for woollies from other survivors.

'The torpedo menace became real for us when two of our crews were sunk in September 1941. Jack Burr, my Best Man who later had two fine victories on the Russian convoys, spent many days in an open boat near Iceland.

'In Merchant ship sinkings the average loss was of one third of the crew. We much admired the brave ship's Officers, many of them had been sunk several times by 1941.

'Histories of the MSFU have concentrated on the battles in the air. I am sad that there seems to be no account of the adventures and losses amongst our so called "ground crews". There certainly were some.

'One typical act of bravery illustrates the sort of thing that I have in mind. RNVR Lieutenant Johnny Shaftoe was knocked unconscious and trapped in his cabin by broken furniture. Pilot Ross Taylor fought him clear and rescued him from a ship which sank in six precious seconds.

'When any of us returned to Speke and met others who had been at sea, there would be great high jinks in the Mess. With ships going to Canada, Gibraltar, Iceland, New York, Philadelphia and later Russia, there was a huge range of different experiences to be exchanged. There were tales to be spun, jokes to be told, pints of beer to be consumed to compensate for weeks on dry ships, and Mess games to be played. It was just a tremendous joy to see old friends safely home, and we behaved accordingly, no doubt much to the embarrassment of the local staff, the CO, George Pinkerton, who loyally defended us and privately sorted us out, the Naval Liaison Officer, Commander Lane, a jovial and extremely bright man from the Penguin publishing family, and the hero in two World

Wars who was in charge of training, once Colonel then Squadron Leader Louis Strange DSO MC DFC & Bar.

'That was the flip side. The nature of the serious side shows through in the last battle fought in a Hurricane of the MSFU far out off the Bay of Biscay. The pilot had not been in action before. The target was the formidably armed four-engined FW Condor. Paddy Flynn, our pilot, had to tackle the Condor at just 200' above the sea. As he concentrated his fire on the enemy, heavy cannon fire blew away his cockpit hood. His aircraft was heavily hit in other places and the ammunition was finished as he turned to look for the convoy. Anxious work with a shot up radio. After 10 minutes flying on an estimated heading he was relieved to see the convoy, but before he could bale out he had to frighten off another Condor. At last it was quiet enough for him to bale out and await his rescue in the sea by the Royal Navy who never failed us once. His first target had been well hit and did not reach its base.

'John Kendal, who flew Spitfires with 66 Squadron during the Battle of Britain, also downed his target. He also then patrolled to guard the convoy, despite worsening weather, and even broadcasted the location of the unfortunate German crew who were safely picked up. When he at last baled out in low cloud his parachute failed to deploy in time and he was killed.

A CAM ship Hurricane of the MSFU.

'In his memory, and to remember the way in which ordinary people responded to great events in an extraordinary way, is this account dedicated'.

The MSFU was disbanded on June 8th, 1943, the threat to the vital convoys over. The following signal was received from the Admiralty:-

'My Lords would like to express their great appreciation of the services rendered by the RAF in providing this valuable defence for our convoys.

'It is with great regret that they are now forced to recommend that this association of the RAF and the Merchant Navy should now be brought to an end'.

Michael Lyne later flew Typhoons over Europe, and survived the war to enjoy a long and distinguished career in the RAF from which he eventually retired with very senior rank. He and Joy are now retired and live near Lincoln. Due to the wounds received when he was shot down over Dunkirk, Michael Lyne missed the Battle of Britain. Nevertheless, as a 19 Squadron stalwart from the dark days of 1940, it was marvellous that Michael could join us at Hendon for the launch of 'Spitfire Squadron' in 1990.

Chapter Twenty-two

Lieutenant Basil King (FAA)

Sub-Lieutenant Basil King.

As early as 1936, Reginald Joseph Mitchell, the genius who created the Spitfire, had considered a naval version of his fighter. He of course sadly died prematurely in 1937. No further interest was shown in a sea-going version of the Spitfire until 1941, but by then the Admiralty considered the need for such a fighter to be urgent for operations off aircraft carriers and flying in the Fleet Air Defence role. Subsequently a number of elderly Spitfires were transferred from the RAF to the Fleet Air Arm for trials and training. What subsequently became Seafires were essentially Spitfires with several modifications enabling them to be operated from an aircraft carrier's deck. These consisted of an arrester hook and four spools for catapult launches, and of course the airframe required some strengthening to cope with the extra loads thus imposed by such rapid acceleration and deceleration. By 1944, folding wings had also been introduced to facilitate the stowage of large numbers of aircraft below deck in the carrier's hangars. As enemy reconnaissance and torpedo aircraft often flew low, the Seafire, equipped with the Merlin engine, would provide a rapid reaction to these low and medium level threats. However, as with the Spitfire, the Griffon engine eventually replaced the Seafire's Merlin, and by the advent of the final Seafire - the mighty Mk 47 which fought in Korea - this 'Spitfire Sister' had also gone through a multitude of marques and modifications. If not for the advent of the turbine engine, one must ask where was the end to the potential of the Spitfire's design?

HMS Battler, an aircraft carrier converted from a merchantman by the Americans.

One Second World War aircraft carrier in service with the Royal Navy was HMS Battler. This ship had started life as a merchantman, but had its hull converted to aircraft carrier configuration in the United States. Battler then became one of the USS Bogue class of escort carriers intended for the protection of convoys, and was commissioned in the RN during October 1942. Upon Battler's arrival in the UK, there commenced a three month period of 'Anglicising' which was completed on March 5th, 1943. On April 5th she embarked four Seafires of No 808 Squadron, and six Swordfish of 835 Squadron. The Seafires comprised three Mk IICs and one LIIC. The Seafire Mk II had been built from the outset at Westlands as a pure Seafire, as opposed to its predecessor, the Mk IB, which was a converted Spitfire Mk VB. In addition to the modifications previously mentioned, these Seafires also enjoyed the benefits of an extra 25 lb of armour plate, and the incorporation of the 'C' wing which allowed the use of four 20mm cannon. Unfortunately the extra weight impositions reduced performance, but the LIIC, powered by the new Merlin 32 with a new four-bladed Rotol airscrew, was intended to remedy the poor performance at low-level. Some LIICs also had clipped wings, like the Spitfire Mk VC, which increased the rate of roll. The disadvantage was the longer take-off run required. The clipped-wing Seafire was, however, lighter on the controls which made it easier to deck-land.

HMS Battler left Belfast for Gibraltar on June 4th, 1943, providing a part of Convoy OS49's escort and ferrying Seafires to the pool being built up on the 'Rock' in preparation for the invasion of Italy. After another similar trip, Battler was back in Gibraltar on August 9th with three other escort carriers: Attacker, Hunter and Stalker. Later these four carriers were joined by a fifth, HMS Unicorn, and made for Malta. On September 8th, 'Force V' left Grand Harbour bound for participation in 'Operation Avalanche', the Allied amphibious assault on Italy. The landings were to take place in the Bay of Salerno, south of Naples, and Force V's Seafires were to provide both low and medium air cover for the invasion; until the beach-head was firmly established, the RAF and USAAF in Sicily were only able to maintain 36 aircraft over the beach-head at any one time, due to the problems created by the extreme range at which such types as Lightnings, Mustangs and Spitfires were operating. For the first four days of the invasion, therefore, the Seafires' presence was essential.

The Seafires of Force V consequently operated over the northern beach-head, the low-level fighters orbiting Capri, ready to repel attacks beyond the beach-head. The high ground northwards beyond the beaches created chaos on the controlling ship's radar screens, so the pilots had to strain their eyes to spot the enemy in the prevailing haze. The first patrol of LIICs reached the coast just in time to drive away six Ju 88s. Thereafter the Luftwaffe relied upon fast FW 190s and Me 109s to undertake hit and run raids. A formation of 12 German fighter-bombers arrived just after noon but were intercepted and turned back by the duty Seafire patrol. At the close of this Italian D-Day, Force V had flown a record 265 sorties, but had suffered severely from deck landing accidents, for the majority of the Seafire pilots were products of the rapid expansion of the FAA in anticipation of 'Operation Avalanche', and had little experience of shipboard operation. At Salerno the pilots faced difficult conditions, including a 'glassy' sea and a lack of wind over the deck; the latter could increase the Seafire's approach speed by as much as 15 knots. The carriers also operated very close together, which, due to the proximity of many other aircraft both taking-off and landing, made it difficult for tired and inexperienced pilots to go round again if their approach was misjudged. On the carriers, undercarriages collapsed, deck hooks were torn adrift, rear fuselages crumpled and airscrews 'pecked' the decks.

One of the Seafire pilots on HMS Battler during Operation Avalanche was Basil King. When he volunteered for the armed forces, his headmaster had written to his selection board recommending that as he was so good at mathematics consideration should be given to training Basil as a pilot. The board agreed, and Basil later found himself in the FAA and at the Naval Air Station at Pensacola, Florida, having arrived there on May 12th, 1942. He made his first solo flight on May 18th. He remembers that his instructor not only taught him a completely new vocabulary, but also how to fly by the 'seat of my pants!' By December 1942 he had completed the RN Fighter Course, although his ability as a pupil pilot was assessed as 'below average'.

Lieutenant Basil King (bare-headed) with other 808 Squadron pilots aboard HMS Battler.

Back in the UK, Basil joined 762 Squadron in March 1943, this being a training squadron. On March 31st he flew a Hurricane for the first time, P2859, and thereafter regularly flew the type on exercises such as formation attacks. On April 8th he completed his first Spitfire flight, in X4657, and thereafter made a number of night landings. By the end of April his assessment as a Hurricane pilot had increased to 'average'.

In June 1943, Basil King joined 10 NOTU, and on the 14th flew his first Seafire, MA984. Throughout June and July a hectic schedule of training flights was flown, including attacks on twin-engined bombers.

On July 27th, 1943, Sub-Lieutenant BAN King joined 808 Squadron. From HMS Battler's decks, Basil commenced flying various patrols and practising air-to-air firing. However, this posed another problem; that of deck landings, of which Basil had no previous experience. However, his flying log book was soon endorsed that his initial deck landings were 'above the average'.

Basil recalls the difficulties of deck landing the Seafire:-

'For some reason I was not given the opportunity to try a simulated deck-landing on dry land at the RNAS Yeovilton, but instead was sent straight to 808 Squadron on HMS Battler without any experience. My CO was not at all pleased. How I came to envy the RAF pilots who could put down on dry land. We had to approach the narrow deck of the carrier which left no room for error. Because of the Seafire's approach angle, our view of the deck was virtually nil - we could only see about 2' of it and the Batsman. He used coloured bats, one in each hand, and gave you signals to let you know what to do, to tell you whether you were coming in okay. Fortunately I landed safely on most occasions'.

Above: A Seafire, arrester hook and flaps down, eases onto HMS Battler's deck.

Left: A Swordfish approaches HMS Battler's deck, a photograph which gives some idea of the difficulties involved.

Seafires preparing to take-off from HMS Battler.

A Seafire being pushed to the end of the flight deck in preparation for take-off. Note the escort destroyer adjacent.

Despite his inexperience, Basil King survived Salerno. Force V was disbanded at Palermo on September 20th, 1943. By February 1944, Basil was serving with 807 Squadron, but the following month began instructing on Seafires with 731 Squadron. At this time he also flew a wide variety of FAA aircraft: Swordfish, Fulmars, Seafires, Fireflies and Barracudas. By July 1945, his deck landings were 'above average', his general flying 'average'. His last flight was in a 768 Squadron Seafire on October 18th, 1945. In total, Lieutenant King had safely completed 34 deck landings.

During the war Basil married, and after the war, amongst other things, the Kings ran a picturesque pub in Wales, which was a favourite haunt of the 'Z-Cars' cast of 1960s television fame, and more recently, a newsagents near Great Malvern railway station.

I met Basil King in 1994, and it was not easy to persuade him to reminisce about his flying days. He gladly loaned me his flying log book and photographs, but talking about the war was painful for Basil and words did not come easily. However, I am pleased to be able to include a little of his story in this book, as Basil King surely stands testament to those unsung heroes of the FAA who were trained, ready, and there to do their duty, whatever and whenever the call.

Basil King pictured at home in early 1995.
Dennis Williams

Chapter Twenty-three

Flight Lieutenant Ron Rayner DFC

Flight Lieutenant Ron Rayner DFC.

On September 5th, 1992, my second book, 'The Invisible Thread: A Spitfire's Tale' was launched at the Abbey Hotel, Great Malvern. As I prepared to take my seat amongst the pilots present and commence signing, I was approached by a local retired gentleman who told me that he used to be a Spitfire pilot and offered to lend a hand with the signing session. To substantiate his claim he had brought a wartime snapshot of himself; I eagerly accepted his offer and in so doing welcomed another wartime pilot to the fold. Since that time I have come to know Ron 'Cloudy' Rayner well, and have much appreciated his support at various events. I have often sat at Ron's kitchen table enjoying a tea-break, mesmerised by his matter-of-fact, and typically modest, memories of his flying days. In many ways our conversations have been the inspiration for 'A Few of the Many', as talking to Ron certainly impressed upon me how much material would ultimately be lost if his memory was not recorded. Enthusiasts present at some of our slide show and question and answer presentations at the Abbey Hotel will recall, no doubt, listening to several of Ron's fascinating accounts - one humorous example being a night flight on which he flew a Spitfire in a searchlight co-operation exercise, during which he was easily detected for he forgot to switch off his navigation lights! But he is neither a casual raconteur nor a 'line shooter' - absolutely not - for Ron Rayner has shared with us, and fortunately myself in particular, his memories having appreciated the historical significance attached to them, as indeed with the other former pilots whose stories are also told in this book.

The following is based upon a tape which Ron 'Cloudy' Rayner kindly recorded for me in early 1995:-

'I joined 41 Squadron at Catterick in 1941 with some 50 hours flying time on Spitfires recorded in my log book. The squadron was re-forming after the Battle of Britain and the fighter combats of late 1940 and early 1941. The squadron was still using the Battle of Britain period formation which was virtually four aircraft in line astern. No 4, or "Arse-end Charlie" as he was called, was supposed to protect the rear of the formation by weaving frantically behind; as I am sure you can imagine, this slowed the whole formation down as he was travelling a much greater distance with his weaving than the rest of the formation. This continued until we got down to Tangmere. This very formation was one of attack, and very useful if you were attacking hordes of bombers, but of course our role on the south coast was to change completely, so the formation also had to change as we were going to be both attacking and being attacked over France. Therefore the virtual line abreast formation was evolved. This was not a close formation but had sufficient distance between each aircraft so that each pilot could look over and inwards towards the leader of the formation and thereby protect that sector of the formation. In other words he is looking behind to the far side of the formation, so that if you were on the port side you would look out to starboard and protect that sector from 90 degrees right round to 180 degrees. The pilot on the starboard side would be doing exactly the same for the port section. This provided a large degree of protection because directly behind in a Spitfire you could not really see anything - there was a rear-view mirror but it was not really that efficient. In line astern it is very easy to turn, as a formation, to either port or starboard, but in line abreast that is when the difficulty arises. Of course a method had to be evolved which allowed us to turn relatively quickly but still maintain formation, so the leader would give instructions, "Turning port", or "Turning starboard", whatever, and on the former those Spitfires on the port side would go over the top of the leader, and the other two on the starboard side would go below him. You ended up at 90 degrees and in virtually the same formation. Those from the starboard side then transferred to the port side and port to the starboard side. You were therefore still able to protect each other immediately the turn was complete. The leader himself had to ensure that his rate of turn was correct so that the rest of his little formation would maintain their positions throughout the turn. I say all this because over France during the sweeps of 1941 we were going to be the targets and therefore the attack would obviously come from above, because by the time we got over France the German controllers would have been made aware of our approach and deployed their aircraft accordingly at 30,000' or even higher. The foregoing introduction to the sweeps will probably help the reader understand what happened to me on one day in August 1941'.

At 11.30 am on August 31st, 1941 (exactly 20 years to the day before Dilip Sarkar was born!), 41 Squadron, led by Squadron Leader Gaunce, provided 12 Spitfires for a sweep over France. 616 Squadron added a further 11 Spitfires to the offensive formation from Westhampnett.

'We usually rendezvoused over Dungeness or Beachy Head, depending on what your particular squadron was briefed to do, and we then went out across the Channel in layers to protect each other. Our objective on this particular sortie was not to either bomb or strafe, but to entice the German fighters to come up and attack us. We would set our course to sweep the area as previously instructed by the ops room, and of course by then we were on the alert for German fighters, each protecting the other's tail, so in the squadron there would be three sections of four. We would progress along these lines looking out for ourselves and also, perhaps, for those squadrons below us. On the day in question, we were between 25,000' and 30,000' and progressed towards France'.

At 12.20 pm, 616 Squadron ran into 15 plus Me 109Fs at 25,000' north-west of St Omer. Blue Section attacked, and Sergeant Bowen, Blue 2, fired at a fleeting German fighter, and he stated: 'I saw pieces come off the port side of fuselage and wing. Volumes of black smoke poured from the aircraft. The pilot then rolled it onto its back and when the plane started to fall away, the hood came off. It is my firm belief that the pilot baled out and I therefore claim this aircraft as destroyed'. Meanwhile, however, 41 Squadron were about to be bounced, and Sergeant Rayner was to find himself in trouble:-

'Suddenly there was a shout of "BREAK!", which meant that we were about to be attacked. When that shout went up you did a steep turn, as hard as possible, either port or starboard, to get away from whoever was diving at you from above. No use going into a dive to get away, that was hopeless as if you stuck your nose down then the engine would cut. The only other possible action was to half roll and get away that way, but that took a long time, so the best evasive action was to break hard and do a very, very tight turn - when I say tight I mean tight, so that you were virtually blacked out with the "g" force as you executed the turn. By the time that I came out of my turn, I discovered that my canopy had been shot away and dust from the perspex had got into my oxygen mask. The engine temperature was rising rapidly, and after a very short time it exceeded the maximum for safety. Now here was my dilemma: I could see the English coast and I must have had about 25,000' to play with, so I tentatively fiddled about to see how much engine power I actually had left. Then I had to decide, what shall I do, shall I make for the English coast and hope to get that far with my height advantage, or should I bale out over France, over land, or get to the Channel and bale out over the sea? Without having made any decision, I experimented to see how far I could get. Gradually descending, and hoping that I would not be attacked again, I managed to get over the Channel and over the coast. There in front of me was Manston which, despite being in a frantic state by now really, I decided I would try and reach. As I got closer and lower, I realised that I would make it with a certain degree of comfort, and decided that perhaps a wheels-down landing was possible, so I managed to get my undercarriage down. I was streaming coolant, clouds of glycol coming out of the aircraft, and by the time I got over the airfield both the ambulance and fire tender were on the perimeter. As I made my approach and put down they were dashing out after me. I got down without any engine at all, got out of the aircraft which was hardly damaged, in fact, and was greeted by the Station Commander who said "By jingo that was a bloody awful landing you made!" So that was all the greeting I got! I also remember the groundcrews swarming over the Spitfire and collecting the perspex - out of which they made brooches and the like.

'I abandoned the aircraft and reported what had happened to the Intelligence Officer. He said that arrangements would be made to return me to Merston, the Tangmere satellite where 41 Squadron were based. I went into the headquarters and the clerk there gave me a railway warrant, but it was routed through London. All I had with me was my flying kit, Mae West, flying boots, long stockings, and a parachute to carry, so I decided that that was the end: no way was I going to travel like that through London! Eventually I persuaded them to give me a warrant to travel by Southern Rail along the south coast to Chichester, near Tangmere, from where I was picked up by the squadron transport.

'The postscript to this episode is that the next occasion I climbed into a Spitfire cockpit and prepared for another sortie, I noticed that some comedian had crayoned an Me 109 in a head-on attitude on my rear-view mirror!

Sgt Rayner at readiness, Merston 1941.
The newspaper report describes a raid on
a German airfield.

'The Tangmere Wing at this time was of course commanded by the legendary Wing Commander Douglas Bader. As I previously explained, we were not actually flying from Tangmere itself but from the little grass satellite airfield at Merston. Should Tangmere be bombed again, our chances of saving the Wing's Spitfires were obviously greater if they were dispersed in this way - there was also another Tangmere satellite airfield at Westhampnett, which later became Goodwood motor racing circuit. At Merston I remember the dispersal hut there with a stove in the centre. Bader would come along and give us a pep talk, standing in the centre of the dispersal hut by this stove, rocking on his artificial limbs - I do not think it was possible for him to stand still with tin legs - he would make little movements to maintain his balance. I remember him saying on one occasion, "If you follow my instructions in this new formation that we are now flying, nobody will get shot down." That was very encouraging, but shortly afterwards Bader himself had to bale out over France. We then learnt that he had left his legs behind in the cockpit and was therefore not in a very comfortable state. The Germans offered to allow an RAF aircraft safe conduct over France to drop some replacement artificial limbs by parachute. Of course we could not make such an exception for any pilot, so to get round it a Circus was organised involving six Blenheims which were to go out on a normal raid and drop the legs before hitting the target. That way it was not a special trip but Douglas Bader could have his legs back. The Tangmere Wing had the privilege of providing close escort to the Blenheims, and I was personally privileged to be amongst those members of 41 Squadron who flew on that sortie. All I can recall now, though, was hearing over the R/T that the legs had been released from the Blenheim.

'Of course the Blenheims were very vulnerable in any case as they were obsolete. On one occasion we provided close escort to these Blenheims attacking shipping on the Dutch coast. We were attacked and I understood at the time that not one of the Blenheims returned, but years later I discovered that just one had survived.

'After a brief spell as an instructor, I joined 43 Squadron in mid-1942 and began a nomadic existence. The squadron was based at Wittering and had completely packed for a move overseas. We aircrew were taken to Padgate in Warrington and then, late one evening, we were put on a train and went to the Clyde, from where we embarked on the Loynster. For a fortnight we sailed a zig-zag course through the Atlantic, and back again, but one night we found ourselves in the Straits of Gibraltar. We were disembarked from the ship immediately and taken in covered three-tonners to the top of the Rock. There there was an abandoned barracks where we were bedded down for the night.

'The next day we were taken to the garrison theatre and told that the invasion of North Africa, was to commence the following day, and that one squadron would fly into Maison Blanc, the airport in Algiers, and that squadron would be us. We were equipped with Hurricanes with long-range tanks to enable us to make the 500 mile sea crossing to Algiers. If the reception we received there was bad, then there would be no chance of getting back and we would have to fend for ourselves.

'We were allowed to go down to the runway that afternoon, in pairs, and run up our Hurricanes to ensure they were to our satisfaction. Of course these Hurricanes had never been flown before, they had been shipped to Gibraltar in crates and assembled on the Rock. Before dawn the next day we took off, circled the Rock and set course for Algiers. About half an hour out into the Med I discovered that my generator had packed up so I had no radio, no fuel gauge, no gunsight, but fortunately I was No 2 to the Wing Commander, out in front of the formation of 18 aircraft, so I managed to stick close to him and signal that I had no communication. Eventually the Wing Commander and I landed in formation on the runway at Maison Blanc before the rest of the squadron - fortunately there was not a hostile reception so the Wing Commander signalled for the rest of the squadron to land. A little while later we were greeted by the commander of the RAF's Commando Servicing Group who were there to re-fuel and re-arm us.

'From Maison Blanc we patrolled the Mediterranean and often escorted the "Aurora", a cruiser, on raids against German shipping bringing supplies to the Tunis area. We would take the cruiser out from Algiers just before dusk, but return at nightfall, landing in the dark on the flarepath. Of course the Germans soon realised what was going on so they waited for us and bombed as we were landing. We had to disperse our aircraft as quickly as possible and dive into the nearest irrigation ditch for cover. This went on for several days until we were leapfrogged by Spitfires as landing strips had by then been prepared further inland. We then joined in the leapfrogging until we eventually made Tunis after the army had gone through some extremely bitter fighting, as did the Merchant Navy who were bringing supplies in along the coast. The Eighth Army, however, met up with the First Army, and thousands and thousands of German prisoners were taken and massed on the plains at Tunis.

'From North Africa we flew to Malta, which was then relieved. When we landed on the island our aircraft were put into dispersals and we then went to live in buildings surrounding the bay. This was quite a treat for us having lived for so long under canvas. It was May, 1943, and the Allied forces were amassing for the invasion of Sicily as a prelude to landing in Italy. From Malta we flew on bomber escorts to Comiso in southern Sicily.

On July 10th, 1943, the invasion of Sicily commenced, "Operation Husky", and on that day we actually landed at Comiso. I remember it well as I parked my aircraft in a dispersal area adjacent to a runway, which was an established airfield - my Spitfire was dispersed next to a Stuka with Italian markings which had tipped over on its back with the two dead crew members still hanging in their straps, right next to my aircraft!

'In Sicily we started the slog up the western coast, and flew patrols of Augusta, Catania, eventually landing at the latter. From there we began escorting the American daylight bombers attacking targets in Italy itself. We were escorting Mitchells and Bostons, and I must say that the American pilots were extremely brave - they would be flying along in formation (we would be weaving above them) and although the anti-aircraft fire would be bursting amongst them they would still maintain tight formation. Very creditable. In addition to our escort work, we ourselves were attacking the retreating Germans who were escaping up the coast to Messina, so we were strafing the equivalent of our tank landing craft as they tried to make the mainland.

'We were then transferred to an airstrip which had been made for us on the northern side of Sicily, and we continued the patrols of Messina and Augusta. Eventually we arrived at Falcone, again a strip prepared for us by the army engineers.

'It was in Sicily that we received our Spitfire Mk IXs. They were marvellous, absolutely incredible. I remember that on my first flight in a Mk IX, an air test, I went up to 35,000', just for the joy of experiencing what it was like to operate a Spit IX at high altitude. It was definitely a different aircraft altogether at high altitude to the Mk V, it was really something. We had only received a certain number of IXs, so we actually flew a mixture of Vs and IXs, so much so that the IXs were not even painted with an individual aircraft letter, they were just given a number. My personal aircraft was still a Mk V, and I always flew FT-J.

43 Squadron's Spitfire Mk IXs at Catania, Sicily. Ron's aircraft was FT-J.

'On September 8th, 1943, we were assembled and told that the invasion of Italy was to commence the next day. Our role was to support the army who were going to land on a beach in the bay of Salerno. On September 9th, therefore, Salerno was our patrol area, about 170 miles across the sea from our base at Falcone. We patrolled the beaches, milling about with German aircraft attacking the ground forces, and whilst the navy shelled the German positions. In addition the FAA also supported the army, their Seafires patrolling from their aircraft carriers (*see Lieutenant Basil King's story*). This went on until September 15th, by which time the army had secured the bridgehead, and a landing strip, called

"Roger", had been pushed up parallel to the beach at Salerno. We were then able to land at Salerno itself, but that was fraught with danger as not only were the Germans still shelling us, but the trajectory of our own artillery also went across the airfield!'

The Salerno beach-head snapped by a member of 152 Squadron's groundcrew, Ray Johnson.

The Allied invasion of Italy, at Salerno, is very much an unsung D-Day of the Second World War. In contrast to the landings in Normandy on June 6th, 1944, the Luftwaffe did get up in force over the bay of Salerno. Although the British troops had fought in North Africa, their American comrades were untested. The Italian coastline at Salerno was defended by combat experienced German soldiers, including many tough and feared paratroopers. For several days, the success of 'Operation Avalanche' really did lie in the balance.

At 1310 hrs on September 16th, 1943, six of 43 Squadron's Spitfires, led by their Polish CO, Squadron Leader Horbaczewski, had patrolled the Salerno beaches but upon returning to airfield Roger they spotted 12 FW 190s approaching from the south at 2,000'. The Spitfires attacked, and Flight Lieutenant Rayner reported:-

'Closing on one of the enemy aircraft he turned to the left and I carried out a deflection attack on him, firing two bursts of about two seconds each. Strikes were seen on top of the engine but I then broke off the attack because of another FW 190 which was attacking me. Squadron Leader Horbaczewski saw the enemy aircraft I attacked crash near Eboli'.

Squadron Leader Horbaczewski claimed two of the 190s destroyed in the fight, and in addition to Flight Lieutenant Rayner's 190 destroyed, Flying Officer 'Dizzy' Deuntzer claimed one as damaged. No Spitfires were lost.

German records indicate that II/JG77 lost two Me 109s and an FW 190 on the day in question, but details are vague. However, II/SKG 10, a fighter-bomber unit, suffered the loss of their Kommodore, Hauptman Wiglev von Wedal, who was killed near Salerno. Whilst 'Horby' also submitted claims for destroyed FW 190s, the fate of Flight Lieutenant Rayner's victim was conclusive and witnessed by Squadron Leader Horbaczewski himself to 'crash near Eboli'. It is possible, therefore, that it was Von Wedal whom 'Cloudy' Rayner met that day in the wartorn Italian sky.

Over Salerno, however, the Allied fighters faced another menace, in addition to the Luftwaffe, as Ron Rayner remembers:-

'Because the Americans were completely new to battle conditions, they shot at every aircraft in the sky regardless of whether it was German or Allied. Unfortunately on one occasion when we came in to land at Roger one of our Spitfires was shot down by these trigger happy people. Very easy to be critical, but they were absolutely scared stiff of course, as everybody is in battle.

'We continuously patrolled the battle front, making sure that the army was not troubled by the Luftwaffe too much. Eventually the Germans got the message that we were not going to be pushed out of Salerno and so the pressure started to ease off as the army pushed inland and north towards the town of Salerno and then on to Naples. I notice in my log book that on September 19th, 1943, we made our first offensive sweep over the airfield at Foggia, which was really a gesture just to show the enemy that we were in command.

'My stay in Salerno came to an abrupt end on September 22nd, 1943. I had been on patrol and when I landed began to shiver. On our way back to our dispersal encampment, I sat on top of the 15 hundredweight truck's engine to try and get warm, shivering quite violently in what was a scorching hot September. When darkness fell I was beginning to feel really ill. Then we had an alert that the Germans had launched a counterattack with paratroopers, so we all had to dive into slit-trenches. That is the last I remember. I passed out completely, only to discover two days later, when I came round being sponged with ice-cold water at a field dressing station, that I had malaria. I was then evacuated in a hospital Dakota to Tripoli.

'I returned to continue flying Spitfires during the remainder of the Italian campaign, and later became a flight commander on 72 Squadron. The fighting in Italy for what were just small hills was intense. I once walked over one with the squadron padre and found it littered with bodies. Truckloads of bodies were also driven past our landing strips as the battlefields were cleared. For us it was a time of living in tents, often in deep mud - very uncomfortable to say the least. We were largely engaged in ground attack against the German army, and strafed convoys of their motor transport and armour. This entailed flying very low, and once I returned to our base trailing a length of telegraph wire from my wing tip - the airfield cleared rapidly!

'By March 1945 we were still attacking German army positions in support of our advancing soldiers. One day that month we were ordered off to drop what were described to us as "fire bombs" on some German positions. These bombs had been made up in drop tank shells. Off we went and dropped them accordingly and watched rivulets of fire running into the enemy positions. On reflection I believe that this was napalm, and possibly the first use of it. During a strafing sortie I also had a narrow escape when a shell came up through my Spitfire's wing root - just three feet from my seat; there was no armour plate beneath the pilot!'

Ron's 72 Squadron Spitfire Mk IX, Ravenna, 1945. A flak shell came through the wing root during a strafing attack; just 3' to the left and it would have gone straight into the pilot's seat. Here Ron's groundcrew pose with the damaged aircraft which he managed to land safely.

Two months later, by which time 72 Squadron was based at Klagenfurt in Austria, the Second World War, in Europe at least, was over. Soon 'Cloudy' Rayner was able to go home, becoming a jeweller, family man and keen yachtsman in Wales before eventually retiring to Malvern. For his sustained period on operational flying, however, Flight Lieutenant Rayner was awarded the DFC.

In more recent years, Ron Rayner returned to RAF Hullavington, where he had made his first Hurricane flight many years before. On that occasion he was moved when a serving senior NCO asked to shake his hand, 'having never met anyone before who had won the DFC'. Ron had certainly earned the silver cross with its diagonal striped ribbon, and that nobody could deny.

Flt Lt Ron Rayner DFC proudly displays his medal and squadron crests at home, early 1995.

Dennis Williams

Chapter Twenty-four

Flight Lieutenant Bob Poulton DFC

Sergeant Bob Poulton pictured in 1940.

Whilst researching the 'life' of Spitfire P8047 'The Malverns' in 1987, I traced Flight Lieutenant Bob Poulton DFC who had flown the aircraft at Manston whilst serving with 74 Squadron during 1941. Our protracted correspondence led to a meeting in August 1988, after which Bob became a patron of the Malvern Spitfire Team. The research for this book provided a good excuse for us to get together again, and on an untypically fine day in December 1994, I made the three hour car journey to Bob's home in a remote Cornish village. From Bob's directions I knew that I would be passing a Post Office, so I took my mail to post there. So small, however, was the village concerned that the Post Office turned out to be run from the living room of an elderly lady's cottage! In conversation I mentioned that I was visiting Bob Poulton, and went on to explain that I was an author writing a new book, a part of which would be about him. 'But he seems such an ordinary man, I often wondered whether there was anything more to Mr Poulton'. Indeed there was, I told her, indeed there was.

Bob Poulton was born on September 19th, 1918, in Dorking, Surrey. Sadly, the following month his father was killed in France. In 1927 Bob was sent to the London Orphan School in Watford. He left that boarding school in 1934, at the age of 16, to work as an assistant to the antiques buyer at Marple and Co in London. In 1938 he joined the RAFVR and began flying at Woking. Called up in September 1939, he was first posted to No 1 ITW at St John's College, Cambridge. There Bob shared a room with another young pilot, James Edgar Johnson, who was destined to become the RAF's top scoring British ace by the Second World War's end. At ITW, Bob remembers that 'they didn't really know what to do with us, we drilled

Line up at No 1 ITW, Cambridge. Sgt Poulton is extreme right. At extreme left in the rear row is Sgt James Edgar Johnson - later to become the RAF's top scoring British pilot and a legend.

and played football, etc. by day, but that was about it'. Eventually Bob flew a Spitfire for the first time at 7 OTU, Hawarden, was commissioned in August 1940, and joined 616 Squadron at Kirton-in-Lindsey the following month. There the squadron was a 'C' unit and was providing further training to replacement pilots prior to their postings to 11 Group squadrons. Later the same month Pilot Officer Poulton joined 64 Squadron at Leconfield, flying south to Biggin Hill with that unit for the closing stages of the Battle of Britain. In November 1940 he was transferred to 611 Squadron at Digby, but a few days later joined 74 'Tiger' Squadron at Biggin Hill where Bob became a contemporary of Roger Boulding, whose story is also told in this book.

74 Squadron was a fighter squadron *par excellence*, and had been so even during the Great War. It had received Spitfires in February 1939, and had fought the Me 109 during Operation Dynamo whilst flying from Hornchurch. In August 1940 one of the squadron's Flight Commanders had become its Commanding Officer; the South African Adolph Gysbert 'Sailor' Malan, undoubtedly one of Fighter Command's most outstanding fighter pilots and leaders throughout the Second World War. Bob Poulton recalls that 'he was good, very, very good indeed'. By the time that Pilot Officer Poulton reported for duty, the squadron had already been heavily engaged during the Battle of Britain. Now it found itself still making contact with the Luftwaffe, largely enemy fighters engaged on sweeps of southern England. In January 1941 the squadron left Biggin Hill for Manston. On March 4th, flying as No 2 to his Flight Commander, Flight Lieutenant John Freeborn DFC, Pilot Officer Poulton shared a Do 215 probable which the pair had attacked

over the Channel. On May 7th, Bob encountered the Me 109, as his combat report relates:-

'I was White Leader patrolling Canterbury below cloud at 2,000' with one section of 'B' Flight when we were ordered to Manston. There four Me 109s were sighted flying low down over the sea just off Westgate. I went down to attack. As I was getting into position to attack one of those four, another Me 109 went past me heading east, out to sea. I opened fire on this E/A and gave it a three to four second burst from about 150 yards dead astern. The E/A climbed up into the clouds still heading east. I climbed up behind him and upon coming out of the clouds found myself about 400 yards behind him. I closed to about 200 yards and opened fire, again from dead astern. The E/A turned to the left and I closed to approximately 50 yards, finishing off with a quarter attack. Black smoke and glycol poured from the E/A which turned on its back and plunged down through clouds, bursting into flames before it hit the sea and disappeared. It took me about 10 minutes to reach the coast again and upon reaching Margate I sighted three Me 109s circling over the town. I opened fire at one of them and delivered a four second burst from astern. I saw no effect from this burst and had to break off the engagement as my ammunition was expended'.

June 1941 saw an increase in Fighter Command's offensive operations over France. Over Gravelines on June 24th, Bob Poulton claimed an Me 109 probable. On July 3rd, 74 Squadron flew as part of the Target Support Wing for six Blenheims conducting a 'Circus' to Hazebrouck. Over the target Bob Poulton's Yellow Section was bounced by six Me 109s from above:-

'I pulled sharply to port and saw one of the E/A diving in a gentle left-hand turn, straightening out into a dive back in the direction from which the E/As first appeared. I followed, but at first made no impression in respect of the distance

From left: Plt Off Bob Poulton, Flt Lt John Freeborn DFC, Sqn Ldr Baker, Flg Off Woods, and Plt Off Tony Mould, all of 74 Squadron pose at Gravesend, 1941. The Spitfire is P8388, 'Black Vanities' and was presented by the Black family of London Palladium fame.

between us. At about 2-3,000' I got within range and fired a three second burst of cannon and machine-gun from 100 yards astern. The port wing of the E/A broke away at the root and the aircraft spun down into a small wood. I then came down to ground level and flew at that height all the way back to the coast. I claim one Me 109E destroyed'.

At around the same time, however, Pilot Officer Poulton 'put up a black' when he was reported for low flying, having taken his groundcrew for a 'flip' in the station's Magister. This resulted in him being transferred to No 1 Delivery Flight at Hendon. In August, 1941, Bob was Court Martialled for the offence but was found not guilty! Consequently, however, he was posted to instruct on Spitfires at 53 OTU, Llandow. Bob recalls that 'it was a bit hairy as the aircraft were all old ones'. The Station Commander was Group Captain Ira Jones, a distinguished Great War scout pilot with 74 Squadron. Bob feels today that old Ira Jones looked after him, in a sense, due to his 74 Squadron connection.

Bob Poulton pictured whilst a flying instructor.

There were dangers, even at OTUs: on February 15th, 1942, Bob, by then a Flying Officer, was involved in a fatal mid-air collision:-

'It was an exercise with the local Home Guard who were supposed to be attacking the airfield. The briefing was not good and most pilots went off on their own to find the "enemy". Unfortunately Flight Lieutenant Pickering and I attacked a Home Guard convoy simultaneously. He made a run along the column and I did an attack from 90 degrees. We never even saw each other and I hit him just behind the cockpit. His aircraft was cut in two and went straight in, he was killed outright. My aircraft was badly damaged but I managed to control it sufficiently to land straight ahead in a field. I only suffered a couple of bruises'.

The incident illustrates that flying is a hazardous business even away from operations. Many wartime airmen perished in training accidents before ever meeting the enemy. Flight Lieutenant Pickering had flown Spitfires with 66 Squadron during the Battle of Britain, however, and had actually survived having been shot down twice, once by the German ace Major Werner Mölders. It was particularly tragic, therefore, that he should have lost his life in this way.

In March 1942, Bob was promoted to Flight Lieutenant and in March joined 611 Squadron flying Spitfires at Drem. In May the squadron moved south to Kenley, and the following month to Redhill. During June Bob was injured in a car accident and was admitted to the RAF Hospital at Ely. Fit and well, Flight Lieutenant Poulton was posted to 64 Squadron at Fairlop in September, and again the squadron had a nomadic lifestyle, in quick succession moving to Harrowbeer then to

Predannack. In January 1943, 64 arrived at Hornchurch where it remained until April. That month Bob was awarded the DFC for his sustained efforts on operations over a protracted period. During the same period certain pilots, including Bob, also made several deck landings in Seafires on HMS Argus. In July, 64 returned to Kenley and thereafter was constantly flying offensive operations over France, often providing long range bomber escorts. These flights were made possible due to the new auxiliary 'slipper' tank which contained an extra 45 gallons of fuel. Flight Lieutenant Poulton and Flying Officer Harder flew a two and a half hour fuel and oil test with the new 'drop tanks' on January 8th, 1944.

A veteran at 25 years old - Flt Lt Bob Poulton DFC.

Flt Lt Poulton with his Spitfire Mk IX.

On January 14th, 1944, 64 Squadron flew on Ramrod 453, acting as close escort to 54 Marauders attacking targets near Fruges. The bombers were divided into three boxes of 18, and 64 and 611 Squadrons found them very hard to protect. Near Abbeville, Flight Lieutenant Poulton's Spitfire developed a glycol leak and turned back, accompanied by Flight Sergeant Thorne:-

'I was leading a section of four aircraft doing close escort for Marauders who I think were bombing V1 rocket sites. Not far inland my Spitfire Mk VB, which had clipped wings, developed a glycol leak and of course began to overheat. I turned for the coast hoping to bale out over the sea and get picked up. The engine soon seized up. I kept heading coastwards but realised that I was not going to make it and so decided to bale out. I had difficulty getting out and somehow managed to get my leg trapped between the seat and side of the cockpit. I eventually got out pretty low and my parachute opened just in time to break my fall. I came to in a field surrounded by German troops who gave me first aid and sent me off to a village called Gamaches. There I was taken to a German military hospital where they patched me up and set my broken right leg. After a week there I was taken to a Luftwaffe hospital at Amiens where I remained for two months. I had two operations on my leg but the break would not join. The treatment I received was good but limited as supplies were short. The hospital, however, was next to Amiens jail which was bombed by our Mosquitos to release French Resistance people held there by the Gestapo and under sentence of death. The hospital was also hit and many German patients were killed - me very frightened and not very popular'.

Dogfight! Sqn Ldr Michel Donnet DFC, a Belgian and CO of 64 Squadron, and two of his pilots 'in action'.

The squadron had actually believed that Bob had been killed, as the Operations Record Book explains:-

'Flight Sergeant Thorne thinks that Flight Lieutenant Poulton, overcome by fumes, went straight in, as Thorne saw him roll over onto his back at 2,000', but though he saw something come out, he did not think this to be Flight Lieutenant Poulton but actually the aircraft's hood. Sickening luck to go out like that after all this time on operations'.

In June 1942, Bob had married a WAAF, and on January 14th, 1944, Mrs Poulton received a telegram informing her tersely that her husband was 'missing' from operations. It was to be several weeks before news of Bob's survival and capture reached home.

The telegram reporting Bob missing.

Bob's 'Caterpillar Club' membership card, available to all whose lives had been saved by an Irvin parachute.

In March 1944 Flight Lieutenant Poulton DFC travelled by train to Paris, and later to Dulag Luft at Frankfurt, an interrogation centre. En route to that location, 'a daylight raid by the Americans took place so I took shelter under Frankfurt station with my guards. There were many civilians there too, and again me not very popular'. From Dulag Luft Bob travelled to Stalag Luft 1, 'four days in a cattle truck with broken leg in plaster - not nice'. By September, Bob's leg had yet to mend, so he was sent before a Swiss Red Cross Commission who passed him for a repatriation exchange. In January 1945, Bob began the long journey home, but whilst on Berlin railway station there was a raid by Mosquitos, 'again, not very popular'.

Back in England, a major operation was undertaken on Bob's injured leg at RAF Weeton Hospital near Blackpool. Afterwards came a long spell of both recuperation and rehabilitation. In April 1946 Bob was granted a 20 % disability pension and released from the RAF. His war was over, 'we no longer want you, goodbye'.

Bob Poulton sketched by a fellow prisoner of war in Stalag Luft 1, October 1944.

Bob Poulton then worked in radio and television with a pre-war friend, but in May 1951 applied to rejoin the RAF and was granted a Short Service Commission as a Flying Officer in the Air Traffic Control Branch. The same year, whilst stationed in Germany with the 2nd TAF, premature death struck Bob another blow when his wife died of polio. In January 1952 Bob came home and served at Odiham, being promoted to Flight Lieutenant in September. In March 1954

Bob married Anne, and after serving both at home and overseas finally left the RAF in September 1968, 30 years after initially having joined the RAFVR.

Bob Poulton's association with aviation was far from over, however. In January 1970 he joined Airwork Services as air traffic controller at the Army Air Corps base at Middle Wallop, Hampshire. In September 1983 he eventually retired, and is now 'an OAP'.

As a reminder of his flying days, on Bob's fireplace is an especially superb trophy - a highly polished wooden propeller blade with gleaming brass leading edge, into which has been set the clock from the instrument panel of the Spitfire in which Bob survived the mid-air collision at Llandow. Like its owner, the trophy really is something.

In total, Flight Lieutenant Bob Poulton DFC destroyed two Me 109s, probably destroyed a third, and shared half a probably destroyed Do 215. One of the Few, he had flown Spitfires for the majority of the war, was awarded the DFC, had been wounded and captured by the enemy, and spent over a year as a prisoner of war. I do not think that Bob Poulton is an 'ordinary man' by any means, but appearing to be so is perhaps a part of his charm.

Flt Lt Bob Poulton DFC RAF Retd pictured at his home in late 1994. He is holding the propeller blade and Spitfire clock described in the text.

Chapter Twenty-five

Flight Lieutenant Kazik Budzik VM KW

Flight Lieutenant Kazik Budzik KW. Note the Polish pilot's flying badge - a silver eagle in flight and clutching a laurel wreath in its beak.

On September 1st, 1939, began the conflict that was to consume the world in flames for the second time this century. Fast moving German armour and troops were supported by modern fighters which cleared the skies for screaming 'Stuka' dive-bombers to pound the enemy ahead of the advancing army. Facing this overwhelming strategy was the Polish cavalry; horsemen against panzers, and the air force; biplanes against Me 109s. The struggle could only end in disaster for the gallant Poles who fought valiantly against awesome odds. By September 14th, the Polish air force had lost some 90% of both its aircraft and aircrew. Unable to continue operations, plans were quickly made for a withdrawal. Three days later the Poles flew their remaining airworthy machines over the border into neutral Roumania. The air war over Poland therefore ceased on that day.

On September 3rd, 1939, Britain and France declared war on Nazi Germany following Hitler's invasion of Poland and subsequent refusal to withdraw his troops as per the Allied powers' demand. Positioned in western Europe, Poland's new found Allies were unable to offer any practical military assistance, but at least those Polish sons who escaped the chaos and new oppression in their homeland knew that sanctuary existed in both Britain and France where other free people were prepared to stand against Germany. The Polish Air Force carried out a plan drawn up on September 5th, in which the air force flying training schools, experimental establishments and workshops evacuated their personnel to Roumania without casualties. Both German and Russian influence was high in Roumania, however, so the Poles decided to continue westwards. Many more escaped independently, the majority by boat and via Constanta, Beirut, Malta and Marseilles.

Eventually the Poles reached France and from March 1940, Polish pilots began joining French Air Force squadrons. Once more, however, the hapless Poles were to be on the losing side, forced again to flee the Nazi invader following the blitzkrieg in the west in May 1940. The Poles were disappointed with the speed of France's capitulation. No means of escape was overlooked by the Poles as they desperately tried to get to England, by various means and adventures, from where they finally hoped to make a worthwhile stand against Hitler.

In the United Kingdom the Poles were shunted from camp to camp. In another new country they had to learn a new language. Polish airmen continued arriving in England throughout the summer of 1940, and indeed until as late as October. Some Polish fighter pilots were rapidly trained on the RAF's modern fighter types and posted as replacement pilots into Fighter Command squadrons. Two all-Polish Hurricane squadrons were formed, albeit with English officers in charge, and No 303 'Koszciusco' Squadron at Northolt became Fighter Command's top scorers during the Battle of Britain with 126 enemy aircraft destroyed despite only having been operational for just four weeks of the conflict! Of the 141 Poles in total that swelled the ranks of the Few, 29 were killed in action that summer. Not only had the Poles shown the RAF that they were possessed of great skill and courage, but also that they were imbued with such a hatred of the enemy which undoubtedly inspired them to exceptional feats of arms. After the Battle of Britain more all-Polish national squadrons were formed, and so the Polish air force again became organised to continue the struggle both better equipped and from a more stable environment.

Kazimierz Budzik had joined the Polish Air Force as an officer cadet before the war. Military service was in his blood, as both his father and brother were regular career officers in the Polish army. Upon the outbreak of war he was undergoing training at the Fighter School at Ulez, from where he was evacuated with his unit. Via Roumania and Syria he arrived in France where he received further training in the French Air Force. Before he could fly to battle in a Dewoitine, France collapsed and 'Kazik' was on the run again. In June 1940 he arrived in England and joined the RAF.

Initially serving with the ATA at Maidenhead, Pilot Officer Budzik began training to be an RAF fighter pilot and flew a Spitfire for the first time at 61 OTU, Rednal. In August 1941, over a year after arriving in the UK, he reported for flying duties with 303 Squadron at Speke. A month later he joined 308 'City of Krakow' Squadron at Northolt. 308 comprised a part of the Northolt all-Polish Wing, and the squadron was constantly participating in the Fighter Command Offensive, flying daylight bomber escort flights, sweeps and the like. Kazik Budzik flew on numerous such sorties, and makes an interesting observation concerning fighter formation tactics:-

'I have no doubt that during the early part of the war the Polish formations were superior to those used by the British squadrons who flew in tight vics of three where each pilot has to be constantly aware of his neighbour's position to avoid collision. In that kind of formation you just cannot concentrate on searching for the enemy. They also flew in line astern, watching each other's tails. I have seen Me 109s latch onto the end of one of these formations and shoot a couple of aircraft down before disappearing, the rest of the formation oblivious to what has happened. Our formation was loose, stepped up, and in line abreast, just like the Germans. You were far enough away from your neighbour not to have to worry about collisions and so could search for the enemy. Each Spitfire was also stepped up, according to the sun's position, each aircraft therefore covering the other. Again just like the Germans, in combat our four aircraft broke into pairs. It was adopted by the RAF who called it the "Finger Four", the Germans of course called it the "Schwarm". It was certainly the safest formation to be in'.

An interesting observation. One wonders whether such tactics had contributed to 303 Squadron's meteoric Battle of Britain success? Of course what is perhaps not properly appreciated is that, having seen combat in both Poland and France, some of the Polish fighter pilots were actually more combat experienced than their RAF counterparts during this early part of the war. Kazik continues regarding his feelings on being a new pilot, and of the life in general:-

'When I first commenced flying operationally I could fly a Spitfire - but flying and fighting in one is a very different matter. On my first trip with 308 Squadron I was detailed to fly as No 2 to the CO, Squadron Leader Marian Pisarek. Someone said to me, "Pisarek is the best there is. Go where he goes, do what he does, watch him like a hawk and you will be alright, you will come home.' I took that advice and on my first few trips I stuck to Pisarek's tail like glue, all the way to the target and back again. I was so intent on following him, though, that I saw virtually nothing of what was going on around me. The more experienced pilots could both fly and fight and search the sky all at the same time, that is why they were so successful.

'The most successful pilots were those who would hold their fire until they were so close to the enemy that they could not miss. My problem was always that I opened fire too early, I was just unable to keep calm enough for all this sneaking up behind people - I just wanted to let them have it immediately I saw them!

'The Polish squadrons were sometimes criticised by the British for using Polish over the R/T in a dogfight. I think that this was a little unfair as we could not speak English all that well anyway. When you have a split second to warn a comrade of danger then instincts take over and you just do not have time to convert your thoughts from Polish to English.

'It was strange going off to war for an hour or so, then coming back to clean and comfortable living conditions with good food in the Mess. It was strange being shot at one minute but being back in London the next, possibly having a drink in a pub just a short while after escorting bombers to a target in France. People have got the impression that we fighter pilots had it easy, but what they fail to consider is that we flew long tours of operational duty. That type of flying in those circumstances caused great stress but I do not think people generally appreciate that'.

After his first tour of operational duty, Kazik Budzik flew briefly with the Air Fighting Development Unit at Wittering during May 1943. The following month, however, he resumed operations with 306 'Torun' Squadron, another Polish Spitfire unit. From September 1943 onwards the squadron flew an increasing number of sweeps over enemy occupied Europe, and Flying Officer Budzik flew on most of these. In May 1944 he was posted to 317 'Wilno' Squadron with whom he flew numerous offensive sorties in the build-up to D-Day. On the great day, June 6th, 1944, 317 Squadron flew four separate patrols over the invasion beaches. Kazik recalls:-

'We must have been amongst the first fighter aircraft over the beach-head as dawn was just breaking upon our arrival. The invasion armada was enormous. Most of the landing craft were still in the sea, heading towards the beaches, it really was quite a spectacle. There was flak everywhere though, mostly from the fleet, and that was quite frightening. Watching the start of Europe's liberation was a fantastic experience, particularly the naval bombardment. You could see the guns fire and the shells landing on the coastline, getting further inland the more our troops advanced. It was amazing'.

As the Allied ground troops advanced they required support from the air to neutralize German strongpoints and other stubborn pockets of resistance. The air over Normandy became full of Allied fighter-bombers; Spitfires, Mustangs and rocket firing Typhoons, all ruthlessly seeking out German military transport, armour and troops as the enemy was pushed towards the Seine and out of France. With bridges blown and under constant attack, the German army was eventually forced to retreat via the Falaise Gap, and there, in that beautiful French countryside, the carnage really began. Formerly quiet country lanes reverberated as aero engines howled overhead as the Allied fighters strafed, dive-bombed and rocketed the retreating German columns. Kazik flew many sorties during this period, his log book noting the destruction of numerous enemy military vehicles and armour.

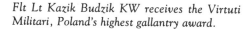

Flt Lt Kazik Budzik KW receives the Virtuti Militari, Poland's highest gallantry award.

That same medal today, the backdrop is Kazik's silk neck-scarf.

On August 17th, 1944, 317 Squadron was strafing enemy transport in the Lisieux area, so low did the Spitfires fly in fact that one aircraft was damaged by steel cables! However, the squadron was bounced by five FW 190s which came down out of the sun; despite aerial superiority being overwhelmingly Allied, the German Jagdwaffe had continued to fly in support of the German army from bases around Paris. The Germans failed to score in this instance, although the Poles damaged five of their assailants, one by Flight Lieutenant Budzik:-

'After the attack I climbed up to 4-5,000' to look for more Huns. Whilst making a turn I saw a lone 190 flying very low and to the east. I put my aircraft into a steep dive and went after it, closing range to 700 yards. Our height was virtually zero. Flying in the enemy aircraft's slipstream I fired one burst but saw no result. I closed to 500 yards but fired repeatedly without result. I then fired again from 300 yards and saw strikes on both wings. That burst exhausted my ammunition, so I turned back and re-joined the squadron'.

In October 1944, Kazik was posted back to 308 Squadron, this time as Commander of 'A' Flight. On October 29th, the squadron flew an 'armed recce', during which Flight Lieutenant Budzik was shot down by light flak near the Breda-Dordrecht bridge in Holland:-

'It was a low-level attack, strafing, and I was leading four aircraft. I cannot remember the exact target but it was probably a flak position or something like that. Anyway, I went in first so got hit first, turned back and crash-landed safely.

There were another four Polish Spitfires not far away doing a similar job, but their leader, Flight Lieutenant Krzemanski, was also shot down by flak as he went in first. He was sadly killed whilst I came out in one piece. I actually forced landed in "no man's land" and was told this by a Dutch woman - the Germans had gone but the Allies had not yet arrived! When the latter eventually did, I was a guest of the 49th British Division, I remember that the soldiers had a bear motif on their sleeves. I spent a pleasant evening in their Officers' Mess before returning to the squadron'.

Flt Lt Budzik poses with his 308 Squadron Spitfire Mk IX, ZF-A on October 29th, 1944. Just a few minutes later he was airborne on a strafing sortie but was shot down by light flak near the Breda/Dordrecht bridge on Holland. He crash-landed ZF-A but was back in action two days later.

Just two days later, Kazik was back in action. On November 6th, however, he was again shot down by flak, whilst leading the squadron on an attack against a train on the Zwolle-Mardewijk line. Having located their target the Poles dive-bombed the train and caused many direct hits. The Spitfires then proceeded to strafe the train and set several cars on fire. The flak was both intense and accurate, and again Flight Lieutenant Budzik, the leader, was hit. Fortunately Kazik controlled his Spitfire Mk IX sufficiently to make another safe wheels-up forced landing, this time near Gorinchem. Just a few days later he was up again, flying an 'armed recce' over the Arnhem area.

In April 1945, one month before the war in Europe finally came to an end, Flight Lieutenant Budzik was posted from 308 Squadron to learn how to instruct.

In May he became an instructor at 61 OTU, now based at Heston, the very unit with which he had himself flown a Spitfire for the first time way back in 1941. The wheel of fortune had turned full circle. Kazik Budzik had survived the Second World War.

Kazik's flying days were not quite over, but he was less than impressed, having survived for so long as a combat pilot, with the prospect of life as an instructor. He was relieved, therefore, to be posted back to an operational squadron in September 1945, this time as a Flight Commander with 309 'Ziema Czerwienska' Squadron flying Mustang IIIs. In February 1946 he moved to command a flight in 303 Squadron, which was equipped with Mustang IVs. His final flight was a 'formation' practice in a Mustang IV on November 4th, 1946. Kazik Budzik had hung up his flying helmet and parachute for the last time.

But what after flying for a man like Kazik Budzik who had experienced all the highs and lows of an operational fighter pilot for over six years? Whilst instructing, Kazik had met a young administrator in the Polish Women's Air Force, and upon demob he and Helen were married. From his mother in Poland, however, he was warned not to come home with Stalin and Soviet Russia now in control, but instead urged to find himself a new life in England. He discovered too that both his father and brother had been amongst those Polish officer prisoners of war massacred by the Russians during the Katyn Wood atrocity. The Budziks made a new life for themselves in Nottingham, near to Helen's wartime station at Hucknall. Kazik became a British Citizen and found employment - as a bus driver. Appreciating that his family in Poland were virtually minor aristocracy, and that driving a bus is in no way comparable with flying Spitfires, one wonders how a man like Kazik Budzik coped: 'Yes, I suppose it was a bit degrading, and it was not exactly either what I wanted to do or was used to doing, but I had a wife and soon two children to support. Times were hard and I was grateful to have a job'. Kazik retired as a bus driver in 1984, and has since exchanged his Spitfire for a Skoda motor car!

For many years Kazik did not discuss his wartime experiences, believing that he was 'just one of hundreds of thousands of Allied airmen just doing my job'. Living in the northern Midlands in Nottingham, and with a growing family to support, he and Helen were unable to travel to London and attend the Polish Air Force Association's reunions. He therefore closed the door on this important chapter of his life. In early 1988, however, I traced Kazik in connection with my interest in the life of another Polish airman, Flying Officer Franek Surma, who largely became the subject of my second book, 'The Invisible Thread: A Spitfire's Tale'. The Budziks' kindness and warm welcomes during my research trips became legendary, and needless to say ourselves and families have since become close, despite the years and miles between us. Unlocking Kazik's memory after all those years was like a dam bursting, as the memories came gushing forth. As we sat for hours in his sitting room talking of long past times, he was back in his Spitfire, left hand pushing open the throttle and right hand controlling the stick as he related many stories so nearly forgotten. Like so many others in this book, I found his modesty almost overwhelming, this retired bus driver with both the Polish Virtuti Militari and Cross of Valour to his credit. Still in a wardrobe was Kazik's RAF tunic, resplendent with 'wings' and medal ribbons; it still fitted, and other souvenirs were close to hand; his flying log book, white silk scarf and shatterproof sunglasses. Although now 75, Kazik Budzik remains possessed of enormous energy and his bright alert eyes flash and sparkle as he remembers his Spitfire days.

At the launch of 'The Invisible Thread', Kazik and Helen both joined us at the Abbey Hotel in Malvern. Outside, a Spitfire Mk XVI was on show. Without a second thought, Kazik, an OAP and grandfather, leapt onto the wing, slid back the hood and jumped into the cockpit with the agility of a teenager. He sat there completely at home and familiar with the 'office'. There is no doubt at all in my mind that this marvellous old character could have taken the thing off there and then - in fact, I am more astonished that he did not!

Now a retired bus driver, Flt Lt Kazik Budzik VM KW RAF Retd is pictured here on the occasion of him opening the Malvern Spitfire Team's exhibition, 'Spitfire!', at Tudor House Museum, Worcester, in 1988.

Chapter Twenty-six

Flight Lieutenant Tony Minchin

*Flight Lieutenant Tony Minchin. Note the RAF
Volunteer Reserve 'VR' letters on his tunic.*

In 'Through Peril to the Stars', which told the stories of 11 wartime RAF fighter pilots who failed to return for one reason or another, I wrote about Squadron Leader Tommy Drinkwater DFC. 'Drink' was a unique airman who had first enlisted in the air force on February 25th, 1936, as an 'Aircraftman 2nd Class/ Aircrafthand under training'. In June 1941 he joined 234 Squadron as a Sergeant Pilot flying Spitfires. On November 11th, 1943, Flight Lieutenant Drinkwater destroyed 19 Squadron's 100th enemy aircraft. On April 11th, 1944, Squadron Leader Drinkwater DFC took command of 122 Squadron, a Mustang squadron which was a part of 122 Wing at Gravesend. On April 19th, 'Drink' led his new squadron on a Ranger to attack an enemy airfield, during which enemy aircraft were damaged on the ground by the 122 Wing Commander Flying, Wing Commander Johnstone, and Flying Officer Minchin. On May 18th, Squadron Leader Drinkwater, a married man for just two months, was shot down and killed by flak during a Ranger to the Tours-Nantes areas. He was buried as an 'unknown British soldier', but after the war was identified by a pair of cuff-links which were a present from his wife.

Whilst writing Squadron Leader Drinkwater's story, I had no idea that 'Flying Officer Minchin' of 122 Squadron actually lived just a few hundred yards away from myself on the eastern slopes of Malvern's North Hill! I was pointed in Tony Minchin's direction by another local pilot and former member of 122 Wing, Peter Taylor, who had met Tony by chance in Malvern at the launch of 'The Invisible Thread' in September 1992 - he had not seen the man since 1945 and had no idea that Tony lived in the same area! I quickly made contact with Tony, and recall that on one of our first meetings we sat on the terrace of Tony and Dorothy's home, enjoying their fantastic and uninterrupted panoramic view of the Severn Valley, across the City of Worcester to the Cotswold escarpment, talking of Tony's flying days. During this conversation Tony described a low-level chase between his section of Mustang III fighter-bombers and an Me 109G, which ended in disaster for the latter, and produced as a gift to the Malvern Spitfire Team his escape kit, the seal unbroken, containing a variety of useful items for the downed pilot, from Horlicks tablets to amphetamines! Tony had joined the RAFVR and had been trained overseas under the auspices of the Empire Air Training Scheme. After eventually returning to England he was posted to 122 Squadron at Gravesend on March 29th, 1944. At that time, the Allied air forces were attacking anything German that moved either in the skies over France or on the ground. It was the preparation for D-Day, and a hectic time.

When asked to contribute material to this book, Tony's enthusiastic response was to produce the substantial diary that he actually recorded at the time. I received the document late one night, but so fascinating did I find its contents that I read all of it before retiring. As a direct contrast to the other accounts in 'A Few of the Many' which are recollections made across the span of half a century, I have reproduced below in full Tony's diary, as it is a contemporary account. It is a superb record of squadron life, flying and fighting in 1944, and gives a real feel of what it was really like to be there and a part of what Peter Brown refers to elsewhere in this book as the 'Great Adventure'.

March 29th, 1944.

I have arrived at last, with Garry, at a Squadron. What a time it has taken. Training in England, finishing in Canada, a period of instructing in Calgary, then home and still more waiting. Advanced training again - a bad crash which set me back some time, and finally the long expected signal from Air Defence Great Britain posting me to Gravesend on a Mustang Squadron.

We both reached the Mess at lunch-time and strolled into the ante-room for a beer. A number of scruffy, tired looking pilots clad in flying boots were already mug in hand talking about the morning's flying and smoking hurriedly. We ordered two "halves" very unobtrusively and sat back watching. After a few minutes, during which time nobody took the slightest interest in us, a young Squadron Leader came up and asked if we were the two new pilots for 122 Squadron. We said we were; then he introduced himself as the CO, Ian Morvin. He chatted very informally for a while, asking if we were fixed up in our billets all right and if we had met anyone else. Then he brought over the two Flight Commanders, Alan Pavey and Johnny Major, also two very pleasant "types".

In the afternoon, Garry and I went down to Flights to gather some "gen" and meet the other members of the Squadron. Alan Pavey then showed us the intricacies of the Mustang III and said we would probably have our first "flip" on the following day.

After tea over to Cobham Hall, a very palatial mansion set in beautiful grounds and belonging to Lord Darnley. This was to be our quarters.

That evening the CO and some of the boys invited us down to the "local" in Cobham village for a few beers. There we all got to know each other better under the mellowing influence of best bitter. It was quite a party and it was 1.30 am when the CO drove Garry and me back in his Jeep. By that time we were all for the Squadron life and felt most at home!

March 30th.

Had my first trip in a Mustang today and must confess hadn't much of a clue. It is quite unlike the Spitfires and Hurricanes I have previously been flying, in fact for most of the time it flew me, and I was beginning to wonder how I was going to bring this mass of screaming horsepower safely down to earth again. However, it turned out all right though the landing was too fast.

Mustang III of Plt Off Pete Wass of 19 Squadron, also based at Gravesend and a part of 122 Wing. Note the auxiliary fuel or 'drop' tanks used to extend the Mustang's range over enemy territory. When their fuel had been used, the tanks were jettisoned and therefore discarded.

Mustang Mk IIIs of 19 Squadron.

April 6th.

For the last few days both Garry and I have been feeling our way slowly and, by observation, gradually absorbing the atmosphere and spirit of the Squadron. We have been careful not to intrude as the old hands resent a newcomer becoming "one of the boys" too quickly. Soon we shall automatically find ourselves part of the rest.

Much hard flying has been done, practising attacks on each other with the cine gun and formating with other aircraft. The whole squadron has been "non-operational" for a week, but a couple of days ago the boys went out on an escort job to Fortresses and Liberators bombing targets in Hannover. It was quite a thrill to see them all roar across the aerodrome in lines of four abreast for the take-off with a 62 gallon drop tank under each wing, looking like a silver bomb. Four hours later they all returned safely with stories of the bitter cold at 30,000', the flak over the target and on the way in, and the seemingly good bombing results - large fires and dense pillars of black smoke climbing thousands of feet into the sky.

Today I realised the stark reality of operational flying. The boys went out over Germany, led by Ian Morvin, on a low level "beat up", shooting at any worthwhile target that came in their sights as they tore across Hunland just over the tree tops at 300 odd mph. From Brunswick they "swept" a large area and came back smack over the Ruhr. It was then that the CO was hit by light flak in his glycol tank. He immediately started streaming white smoke and everyone was telling him to pull up and bale out. For some unknown reason he carried on until finally, overcome practically by the fumes, in his cockpit he tore off the hood and jumped while still only 100' above the ground. Naturally his 'chute failed to open and his body hit the deck with a fearful impact. And so we lost our CO.

The tragedy was lessened somewhat by the success of the day's trip. During "de-briefing" it came out that considerable damage had been done to small factories and innumerable trains, barges and motorised vehicles. That night we all went to the "local" and had several beers. It was the quickest and easiest way both to celebrate and forget.

April 9th.

My first "Show" and it is Easter Sunday. A withdrawal escort to "Forts" and "Libs" bombing Bremen. We were given all the "gen" in the "briefing" tent: the way in, the way out, where to rendezvous with the bombers, and the heavily defended flak areas en route. Instructions were given in case anyone was forced down or had to bale out over enemy territory. Call signs and radio aids were jotted down. Escape packets and wallets containing Dutch and French currency to facilitate evasion in case of misfortune and finally - "Good luck!"

There was a decidedly "coiled up" feeling in my stomach as I strapped myself in the cockpit. Two or three times I checked everything: oil, fuel, glycol, temperatures and switches. Against "chocks" I opened the throttle gradually, checking boost, revs and magnetos; then pushed it wide to the "gate" until the aircraft was quivering under the unleashed power of the Merlin engine. Back with the throttle until there was only a smooth tick-over. Press the button and call up control to test the radio: "Receiving you loud and clear". Test oxygen; the mask must fit snugly over the contours of the face. Wave away chocks and taxi out for take-off with the rest.

Once safely airborne, vital actions completed and settled and comfortably in formation, the tense feeling wore off somewhat. We climbed steadily up through some patchy cloud into the brilliant sunlit world that has no part of the earth beneath. Across the North Sea looking cold and grey through the breaks in the cloud and climbing higher into the blue crystal heavens all the while. In the distance the line of the Dutch coast appeared, becoming more sharply outlined every minute. At 29,000' we levelled out and crossed over land. Soon I became aware that I was under fire - my baptism of fire. Innocuous looking black puffs appeared to the sides of the formation and slowly mushroomed out. I watched fascinated feeling like a spectator rather than a target, until it crept nearer and now in the centre of the black could be seen an ugly red flash and a faint thud came to my ears through the padded helmet. By now the Squadron was taking evasive action and soon the flak was left behind.

On past Münster where another outburst of flak welcomed us and finally to Bremen itself where the last of the bombing was in progress. Consistent heavy flak here aimed at the bombers, but we kept to one side. The results so far as one could see were good. Most of the target area was obscured by black smoke, but several fires were seen and the general impression was that it was most unhealthy down there.

Back with the "big boys" weaving continuously up and down the "stream" and feeling a bit tired and cold. The remainder of the trip was quite uneventful and I landed 3 3/4 hours after my take-off time. Into Intelligence for "de-briefing" during which we swallowed gratefully mugs of steaming coffee and inhaled deeply on our cigarettes. Then back to the Mess for a nap in a comfortable armchair before changing for the evening.

April 10th.

A quiet day with some low level practice bombing in the morning.

April 11th.

Another escort job today, to 620 Forts and 240 Libs bombing Magdeburg. More heavy, accurate flak encountered and the thick vapour trails left by the bombers formed a milky cloud substance all the way to the target. Four rocket firing Ju 88s were sighted attacking a rear formation of Fortresses, one of which blew up in mid-air. No attack was made as they were too far away from us. $4^1/2$ hours in the air.

April 12th.

Yet another bomber escort - penetration cover for Forts and Libs bombing the Ball Bearing Factory at Schweinfurt. Heavy flak over the target and two Me 109s spotted diving away from a box of Forts. Two of the boys peeled off after them, but failed to catch them. 3 3/4 hour trip.

We lost Pete Heller the other evening off the Dutch coast. Shot down by flak ships.

April 14th.

Formation practice, dive bombing and ground attack on dummy targets off the Thames Estuary.

April 15th.

We all moved early this morning to our new base on the south coast - Ford aerodrome near Bognor. Tent life has now begun and we are learning to become thoroughly mobile and self contained, capable of moving off at very short notice. This is for when the Second Front starts and we move over to the continent.

April 19th.

A marvellous Show today. A Ranger operation to Lyons. This is a beat up of airfields and generally shooting up of anything enemy. The Wing Commander led us. Wing Commander Johnstone is one of the best; a quiet, confident leader, he inspires confidence and the will to follow him anywhere.

We flew high level to Besançon then suddenly flipped over on our backs and came screaming straight down from 15,000' to deck level, flattening out then and fanning out in a long, loose line abreast travelling like bats out of hell. I was with the "Wingco" and we took in Lyons, Dijon, Saint Dizier, and Rheims shooting hard as we flashed over the Hun aerodromes. I spotted a Ju 88 parked on one 'drome with several men working on it. As we approached I opened up with all four guns and sprayed the aircraft. The little figures that were men crumpled or skeltered madly for cover. We were past; a second before they could reach their guns.

Onward up north over the peaceful looking countryside of Occupied France. Sometimes a peasant would pause in his work, look up and wave as we skimmed a few feet over his head. It was hard to believe that this was part of war torn Europe. We were soon to be rudely awakened though, for as we neared a fair sized town a stream of red "golf balls" flashed across our path coming almost horizontal as we were so low. The Hun gunners were really on their toes there, and I, being nearest the town, felt distinctly naked. It took some furious weaving

With Luftwaffe front-line bases within range of Allied fighter-bombers, the end was in sight. These scenes of devastation show the effect of strafing on such airfields and as described by Tony Minchin.

to keep out of the way of that glowing tracer and it was all over in a few seconds, though it seemed long minutes to me.

Light flak such as 20 or 40mm is always deadly stuff to come up against: "golf balls" as we call it, but not much of a game.

April 20th.

Practice dive-bombing in Pagham Harbour this morning. One of our boys, an Australian, never pulled out of his dive and went straight in. He was a decent type and very keen too.

April 21st.

Had the afternoon and went into Bognor. It was a beautiful spring day with a touch of summer in the air as well and the countryside looking as only the countryside could look in Sussex on such a day.

Saw "Goodbye Mr Chips" which I have hitherto always missed: a most moving film and superbly acted by Robert Donat and Greer Garson. In the evening to the "Victoria" where I ran into "Chips" Carpenter whom I have known at Montford Bridge. Heard that "Shortie" Learn, a Canadian, I also knew is dead. He was with Pete Chappell on a Spitfire IX squadron.

I joined up with "Chips" and some of his pals who had cars and we all cleared off on a pub crawl. Had a most pleasant evening and drove back with gay abandon onto the aerodrome.

April 22nd.

The CO - Squadron Leader Drinkwater, a Cornishman from St Mawes, sent me up to practise dog fighting and cine gun attacks with another chap, a very strenuous afternoon's work.

April 24th.

A Show on today. Penetration cover for Forts and Libs bombing Friedrichshafen. Uneventful except for heavy and persistent flak over Strasbourg which made us all weave madly. My Airspeed Indicator and Rev Counter went unserviceable, so I had to be guided in to land. $4^1/2$ hours in the air.

May 2nd.

Have just returned from a week's leave. Hugh Gillett flew me to just north of Plymouth in a Mosquito, so it was no time before I was home. What bliss it was to sleep in a feather bed and loll around in the sun without the tension of impending "ops". I did nothing of real interest for the whole week. Just relaxed mentally and physically which was what I needed.

Two days before expiration of my leave I did go up to London and met "Tich" and Derry. We had a pretty moist and very cheery evening chiefly at my Belgian Club "Chez Maria" in Park Lane. Next day I managed to get in to see "Panama Hattie": quite a good show and amusing which was the chief thing.

Arrived back on the Squadron about 9.30 pm, found Garry in the Mess tent and got all the latest gen from him. The Squadron destroyed six He 111s in the air during a Ranger operation near Dijon. It seems they planned an attack on a Hun airfield where they knew there were He 111s. The boys arrived on the spot just as the six Heinkels were coming in to land, so they sailed in and shot the lot down in turn. They were actually queuing up for the last one! A couple more were destroyed on another Show and several damaged on the ground. Jack Crosslan was hit by flak and baled out over France. A good week's work, it would have to happen while I was away.

May 6th.

The last two days have been quiet with only practice flying to fill in the time. Today, however, four of us did a wizard show: a Ranger operation to Fürstenau. We set out for Coltishall, refuelled there then made off over the sea about 4 pm. We flew over the North Sea at zero feet, through rain squalls until we sighted Heligoland; then a turn south. Before we reached the Frisian Isles a German merchant convoy appeared in view. We jettisoned our drop tanks and sheered off a bit - marking their position though. Keeping flat down on the water we flew between the two easternmost Frisians. Soon after crossing inland we came to a Hun aerodrome around which was flying a Fieseler Storch - an elementary German trainer. We could do nothing with it going at our speed though we opened up. A quick spray at some Ju 88s parked round the edge of the field and we were on our way as some nasty flak was coming up from the airfield. North of Löningen we thoroughly strafed another aerodrome. Pete Steib destroyed a Ju 88 on the ground. Later on, flying west, Sandy Leish and myself attacked a goods train and brought it to a standstill with smoke pouring from it. We crossed out to sea just by Ijmuiden and so home as it was getting dusk. Nearly four hours in the air.

May 7th.

Up early in the morning to escort Forts bombing Berlin. A long, cold trip, but fairly uneventful except for the usual flak welcome. Over four hours in the air.

May 8th.

First dive bombing Show today. With a couple of 500lb bombs each we set off for the marshalling yards at Busigny. Crossed into France about 6pm, found the target just north of Saint Quentin and peeled off to bomb. Very successful and little flak.

May 9th.

Up at 6am for a Sweep on aerodromes near Metz and Wiesbaden to lure the Hun into the air. The Fortresses were going in to bomb after we had scoured the area. After I had been flying for over an hour I suddenly realised that my electrical system had gone. Result - no guns, no sight, no RT no bloody good. I about turned very smartly and beat it for home as hard as I could go, keeping a very sharp look-out for Huns who might be tempted to attack a lone wolf.

May 10th.

Yesterday Hugh Gillett was hit by flak over Germany and was last seen heading for the deck in a steep glide. Gerry Germain has also gone. He went up to Denmark on a four man Ranger, was attacked from behind by an FW 190 and shot down in flames. Sandy Wheeler and Digger Watson, both of whom I knew before, have arrived as replacements. We need them.

Was up this morning at 4 am, very cold and weary to prepare for another Show. Took off at dawn for Manston where we had breakfast and refuelled; then off to act as withdrawal cover for Fortresses west of Hannover. Shocking conditions, a white cloud substance from 11,000 to 30,000' and of course by the time we had struggled up through that muck there was no sign of the bombers. I had to come back alone again as I lost the rest in cloud - my fairing doors being down. Put the aircraft into a shallow dive at 30,000' and it was 10,000' before I came out of cloud. I was beginning to get a bit worried as I'd no idea where I was. Fortunately the Zuider Zee came into view and I was able to set course from there.

May 11th.

Shall be glad of a rest soon. In the afternoon a dive bombing Show came up - the marshalling yards at Monceau just west of Charleroi. As we were going into bomb the swines started throwing up a lot of flak which I didn't see until I felt a colossal thud on the aircraft and just saw a lump of flak ricochet off my cockpit hood, about six inches from my head. Thank God these hoods are bubble shaped or that piece would have come straight in and it would have spelled "Finis!" However we went in and hit the yards successfully. When I landed I found that piece of flak had come through the propeller nicking it and also tearing away two of my port exhaust stubs before bouncing off my canopy.

May 12th.

Up before dawn again and off to Manston for breakfast and refuelling. We picked up over 1000 Forts and Libs north of Schweinfurt and brought them back without much trouble to the coast. They had been bombing Fulda.

In the evening, though tired, went into Bognor for a few beers to help me relax. Met George Woodward whom I was trained with in Canada: he is stationed nearby on a Spitfire Squadron. Later in the evening I bumped into Roger Borne, a free French pilot who was also trained with me in Canada. He is also with a Spitfire Squadron. It seems that most of the fighter types are now collected on the south coast.

What a week this has been. Out on long, tiring ops for the last seven days without a break. It has been great while the show was on, but afterwards it leaves one a bit limp. On the other hand being pretty constantly on ops keeps one in form as it were and in the right mood. Too long a rest, I think, between Shows is bad.

May 13th.

Oh luxurious day - no ops to worry about and a long lie in this morning. I really needed this rest. Had a very lazy day and popped into Bognor again about 6 pm with Chris Lyerrod, a Norwegian pilot on the squadron. Again I met somebody I knew at the "Vic": Peter West who was at Hurstpierpoint with me. He is stationed nearby on rocket firing Typhoons.

May 14th.

Another day off. The squadron was released from ops for the day as we are all moving to a new base near Chichester. It was late in the evening when we flew kites over and on arrival there were tents to be put up and a general settling in to be effected. It was after 11 pm before I hit my camp bed feeling very tired and dirty.

May 15th.

Up at dawn for a dive bombing Show on the marshalling yards at Chaulnes, west of Quentin. Considerable cloud most of the way to the target, but we managed to find a break and went in. The whole thing was a farce as some of the bombs stuck and the ones that did go down failed to explode. Something very peculiar there. The Engineering Officer will probably have to stand a bit of a rocket.

Into Chichester on the back of Artie Lee's motor bike in the evening. Just time for a pint, a film and back for late dinner.

May 16th.

No Show for me today, though of readiness from dawn till dusk.

May 17th.

Some of the boys went off on a Ranger to Denmark led by the "Wingco". Secret Service gen had informed us that there would be an assortment of Hun aircraft flying in the Aarlborg area in the afternoon of the 17th. The Show was carefully worked out and timed to the minute. The boys arrived on the scene and ran into a really mixed bag. Followed a hectic party during which we destroyed seven of their aircraft and badly damaged several more. We lost two pilots. The aircraft encountered included Ju 88s, Ju 188, Ju 34, He 177, Arado 196, FW 190 and Me 109s.

May 18th.

Squadron Leader Drinkwater, our CO, organised a four man Ranger to Bordeaux and back of Paris area. I suppose he was inspired by yesterday's success. Anyway they saw nothing and ran into a heap of flak. The CO was killed and Harry Cush, a really stolid Canadian from Calgary came back quite unmoved with two big flak holes in his wings plus a bullet graze across his neck.

A bad business that. Two of our COs have now gone in as many months. These Rangers are all very well - bags of fun and all that, but they can be pretty costly if something goes wrong. We usually hope to catch the Hun napping on Shows of that sort by going really deep in where least expect a single engined fighter to appear. Fortunately we have a very long range with our extra drop tanks.

May 19th.

Bad luck always seems to come at once. The squadron took off on an escort job this morning and climbing up in formation through thick cloud two aircraft collided. They both burst into flames and Sergeant Russell was killed. Pete Steib in the other kite managed to bale out but broke his ankle in the process. Pete was back with us in a few days as the incident had taken place while still over this country.

Spent a depressing afternoon sorting out the CO's kit and packing it. He had only been married a couple of months too. I'm glad I don't have to go and see his wife about it.

May 20th.

Today the squadron moved to Southend for a week's rest off ops. We could do with it judging by the last few days' misfortunes. We arrived about 4 pm and as soon as we were fixed up in our quarters - a very pleasant Georgian type mansion - made preparations for going to town. After a much needed bath and change of clothing I was ready for anything. Our new CO arrived - a New Zealander - Squadron Leader Joyce DFM, he seems OK but time will prove that. After tea there was a general rush into Southend: It seems quite a lively spot - the Palace Hotel on the Front appearing to be the nucleus of the night life.

May 21st.

We have arranged a very good flying schedule for our week here. Each Flight takes it in turn to fly afternoon and following morning, 24 hours on and 24 hours off. Several of us went up to London like a shot this afternoon. A bit quiet being Sunday but after fixing up rooms at the Strand Palace we adjourned to the Grosvenor House Sunday Officers' Club where a tea dance was in progress. Some quite attractive "popsies" thereto, so we decided to enjoy ourselves.

In the evening to "Chez Maria" where several drinks were consumed in addition to a large steak and chips. A little ribald repartee with old Maria herself and then off most hilariously to the Mayfair. There, propped up against the bar was Pete Chappell. We were glad to see each other again so that called for a small celebration. Pete apparently has recently had a very narrow squeak flying hide and seek with several Huns, only escaping by popping into a large, woolly cloud.

May 22nd.

Arrived back at Southend around mid-day, just in time to fly. Put in some low-level and dive-bombing practice.

Into Southend again this evening where I was invited to a private party with one or two of the boys. There was a barrel of beer and plenty of sandwiches in the house so the whole thing was quite a success. About 4 am, having finished all the beer, we left.

May 23rd.

Awoke feeling like a log, but had to stagger up and get ready to fly. Tried some air to ground firing, which was not very successful.

Off in the afternoon and into Southend again to see a "flick". Stayed the night at the Cecil Hotel after going to a dance in the evening at the Palace.

May 24th.

Wired "Tich" to meet me in London Thursday afternoon; hope he can make it. A little flying during the afternoon and a quiet evening for a change. Also must nurse the bank balance a bit.

May 25th.

At mid-day up to London where I met "Tich" at the Strand Palace. We made quite an evening of it going to the Mayfair and the Chez Maria. Rather expensive and rather moist; but it was good to see the old boy again.

May 26th.

A little dive-bombing practice in the afternoon and a quiet night. This is a heavenly place and it would be great to be stationed here. The Mess is really a fine old house, Georgian style, white with green shutters over the windows. Outside the dining room is a pillared loggia overlooking the beautifully kept lawns and gardens. It is all so peaceful too. This evening it seemed particularly so. I sat outside in the warm, soft air and the stillness was only broken by the lazy chirping of an occasional bird. I let the soothing beauty of it all flow over me in waves. I'm afraid going back to the airfield and ops after this week of ease and comfort will be rather hard. Still it has been a wonderful break. In surroundings such as these war seems even more stupid and futile. Back on the airfield with the ops atmosphere all around one becomes used to the idea and, to a certain extent, I think, hardened so that even the deaths of one or two members of the squadron leave one comparatively cold. One merely thinks - "what damned bad luck, he was a good bloke too, but thank God I'm still here!"

May 27th.

A completely negative day in every respect.

May 28th.

Down to Flights in the morning to get all the gen on the new Gyro Sight which some of our aircraft are having fitted. It seems to be an absolute "pip" and once one knows how to work it and can get a Hun in the sight, that Hun should be dead meat.

Back to Funtington in the afternoon, our pleasant week having come to its conclusion.

May 29th.

Today has been a regular heat wave and I have been flying through it all. A Fighter Sweep in the morning to the Paris area and another in the afternoon around Cambrai. Nothing especial except for flak which was pretty hot, but not as hot as the day. Strapped in the cockpit with Mae West and parachute on it was like being in a super hot house. I spent the day in complete saturation.

May 30th.

While the boys went off on a Liberator escort job in the morning, I went out with Johnny Major in the Jeep for a swim. We found a place near Bosham where we could splash around in about six feet of water. In the afternoon, as it was still very hot, a squadron bathe was laid on and we all drove over to Thorney Island aerodrome; a rocket Typhoon base and bathed in the sea; marvellously refreshing.

On Thorney aerodrome there are several intact Hun aircraft which are flown to various 'dromes in the country to show pilots what they are like close up and how they behave in the air. We looked over an FW 190 and agreed it was a damn good aircraft.

May 31st.

Briefed this morning for a dive-bombing Show on St Just-en-Chaussée with a couple of 1000lb bombs slung under the aircraft which seemed to us like flogging a willing horse. We have never done that before and were wondering how the extra weight would affect the aircraft during take-off and during the dive. However, the "Show" never came off owing to hazy conditions, which was probably just as well. Anyway, I distinctly heard several sighs of relief.

Lance, Garry and myself popped into Portsmouth for a quiet evening at the pictures followed by a good meal at the "Cut Loaf" in Southsea and the odd noggin at the "Barley Mow".

June 1st.

Up at 6 am in readiness for a Show which never came off - due to bad haze again.

June 2nd.

Nothing doing until 6.30 pm when we went off on an Armed Recce in the Dreux, Nogent area of Normandy. Saw no military transport to shoot up and apart from flak from Rouen the trip was uneventful. Had some more trouble with my damn nose: the pain is coming on at lower altitudes just recently. I suppose I shouldn't be flying at all the state my sinuses are in, but I would be more than fed up if I had to leave the squadron - especially just now when invasion is very much in the wind. I just can't miss that.

June 5th.

For the last two days there has been a tense excitement, the aircraft have been specially painted with black and white stripes and we have done no ops; moreover no-one has been allowed on or off the airfield.

Tonight in the Mess Tent we were all drinking beer, a bit on edge, when at 9 pm, Wing Commander Johnstone summond us to the Briefing Tent. When everyone was seated he looked around, grinned, and said: "Well chaps this is it - 'D - Day' tomorrow!" Then he got down to business, unfolding various maps so showing the beach-heads to be invaded in Normandy, the dispositions of British, Canadian and American troups; times of landing and finally our part in the operation. Group Captain Jamie Rankin also said a few words before wishing us good luck.

It was a very tense two hours or so with everyone wondering just what was going to break loose the next day. An operation as gigantic and ambitious as the one we were listening to was fraught with all kinds of possibilities. Would our troops force a successful landing without suffering too heavy casualties? Would hordes of Hun planes come up over the beach-head area in a desperate effort to thwart the invasion?

The scene in that Briefing Tent will always be imprinted on my memory. The Wingo and Jamie Rankin calmly explaining the working of this vast undertaking;

the maps and charts round the walls covered with coloured lines and code words; the expectant look on all faces - wondering, wondering all the time just what they themselves would be up against in the morning. It was midnight before I rolled into my camp bed.

June 6th. 'D - Day'.

Was awakened at 3.30 am and told to stand-by aircraft at immediate Readiness. Trying to clear the mists of sleep from my brain I struggled into clammy clothes and flying boots, stumbled out into the chill pre-dawn and made for my aircraft. Several of us remained at Readiness until well after dawn had broken, but no call came through. Apparently the landings had taken the Hun by surprise and so we were not immediately required. A little later we were called escort for the mass of shipping that was moving to the beach-heads; still no Huns appeared in the air.

Just before dusk a continuous stream of Gliders towed by Stirlings and Halifaxes passed over us carrying troops and commandos to areas behind the beach-heads. The initial invasion seems to have come up to expectations and high command is well pleased. From the aerial viewpoint though, the day has been a big anti-climax.

June 7th.

Roused again at 3.30 am, and this time airborne before dawn. The Squadron flew over to the beach-head where we patrolled up and down off the coast for some time before turning and sweeping right in behind the beach-head to try and find some Huns, but nothing came up. In the grey dawn light everything seemed quiet from the air, except for occasional flashes of gunfire and inland a big fire blazing.

In the Bay of Seine, between Le Havre and Cherbourg, where the landings had been effected a mass of shipping had already accumulated and the secret "Mulberries" were being put in position.

Up again at 5 pm with bombs to strafe and destroy any Hun convoys moving up to the beach-head. We dive-bombed a big convoy of motorised vehicles and blew them sky-high. Lost one of our boys from flak. An hour after landing from that trip I was up again on the same job. We bombed a viaduct - an important line of communication to the battle area - and received some flak for our trouble. By the time we landed it was dark and I was asleep on my feet. Must have been snoring before I hit the pillow.

June 8th.

Thank God for a lie in this morning. I slept until 9 am, had breakfast and was airborne at 11 am. More dive-bombing - this time a marshalling yard behind the beach-head. Afterwards we went down and shot up several Hun military vehicles moving up in the Argentan area. The weather then prevented any further sorties.

A Cingalese pilot has just been posted to us - Flying Officer Talalla DFC.

June 10th.

Booked for another strafing Show with bombs included in the Mortain area.

Bags of Hun military transport carefully camouflaged and concealed by the road sides. Low cloud made dive-bombing difficult, but we had a shot at some shallow dives and scattered the "eggs" amongst the transport. Afterwards we had rare fun and games swooping low up and down over the convoys on the Mortain - St Hilaire road and giving them all we had.

20 Me 109s with RAF roundels and our invasion markings "bounced" some of the boys, who, taken by surprise, had a hell of a job to extricate themselves. Flight Lieutenant Hayward was badly shot up, receiving a cannon shell through his leg, but he turned very smartly on his adversary, shot him down and brought the plane back to land. He had to be lifted out of the cockpit and taken to hospital immediately. Damn good show on his part.

June 11th.

Only slight activity today; restricted by weather conditions. It will be a good job when we get over to Normandy where we won't be so restricted by climatic conditions.

June 12th.

On a dive-bombing Show late in the afternoon east of Dreux. One of my bombs destroyed a train and box cars in a siding. The other bomb hung up for a second or two then fell into a field - dammit.

June 18th.

The boys went out yesterday evening and ran into some Huns - got two for the loss of our CO, Squadron Leader Shaw.

June 20th.

Slack day, but some of these V1s came over and one dropped quite near.

June 21st.

Dive-bombing Show in the Évreux area. Bashed the railway siding successfully. Saw some Huns taking off from Évreux airfield and screamed down to attack from 10,000' but the b_ _ _ s disappeared against the background of countryside.

June 25th.

Yesterday the lads knocked down an FW 190 and landed on an airstrip in Normandy. Today we all took off to our new airstrip in Normandy, B7, near Martragny.

Our base is practically on the Caen - Bayeux road and our tents are pitched in an apple orchard. The natives seem apathetic and unmoved and probably don't care whether it is us or the Hun who are there. Being in the country seems to have left them largely untouched by Occupation.

Bayeux has some well stocked shops with many things difficult to get in England. Some of the young girls seem anti-British; probably those who have been mistresses of German Officers and well looked after.

June 27th.

Out on a Show this evening. Huns were sighted in the Caumont area. I was with Alan Pavey's section and down we went flat out. Through a thick batch of cloud during which I lost the others. I suddenly heard Alan shout over the R/T "we are onto four FW 190s", and a little later "I've got one of the buggers!" Then I saw two aircraft travelling parallel to me and a fair way away, so got closer and underneath. It was two 190s and I squirted at one and hit him, but he broke violently away and they both nipped into cloud. I was livid with frustration.

Alan had the new Gyro gunsight and sent his first Hun crashing in flames, and the starboard wing came straight off the other.

June 28th.

Sunny, peaceful afternoon and I was sitting on the canvas latrine by a ditch at the edge of the airstrip when suddenly seven FW 190s came screaming down with all guns blazing! Talk about being caught with your trousers down! I was off into the ditch only to find out too late that it was filled with a virulent bed of nettles!

June 29th.

Dive-bombing Show near Villers-Bocage. Heavy flak from some woods. Climbed up through cloud and suddenly a burst of flak exploded a damn sight too close for comfort.

June 30th.

Into Bayeux. Nice, clean town with shops full of stuff - meat, butter and cheese, smart hats, dresses and shoes.

This evening a large force of Lancasters came over and dropped a mass of bombs on Mehediot where the 21st Panzer Division had dug in. When the Lancs had finished the area was flattened. One Lanc landed on our airstrip as his rear gunner had been badly wounded by flak.

July 3rd.

Dive-bombing trip on an important bridge over the River Orme just south of Caen. My section completely destroyed it. Some close flak as we went in.

July 5th.

Armed Recce in the afternoon. Spotted a lone aircraft tucking in and out of broken cloud. We crept up behind and underneath him and saw he was an Me 109G. Jimmy Talalla made an attack but overshot and found himself right along side the Hun who had an Ace of Spades emblem on his cowling. He then half rolled and dived vertically to the deck. I thought he would never pull out, but he did just above the trees. Then followed a chase at zero feet. He used every contour of the land, going under telegraph wires etc., making it a difficult deflection shot. Alan and Jimmy took pots at him, but I was behind and as he rose slightly over a small hill I gave him a five second burst from 300 yards. Strikes appeared all over him and he went smack into the deck doing about 300 mph.

July 7th.

Just as we took off on an Armed Recce, Sir Archibald Sinclair and Sir Charles Portal arrived to look over our airfield and talk informally to the pilots. I missed it, being airborne and all we saw was flak.

July 8th.

Dive-bombing Show on railway south of Gacé with some good hits. Air Marshal Sir Trafford Leigh-Mallory paid us a visit at tea-time and chatted with us. At 2 am enemy aircraft dropped some bombs near the runway - not much damage.

July 9th.

Our CO is departing on rest and Ronnie Stillwell from 65 Squadron is coming over as our new CO.

July 10th.

Evening Show at 9.30 pm. Down to Rennes - Le Mans and Alençon. Just as dusk was falling we spotted a number of MET on the road and strafed them, destroying several. Landed back at base 11 pm.

July 12th.

More strafing of MET. After we had attacked Hank Smith was hit by flak and started streaming glycol, so baled out.

July 13th.

Wing Show at 5 pm. Marshalling yards at Challet. I flew No 2 to the Wing Commander and we found the target and hit it successfully. On the way back Alan Pavey went below cloud and spotted two FW 190s, one of which was damaged by him but both escaped into cloud.

July 15th.

40 plus Huns came over the beach-head and were tackled by the Spitfire boys. Four were shot down and the rest made off. One Me 109 being chased by a Spit came screaming across our orchard with his cockpit on fire. He baled out and his plane crashed near our runway.

July 16th.

Moved to B12 near Ellon which has a longer runway enabling us to take off with two 1000lb bombs - dammit.

In the early hours of the morning our own 4.5s had been shelling the Hun from the edge of our orchard. The Hun replied by pumping 88mm shells at our airfield - peppered 26 of our kites and killed and wounded a few of our boys. We hadn't had time to dig in and the shells were exploding in the trees under which were our tents.

July 17th.

Next morning we were digging fox holes like mad! That night we flew the serviceable aircraft back to B9 for safety and brought them back at down ready for Monty's new "push" against the Hun SE of Caen.

July 18th.

At dawn hundreds of heavy bombers came across and by 7.30 am 9000 tons of bombs had been dropped and the army then went in. We did some dive-bombing and Armed Recce patrols.

July 20th.

An Auster flew me back to England for 48 hours leave. Met Josh and Garry in Worthing and had a moist evening. Nowhere to stay so the "popsy" I was with offered to take me home to her parents. They were most kind when they knew I had just come over from France. Slept in and had a hot bath - first for a month

July 22nd.

Had a good breakfast, haircut, shave and shampoo, bought some tomatoes, cucumbers, cherries and raspberries to take back to France.

July 24th.

No aircraft available on 23rd to take me back, so got on a mail-carrying Anson today.

July 25th.

The boys went out this morning, ran into some Huns and got three of them. I went on a dive-bombing Show in the afternoon but after 20 minutes flying my R/T went dead and I came back with Ed. About 5 minutes after we turned back 12 190s bounced Blue Section. Maurice Pinches got one and damaged two more before five got on his tail and put a bullet through his elevator. He spun down several thousand feet and escaped. Flying Officer Walker also shot down a 190. Tony Hargreaves is missing.

July 26th.

Took off for the Dreux area. Huns reported to be in the vicinity. But Ed's R/T went duff and I had to come back with him. The rest of the squadron saw 12 190s above and engaged. I could hear the ensuing dogfight on my R/T and was I mad at missing it. The squadron destroyed six, one probable and four damaged. Ken Galloway was last heard saying he thought he would have to bale out.

July 27th.

The boys were up at 7 am and west of Caen they ran into 40 plus 190s. Alan Pavey took Black Section in and nobody saw him again - I'm afraid he has had it as six 190s were making a head-on attack to him. Garry got back by a miracle - his aircraft was peppered - the right elevator was shot away and undercarriage also shot up, but he managed to stagger back streaming oil and glycol and landed with a burst tyre.

July 28th.

Went into Bayeaux this afternoon with Artie Lee for a hot bath and good meal at the "Lion d'Or" Hotel.

July 29th.

Wonders will never cease. We actually had some "popsies" in the Mess today; English army nurses who have just come over. 80 more are coming, so we will be having regular visits. Great for morale!

July 30th.

Off dive-bombing a close support target SE of Caumont. Took off for first time with 1000lb bomb under each wing. Apart from feeling like a pregnant pig on take-off, the aircraft behaved quite well although I built up to 500 mph in the dive. Fighter Sweep in the evening, marshalling yards at Louye hit with good results.

August 1st.

Barges have been sighted on the Seine. They are carrying supplies to the German army. Our Wing has been given the task of knocking them out.

August 2nd.

Dive-bombing barges with 1000lb bombs. The Group Captain - Jamieson - flew as my No 3. We got some direct hits, but he blacked out pulling out from his dive but came to about 100' from the deck - a narrow squeak.

August 3rd.

"Barge bashing" again. Good results obtained and after bombing we went in and strafed them.

August 4th.

More successful "Barge bashing", but we have lost four pilots whilst dive-bombing, the bombs just exploding upon pressing the electric release button. The weight of the bombs is causing hairline cracks in the wings and the electrical spark just ignites the petrol in the wing fuel tanks. Once the pilot in front of me disappeared in a bang and mass of flame. So no more 1000lb bombs - back to 500s.

August 8th.

Another Armed Recce this morning - some flak. In the evening we had a real party, inviting 50 army nurses from just outside Bayeux. Planes had been flown to England to bring back lobster, ham, pies, trifle, beer and spirits. A platform was erected outside the Mess Tent and a five-piece band played. It was a great success.

'A lapse in the diary due to the unsettled state we are in. Managed to get seven days leave on August 10th and flew to England in a Dakota. Went home to Cornwall for complete peace and quiet.

'Back to France found the boys had been revelling in ground attack. It was the Hun retreat from the Falaise Gap. They have been strafing men and transport trying to escape. Up the next day with the rest in a mad whirl of aircraft, flak and bullets.

'More dive-bombing on shipping. I recorded a direct hit on a steamer in the Seine. Flight Lieutenant Lewis was hit by flak and baled out over the sea, but was soon picked up.

'The day before we had been on a ground attack mission and Flying Officer Thomas had been hit by flak and baled out over the sea. We looked for him until dark, then again at first light. He was spotted off Dieppe and soon picked up by a Walrus.

'The day before we left for another airfield I was on a Fighter Sweep in the St Omer - Hazebrouck area when flak started coming up. I felt a terrific thump and the aircraft keeled over to one side. A lump of flak had shredded a couple of feet of my wing tip. By trimming hard on the aileron I was able to get back OK.

'From St André we moved to Beauvais, 40 miles north of Paris. We made some trips into Paris as there was no activity due to supplies not catching up with us. Attractive girls, beautifully made up and tailored, walked up and down the Champs Elysées. Got back to Beauvais at 8 am the following day having got lost in the dark and having run out of petrol three times, but managed to scrounge some from American transport.

'Next move was on September 9th, to Belgium - an airfield at Grimbergen recently vacated in a hurry by the Luftwaffe. Our billets were in a chateau - best by far we have had. Vastly improved food with the addition of fresh fruit and vegetables.

'The flying was more interesting as we were able to scour large areas in Holland and the Hun didn't know that we were so close. So we piled up a good score of destroyed trains, barges and road transport. There were, of course, the odd losses from flak. Pilot Officer Thorne who had won the DFC back in Normandy, was last seen going in to attack some transport. Several pilots from 65 and 19 Squadrons, which also made up our Wing, were also lost.

'We had a number of cars at our disposal - left by the Luftwaffe and which they had commandeered. So whenever we could we roared off into Brussels where we were greeted most enthusiastically. The proprietor of one well known cafe - the "St Jean Baptiste" came up to the chateau and invited three of us to dinner. We had a wonderful meal and superb wines and afterwards he took us to his archery gallery behind the cafe where many celebrities, including the King of Belgium, had tried their hand with the longbow.

'There was also the unforgettable "Gabrielles". Gabrielle, a wonderful creature, temperamental as only Continentals and film stars can be - laughing and joking one minute and then some little thing would upset her and she would send out a stream of indignant French, and perhaps even throwing a glass or two. We used to drink there until 11 pm when the doors shut and us plus one or two select friends would drink champagne in the house until perhaps 4 am.

'We lived like that for a month, flying by day and whooping it up at night.

'September 17th - the Arnhem landings. We patrolled the area to keep enemy aircraft away from the Gliders and paratroopers. We had several fierce dogfights over Arnhem as the Hun came up to try and stop the landings and bomb the bridge. Eventually as the month drew to a close word came that we would be going back to England to escort our bombers doing daylight sorties for the first time. No-one wanted to return. Not just because of the good times we were having in Brussels, but the flying we were doing. The spirit in the Wing was high. We knew we were good - had been told we were one of the best in 2nd TAF.

'We threw a hugh party at the château before we left, inviting all the friends we had made in Brussels. The guests came in their best finery and were clearly impressed by the superb cold buffet laid on. Champagne, whisky, gin and cognac to drink and it was 4.30 am before the last guest left.

'Up at 6.30 am for a Show into Holland and in spite of the party the night before we had a heyday destroying trains and transport.

'Last Show the next day scouring Utrecht - Amersfoort - Apeldoorn. Bagged numerous trains and in spite of a lot of flak all returned safely.

'Next day - September 28th - the Tempest boys under Wing Commander Beamont took over from us. Back in England we did several escort trips to our

Lancasters including one on October 14th when over 1000 Lanc and Halifaxes bombed Duisburg. Flak over the target was a solid wall, but we all got back.

'Next Lanc escort to bomb the Sorpe Dam. Saw a V2 rocket contrail shooting up from somewhere in Germany - wonder where it landed!

'My last five ops were done from Andrews Field in Essex. Two Fighter Sweeps to the Paderborn area. Saw an Me 262 jet take-off from Osnabrück and attacked. He must have seen us for he opened the "tap" and just left us standing although we were doing over 500 mph in the dive.

'Three more escort trips. Heavy flak over target area in each case but all returned.

'On the last op I couldn't immediately get the wheels up after take-off, but after some jiggling about managed to retract. Then five minutes later the port drop tank cut when I switched over to it. Thought I might have to return but was anxious to

An incredible photograph showing a V1 about to impact in Brussels. The photographer was killed.

Antony Whitehead

complete my last trip so switched on to starboard drop tank. When that emptied I was a bit dubious about the port one, but luckily it worked.

'Conditions were so bad on our return that we diverted to Manston for the night. There I met some old friends; Wing Commander Colin Gray DSO, DFC and two Bars, plus Jeff Smith and Arthur Elcock. Went on a pub crawl to celebrate the end of my Tour'.

The foregoing, written, it must be remembered, by a 23-year-old and at the time of the events described, is amongst the best contemporary material it has ever been my pleasure to 'discover'.

Only two of Tony Michin's diary entries require any additional data from myself.

Firstly, on June 10th, 1944, Tony describes 122 Squadron being bounced by Me 109s painted to represent Mustangs; the reality is that they WERE Mustangs! 122 Squadron was actually mistakenly attacked by 19 Squadron, a tragic error which would be known today as a 'Friendly Fire' incident. During the course of my research I have come across similar claims several times - in every case there is a similar explanation, there being nothing to be gained but everything to lose for German aircraft masquerading in RAF colour schemes; even the famous Rosarius Circus of captured Allied aircraft, used to demonstrate 'enemy' capabilities to Luftwaffe personnel, wore outsize German markings as an extra precaution! It was always just a question, however, of the speed of combat having deceived the human eye.

Secondly, regarding the Me 109G that Tony destroyed on July 5th, 1944, he told me that the Squadron later heard via the French Resistance that the pilot had been an ace, a 'Major Muller'. The Ace of Spades badge on the 109's cowling seen during the combat by Jimmy Talalla, identifies the aircraft as being from JG53 'Pik As'. Lo and behold on the same date, at an identical location and time, 6/JG53 lost Unteroffizier Bruno Ohsenkamp. His Me 109G was Werk Nummer 110260, yellow 7+. This was undoubtedly Flying Officer Minchin's victim as no other Jagdwaffe casualties that day could even be considered as candidates.

If ever one was to fly and survive a tour of operational flying after the Battle of Britain, the period that Tony Minchin flew, March - October 1944, had to be it. During that time he flew in support of the D-Day landings, which must have been an incredible sight, and participated in the Battle for Normandy and the Falaise Gap, watching the German army retreat beyond the Seine. What a sight it must have been too, escorting huge formations of American bombers to Germany itself. Tony also saw 'in anger' two of the greatest technological developments of the war - a V2 missile, and an Me 262 jet. What unique experience.

An Me 262 jet, the revolutionary combat aircraft which came just too late to turn the tide for Germany.

Tony was demobbed in 1946 and became a printer, living in Malvern, Worcestershire, but travelling by motorbike to work in Gloucester. When he left that company Tony had become its Production Manager, but then joined Robert Horn's, a paper manufacturer based in London, as a salesman tasked with opening up the Midlands. This Tony did, becoming Marketing Manager, and by the time that he eventually retired in 1986, Horn's had become a £180 million concern.

Tony Minchin and I share another passion, that of carp fishing, and I look forward to us having time to spend together in the future on the bankside in pursuit of our monsters. It is hard, though, to imagine this very fit and 'with it' 73-year-old gentleman busting trains and zooming about the sky in a Mustang - but then, that is all a part of my personal fascination.

Flt Lt Tony Minchin at the launch of 'Through Peril to the Stars', *Great Malvern, September 1993.*

                                                    Dennis Williams

Chapter Twenty-seven

Leutnant Peter Wulff

Hans 'Peter' Wulff *pictured whilst a Luftwaffe officer cadet.*

I believe that any appraisal of the 1939-45 air war should offer the reader a balanced view of its events, it being likely that the majority of enemy airmen were just soldiers, fighting for their country and not therefore being particularly politically motivated. It is also true to say that there remains an invisible bond between combat fliers of all nationalities, from the Great War to the Gulf Conflict. These men were born to fly, came from similar social and educational backgrounds, and shared a passion for aeroplanes. Of course they had no control over which side of the Channel they were born, and consequently whether their machine was emblazoned with a swastika or cockade. Far too many authors, however, do offer merely the Allied viewpoint. Admittedly it is much harder to obtain information regarding the Luftwaffe. There is firstly the language barrier to overcome, and then the fact that so many German military records were destroyed in 1945, which now causes immense frustration to historians.

Fortunately many individual Luftwaffe units have their own reunion associations, just like RAF squadrons, but the numbers of these are now decreasing in many instances, for obvious reasons. The German fighter pilots, however, formed Der Gemeinschaft der Jagdflieger E.V., and this is a large and thriving organisation which readily offers assistance to researchers.

Der Gemeinschaft der Jagdflieger E.V. was not, however, merely formed for living in the past; after the Second World War, the jagdflieger were used as the scapegoat for failing to prevent the Allied aerial bombardment of Germany, despite their immense bravery against ultimately incredibly overwhelming odds. Those who subsequently applied for civilian jobs in the rubble and chaos of the immediate post-war Fatherland were often rejected out of hand for no other reason than their jagdflieger antecedents. With nowhere to turn, the German Fighter Pilots' Association was formed as a mutual help organisation. Slowly the standard of living was increased, and members were eventually able to take their appropriate place in society. Many former German servicemen, however, preferred instead to make new lives overseas. Martin Drewes is a perfect example. Born in Lobmachtersen bei Braunschweig in 1918, he experienced the thrill of flight for the first time in 1926 over Wangerooge Island. As there were still few opportunities for flying training, in 1937 he enlisted as a Fahnenjunker, or Officer Cadet, in Panzer Regiment 6. On September 1st, 1939, he was transferred to the Luftwaffe and became a zerstörerflieger. In February 1941, Martin joined II/ZG76 'Haifischgruppe' (Shark Group) at Jever, Wittmundhafen. In November, his Gruppe became night-fighters, the unit being re-designated III/ Nachtjagdgeschwader 3. In February 1943 he became Staffelkapitän of 11/III NJG3, and a year later took over as Gruppenkommandeur of III/NJG1. In July 1944 he received the Ritterkreuz, and on April 17th, 1945, just 13 days before Adolf Hitler shot himself amidst the ruins of Berlin, 26-year-old Major Drewes received a telegram from the Führer awarding him the Eichenlaub. By the German surrender, Major Drewes had flown 253 combat missions and had destroyed 50 'Viermot-Bomber', 43 of them by night, and two Allied aircraft by day. In 1991, Martin recalled defeat in 1945:-

'At the end of World War II we were at Husum in northern Germany, officially being "disarmed soldiers", which means that the occupation forces arrived after May 8th, 1945. We then spent several months at the "reservation area" in the Schleswig region. I then spent nearly two years in British Internment camps in Germany, such as those at Westertimke and Fallingbostel. Why? It just depended on the inquiry made by the interrogation officers, who were not always British.

'In 1949, because there were no decent prospects for former fighter pilots in Germany, I got fed up. Without a passport, not speaking even one word of the language, not knowing anyone, without any money or luggage, I went to Brazil. In Germany there were virtually no opportunities for us to fly, to do what we really knew, to be a pilot, but it was not too late to learn other things, to become a professional, to work in finance, administration, as a manager of firms in a country which had inflation. It was very interesting but extremely hard work'.

Other German servicemen who had been captured by the Allies decided to make new lives in the victors' lands. One such man was Leutnant Hans Wulff who had been captured by the British on New Year's Day 1945. Still a prisoner in Britain, after the war Leutnant Wulff was employed as an agricultural worker in Pembrokeshire. There he met a local girl whom he married after his release in 1948 when he became a farmer and eventually a British Citizen. In his new country, Hans became known as 'Peter', which was more anglicised and taken directly from the children's story 'Peter and the Wolf'. More fortunate than many former Luftwaffe airmen, however, Peter started gliding again in 1952, with the Midland Gliding Club at the Long Mynd in Shropshire, and gained his licence to fly single-engine powered aircraft in 1957. He then became the personal pilot of a Pembroke industrialist, beginning 'the happiest six years of my life, during which I was farming just three days a week and flying the rest'.

The Malvern Spitfire Team had the great pleasure of meeting Peter Wulff by complete surprise whilst exhibiting at an obscure event in Herefordshire. Since that time Peter has become a close friend and enthusiastic supporter of our work. Quite rightly he is keen not to glorify war, but as David Malpas remarked to Peter during the launch of 'Angriff Westland' in 1994, 'You are a part of history. Many people would probably like to meet Henry VIIIth, for example, but they can't, but as you are still alive they can meet you.' In 'Through Peril to the Stars', I wrote something of Peter's story in the Postscript, largely concentrating on when he was shot down and captured on Operation Bodenplatte, and his subsequent experiences as a prisoner. On the 50th anniversary of that occasion, New Year's Day 1995, Peter and I spoke further of his wartime experiences which provide an incredible 'view from the other side'. Readers may be familiar with the original documentary 'Memphis Belle', in which a handful of German fighters attack a huge formation of Flying Fortresses again and again, fleeting targets at which hundreds of waist, ball and turret gunners opened up. I often wondered as a child what those German pilots flying in the defence of their homeland were really like, facing formations of 1,000 Allied aircraft by both day and night; getting to know Peter Wulff made me realise that they too were brave and honourable young men.

Hans Wulff's route to a fighter's cockpit was an unusual one, however:-

'My desire, right from the beginning, was to be a jagdflieger. However, I had so many obstacles put in my way. I had started gliding in 1937, before the war, and I had a very, very good instructor. I was not called up until 1941, but my instructor had told me that as I would soon be in the Luftwaffe I might as well start early on aerobatics, so I had winch launches which got me up to over 800'. I both looped and flew by night in my glider, so by the time I actually joined the air force I was quite prepared. My old instructor is now in his 80s but we still see each other a lot. I owe him a great deal, not only flying techniques but also the instinct required to survive as a pilot in wartime.

'I undertook the normal flying training in the Luftwaffe, but at the Luftkriegschule, or Air War Academy, they said that with my ability in both mathematics and navigation I could not go to fighters but to either a bomber or long-range reconnaissance unit. I was very disappointed, but was sent to another school to fly He 111s. After a couple of weeks there, in the spring of 1943 I was posted to the IVth Gruppe of KG53 'Legion Condor' at Orleans, south of Paris. This was the KG53's training Gruppe where we were to receive advanced training on the He 111, particularly in respect of instrument flying and practice bombing. I learnt a lot but still desperately wanted to be a fighter pilot.

'We had an instrument flying instructor who was an awful teacher but an excellent pilot, having flown some 300 missions in Russia, so the trick was to watch him fly but not listen to him. I thought that if I fouled up the training course I might have a chance of being posted to the Jagdwaffe, so when this particular instructor was flying with me one day, sitting next to me reading a book, I deliberately stalled. You can imagine that in a big plane like the He 111 this gave him quite a shock! He was hopping mad. Next flight I thought that I would try something else, so before take off pretended to go right through the procedure but could not start the engines. Again he was sitting beside me reading, and asked what was wrong. I said that I didn't know, I just could not start the engines. I had actually intentionally not switched on the fuel supply. When the instructor checked he went quite mad and went and wrote a recommendation for me to transfer to fighters. However, the Staffelkapitän who sent for me knew that I was trying it on, and he left me in no doubt as to the consequences if I failed the course. The instructor concerned had refused to fly with me again, so I had to complete the course with a fellow officer sitting beside me with the training manual. The exam was eventually given by a Lufthansa Captain who was aware of the situation which he found quite amusing. Anyway, he passed me to fly the He 111 in all weathers.

'We then went to III/KG53 which was resting and re-fitting near Munich in southern Germany. There we flew more training sorties and got used to our new Staffelkapitän, a very experienced pilot. The Geschwader then moved to Russia. En route we lost two pilots due to bad weather. It showed that training is all very well, but there are situations when only experience can save you. In Russia the real war started for me, I made my first combat flight in December 1943. God it was cold in Russia, at night the groundcrews even had to take the batteries out of our aircraft to prevent them freezing. By this time the Russians had turned around and commenced halting the German advance, so my first operational flights were in support of the German army, attacking the Russian front-line troops. This was bombing from 18,000'. I was fortunate to have a very experienced navigator and observer whose job was also being bombardier. He was an Oberfeldwebel who had already flown 60 combat missions in Russia. That experience on board our aircraft made a lot of difference. After returning from my first attack news filtered through that bombs had also fallen on our own troops. As the new pilot I was blamed, the Gruppenkommandeur was adamant about it. My gunner, however, a very keen little chap, had taken photographs of our attack and was able to prove that the pilot at fault was actually the Gruppenkommandeur himself!

'My next flights were to attack targets well behind the Russian lines, military concentrations. On one such flight there was an almighty flash amongst our formation of 20-30 He 111s. I had never seen anything like it before, so I asked my observer whether it had been caused by one of the flak guns which we had sold to the Russians in 1940 and which I knew were very good; he said not, it was a direct hit in an He 111's bomb-bay! All of the aircraft surrounding the one that was blown up were damaged. I realised then just how dangerous flak could be.

Leutnant Wulff's III/KG53 He 111 in formation over Russia, 1943. By then the tide had turned against Germany.

'I enjoyed it more when I was sent off alone at night, train hunting, when I could use my initiative, instead of just following a leader like sheep. The formation leader often changed - sometimes it was the Gruppenkommandeur, sometimes another experienced pilot. One day we had a very senior officer flying with us who had little experience but insisted upon leading the formation himself. Sometimes you would not get it right on the first bombing run so had to go round again, although of course because of flak and fighters this was very dangerous. Can you believe then that on this attack the formation leader went round with 20-30 He 111s 16 times before we bombed! He was a great soldier, no doubt about it! When we landed my neighbour in the formation congratulated us for destroying a fighter, but we were puzzled and knew nothing about it -

apparently a Russian fighter attacked us from below, climbing vertically at the point when we released our bombs - one hit him straight on the nose and the fighter exploded!

'Bombing, however, was not for me. We eventually went to an airfield in Lithuania from where we returned to the Russian Front, flying from huge fields in the Southern Ukraine. There we had to supply 200,000 surrounded German troops. Prior to our arrival the transport planes had actually been able to land within the German held area, but that was soon so reduced that the only way to get supplies in was from the air. We carried ammunition, food and petrol in our bomb-bays and had to drop these from 600' into a specially marked triangle which was lit at night. We preferred doing this in bad weather due to the flak and fighters as we had to go in so low. You then had to fly through cloud and carefully calculate where to descend at about 500'. Once I descended too early and could actually see the Russian troops shooting at us with rifles. We were hit and the port engine lost all its coolant and stopped. I had to drop our load, hoping that we were over German troops by then, before disappearing into cloud and coaxing the remaining engine to get us home safely. Next day we had a new aeroplane, there were plenty of new planes but a shortage of pilots.

'On another flight I complained to my crew that I suffered from a painful bladder when descending quickly. My observer suggested that I should urinate into a condom before we descended, tie a knot in it and hand it to him to throw out with the bombs - this I did, but when he tossed it out with the bombs the slipstream blew the urine-filled condom back inside and it burst all over him!

'We then went back to Lithuania where we began specialising in long-range bombing to hit Russian munitions factories deep behind their lines. Then came a request from Berlin asking pilots to transfer to the Jagdwaffe, it was ordered that those requests should not be denied under any circumstances. I knew that flying fighters was going to be a tough game over Germany, fighting against either the Americans by day or British by night, but it was what I wanted to do so volunteered to go, it was a chance in a lifetime for me. I had to go to Berlin to decide which branch of the Jagdwaffe to go in, either single-engined day or night-fighters, or twin-engined day or night-fighters. If I had decided to go onto twin-engined night-fighters then I would have taken both my observer and gunner with me, but to fly night-fighters meant going back to school, which I did not want to do. Flying single-engined fighters also demanded this, so I decided to fly twin-engined day fighters, loving my two engines which had after all saved my life in Russia. I kept my wireless operator, however, and we joined ZG26 which was stationed at Königsberg on the River Oder, 100 km east of Berlin. We converted to the Me 410 with the Geschwader's Ergänzung Staffel, or Training Squadron, at Sagan, near to the famous RAF PoW Camp from where the "Great Escape" was made. We only had one dual control aircraft for instruction, an Me 210, so training was limited to just one flight with an instructor in the back then off on your own in a single-seater. We started with 15 pilots, all experienced bomber, transport or reconnaissance pilots, but after a week there were only eight of us left, the other seven having been killed in flying accidents. After three weeks we went to our unit, 8/ZG26.

Above left: Leutnant Wulff (right) upon leaving the Russian front to fly fighters in the west.

Above right: Leutnant Wulff bids farewell to his navigator.

Left: After a farewell party, the following morning Leutnant Wulff prepares to fly his He 111 westwards and begin his career as a fighter pilot, albeit looking a little the worse for wear!

'It was not easy being a new boy again but II/ZG26 had a good atmosphere so we soon settled in. The losses, however, were tremendous. Previously I had absolutely no perception of what it would really be like, but it was after all what I wanted to do. Most inexperienced pilots were lost on their first few operational flights, but I was curious, I wanted to see combat. It was incredible, quite a sight, I can tell you, to see 600 or 800 Boeing B17 Flying Fortresses. Without fighter escorts attacking the bombers was not too bad, but once the fighters came with them all the way it became very difficult. On my first flight, before I really knew what had hit me, my one engine was ablaze and the other spitting flames. Never having done it before, I was reluctant to bale out, so I told my wireless operator that I was going to forced land. The controller told us that as we had height they would try to get us down onto an airfield. They gave me a course but as we approached the selected airfield a huge cloudbank approached the field so that I had to guess the last few hundred yards. We belly landed and got away with it. The aircraft was wrecked but we were the more important. We caught the train back to our unit where we could always get a new plane.

'On my second operational flight I was shot down by fighters near Leipzig. I was looping on just one engine but decided that the deck would be the safest place to be, I thought that I may then either find an airfield or land in a suitable field. Six Mustangs came to finish me off, they chased me from behind, but as we were so low, and due to my violent evasive action, they were unable to get a good shot at me. In the Me 410 my wireless operator had the use of two fuselage mounted remote control rearward-firing machine-guns with which he was also able to upset the Mustangs a bit. They then flew together, beside me, and had a conflag about what to do. Separating into two sections of three, I knew what was coming, three were going to attack me head-on and three from the rear. I thought "Christ, I'm not waiting for this", so I just stuck the aircraft down into a huge cornfield where the stooks were still standing. We hit the ground at about 150 mph, it was fantastic, both engines were torn off, but there was no fire, thank God. As we got out of the 410 the Mustangs strafed us on the ground. We ran to a nearby wood where we found armed German civilians, clearly there to get downed American airmen. I thought "this is all I need!" There were several cases where Americans had been shot like this, but those responsible were largely refugees who had lost everything, and I can only consider that they had therefore gone quite mad. There was, however, a case where one of our crews had been shot down over central Germany and were later found with their heads cut off by

Leutnant Wulff in his new aircraft, a II/ZG26 Me 410 'Hornisse' (Hornet).

Leutnant Wulff takes aim through his Me 410's roof-mounted gunsight.

German civilians armed with scythes. The German airmen had been mistaken for Americans as our flying kit was very similar. Because of this we had been issued with armbands bearing a bright yellow swastika, so we were okay. That was certainly one of the black sides to the air war.

Our Staffelkapitän in 8/ZG26 was a "Von", and his wireless operator, formerly on night-fighters, and I were very friendly, he had made me welcome when I joined the unit. One night the Staffelkapitän was returning from the Officers' Mess after a few drinks when he saw a soldier climbing out of the adjacent women's quarters. He shouted "Stop!" three times, as per orders, then shot the man. The "Von" was the crack pistol shot of the unit, but when the body was examined it was discovered that he had been hit in the leg, arm and head. If he had been hit in the head first he would have just dropped, no need therefore for any other shots. If he had been hit in the head second, then no need for the third shot. It was suspected, therefore, that the Staffelkapitän shot him first in the arm and leg, then administered the coup de grâce at point blank range. He was immediately relieved of his responsibilities whilst on the ground. Due to the shortage of pilots, however, he was able to lead us in the air before his Court Martial. One day we took off and attacked some bombers. After the first attack, in which all became separated, we would re-group on a previously agreed side of the bombers and tactically re-assess the situation before attacking again. On this occasion we re-grouped, and the Staffelkapitän began descending in a slight dive. As his No 2, I followed him, you do not let your No 1 go anywhere alone, but he put up his hand, signalling for me to return and join the others, which I did. The Staffelkapitän failed to return from that flight. Later in the day I received a telephone call from my wireless operator friend who explained what had happened. Apparently during the dive, after giving me the signal to leave him, the Staffelkapitän threw his forage cap into the rear cockpit and told the wireless operator to give it to his mother; he then told him to bale out. The wireless operator was unable to understand why, so refused, but the pilot then ordered him to do so. After taking to his parachute, my friend saw the Me 410 dive vertically into the ground under full power. The Staffelkapitän had committed suicide.

'The American and British escort fighters, especially the Mustangs, with such long range, were eventually even able to come to our airfield and attack us as we landed. The powers that be decided that it was futile to continue with the 410 against such superior single-engined fighters, so we became JG6 and converted to single-engined fighters ourselves. When in France and training to fly He 111s, I had made friends with a nearby Fighter School which had in its possession a Spitfire captured in 1940. I kept on and on pestering them to let me fly it, which they eventually did. Similarly, at that time I also scrounged a flight in an Me 109, but we in JG6 were not to get the 109 but the FW 190. Overall we were satisfied with this as we probably preferred the 190 which was better than the 109 up to 20,000', above that the new 109 had the advantage. Such was the urgency of the hour, however, that we twin-engined pilots only had a few hours to convert to singles. We had a two-seater, single-engined Me 108 communications plane in which I had to oversee the conversion and give a little instruction in a dual environment before the pilots went off alone in a 190. Actually the transition was quite smooth.

'By then, August 1944, the Allied invasion was well underway and things looked very bad for us in the west. Every German fighter possible was needed there, so we were transferred to north-east France. As fighter pilots were supposed to be poor navigators, however, a specialist came who was to guide us on the long flight to our new base which was just a country field. I don't know why, but before I took off I got my groundcrew to adjust my seat so that I could sit very low in the cockpit. I did not anticipate fighter contact so did not need to be sitting upright looking over the sides. I don't know why I did it. Anyway, try as he might, Oberst or not Oberst, this specialist could not find our new field himself! I was a Schwarmführer and found a disused airfield. I went down to have a look but saw that there were various posts sticking up here and there. I thought that I could just get in with wheels down, but told my Schwarm to stay above and make belly landings if anything happened to me. I landed but the 190 hit a post and the tail went up and over. The hood was smashed and if I had not been sitting low down I would definitely have been killed. My head was cut badly. The Schwarm belly landed as instructed and the pilots dug me out with the help of a French farmer who turned up with a spade. He did not have to do that as I was an enemy flier, neither did the local doctor have to treat me but he did. I gave him my last cigarettes.

'That night I went to a German field hospital, and then later to a Collecting Point in Belgium. There there were officers from all the Wehrmacht waiting for postings. The front line, however, was getting closer and closer and I was getting very nervous. I spoke to the head doctor and told him that he must post us otherwise we would be overrun and all captured. He said that he had no orders, so I decided to go off by myself. However, what with the partisan activity and retreating troops it was very demoralising. I could have hitched a ride on a tank, but then I saw deserters hanging from trees who had been executed by SS squads as an example to others. If stopped by them how could I prove that I was not a deserter but a wounded pilot trying my best not to be captured by the Allies? As that was clearly impossible, I went back. Then the highly skilled, like pilots and tank commanders, were taken away in a bus to Luxembourg, then southern Germany. Then I went to hospital near my home. I probably owe my survival to that period of 5-6 weeks out of the fighting.

'When away from your unit for more than four weeks, the system was that you would then go to a Collecting Point and be posted therefrom. At this time they were putting together the new Me 262 jet units, and with my extensive twin-engined experience, as both a bomber and fighter pilot, I stood a very good chance of being posted to such a formation. However, I had to balance old friends against the prospect of new, and decided that, especially in war, old friends are more important, so I rang my Gruppenkommandeur in JG6, which was now operating from a small field east of the Rhine near Cologne. It was now the end of October 1944 and half of the original JG6 had already been lost. Anyway, my Gruppenkommandeur sent me a travel warrant and I returned to the unit. We then went to Hagennue, near Hamburg, from where we flew operations against the B17s. We had a Feldwebel posted to our unit who had been badly wounded and captured whilst flying FW190s on hit and run raids on England during 1943. The rule was that repatriated prisoners must not be put back into action, but this chap was absolutely determined to fly again. It was my job to re-familiarise him with flying, to get him back into the air as soon as possible. He was a bright lad and after a few circuits and bumps he was okay. The next day we flew a training exercise with the whole Geschwader of 70-80 planes and I can still hear that Feldwebel's voice now, he was flying beside me and suddenly shouted "I've lost my prop!" and I looked to see his propeller unit going vertically upwards! The Kommodore told him to descend through the cloud and make a forced landing in a field. Someone should have remembered that pilots were more important than planes on that occasion, as the pilot concerned decided to land wheels down - he was killed. I had to tell his widow, which was the worst moment of my entire war.

'Whilst with JG6 we used to have a briefing at 8 am, although the alarm start never came until either 10.30 or 11 am. The pilots could not understand why there had to be a briefing at 8 am, especially as there was always another before take-off, so said to hell with it and stayed in bed. I was Duty Officer so had to be at the 8 am briefing, but was mortified when the Geschwaderkommodore walked in! He asked where the other officers were, so I told him that they must have been somehow hindered, that there must be a good reason for them not attending. He was furious and told me to get the officers together immediately. He went straight into the Officers' Quarters - there were even pilots jumping out of the window to escape him! I said, "Come on, you've got to come," and when we were all together he went mad, saying that there would be no operations that day but instead a Court Martial! Being considered the only trustworthy officer, I was ordered to fly to Berlin and collect the Judge. We talked and I explained the circumstances to him. During the trial, when the Kommodore gave his evidence we all stamped our feet - loudly - and the Judge had to stop proceedings twice to give warnings and bring the Court back to order. I relate this story to indicate that we were not automatons in the German armed forces as is widely, and incorrectly, believed - if we thought that something was wrong we said so!

'We were then transferred to Quakenbrük, still flying against the American bombers, then in support of the Wacht am Rhine Offensive, or "Battle of the Bulge" as the Allies called it and which started on December 16th, 1944. Whilst flying during that period I was suddenly startled to see that a Spitfire had formated on me! We two pilots looked at each other in total astonishment - we could not shoot at each other as we were flying level, but the Spitfire quickly half-rolled away. I shouted "Break", and everyone executed a 180 degree turn!'

On New Year's Day 1945, JG6 participated in Operation Bodenplatte, the Luftwaffe's last offensive which was mounted against 2nd TAF bases in Holland. JG6 was briefed to attack Volkel. However, due to a navigational error the Geschwader failed to locate their target. Instead, Leutnant Wulff shot up a convoy; although such targets were not part of his brief, he reasoned that such a target of opportunity was better than nothing. He then climbed to join battle amongst FW 190s and Me 109s fighting a 'superior number of Spitfires and Tempests'. He shot down a Spitfire, but was then hit himself. Hans Wulff - as he was then - was very low to bale out, but had studied the emergency escape procedure for such occasions written by Germany's famous female test pilot, Hanna Reisch. Following her instructions, he blew off the canopy, undid his straps and, whilst still standing in the cockpit, pulled his ripcord. The parachute deployed and sucked him straight out of the doomed aircraft. On the way out, Leutnant Wulff hit an elevator, however, which broke three ribs and injured his back.

Earlier that morning, Squadron Leader AE Umbers DFC had been leading the Tempests of 486 (New Zealand) Squadron on an armed recce to the Paderborn-Bielefeld area. Over Arnhem, however, the Squadron was recalled to 'mix it with the Luftwaffe' over the Eindhoven area. In the ensuing combat, the Tempest pilots claimed five FW 190s and one Me 109 destroyed, and two 109s and one 190 damaged. Pilot Officer GJ Hooper reported:-

'I was flying Green 4 when flying due west at Eindhoven I saw three FW 190s flying more or less in line abreast in a northerly direction and at zero feet. I was at about 1,000' and went down on the port 190. I closed in to about 200 yards dead line astern and opened fire but observed no strikes. My starboard guns stopped firing but again I fired at almost point blank range. As I passed over the FW190 I saw a puff of smoke come from the starboard side of the cockpit. I pulled up to the starboard and saw the FW190 crash into a field and burst into flames.'

It is believed that the 'puff of smoke' coming from the FW 190's cockpit was actually Leutnant Wulff's parachute.

'Peter' Wulff is clearly very lucky to be alive. He is also a natural pilot who has enjoyed many hours in the air both in powered aircraft and gliders, both military and civil. He has recorded over 50 of each category in his log book, and, since starting gliding in 1937, the only year he did not fly was 1946 when a prisoner of war in England. I can hardly imagine Peter Wulff as a former enemy airman, but rather as a young man who loved flying, a professional airman on the 'wrong' side through no fault of his own.

In August 1994, Peter gave me his 'Legion Condor' cuff title which KG53 members were honoured to wear on their left sleeves; that piece of embroidered cloth, over half a century old, occupies a very special place in my collection and represents a friendship that I value greatly.

Peter Wulff back in the pilot's seat of an He 111. RAF Museum, August 1994.
David Malpas

Peter Wulff signing prints at the launch of 'The Invisible Thread: A Spitfire's Tale', Great Malvern, *September 1992.*

Chapter Twenty-eight

Unteroffizier Paul Moeller

Unteroffizier Paul Moeller, September 1941,
on leave after qualifying as a pilot.

The pilot donned his straw-coloured schwimmveste and summer issue flying helmet, and climbed aboard the drab-painted and swastika-emblazoned He 111 bomber. Within the confines of the narrow fuselage, he stepped over the engineer's seat, built as an integral part of the cabin bulkhead door, and through into the glazed cockpit. He slid easily into the pilot's seat, suspended above perspex panels and giving a helicopter-like impression, and placed his feet firmly on the rudder pedals. He noted with satisfaction the elevators' response as he moved the U shaped joystick. Another man then entered the cockpit and unfolded the navigator's seat to the pilot's right. Players in a scene repeated countless times during the Second World War, the pair said nothing as they absorbed the atmosphere. This He 111H-23, however, was not to take off on an operational flight that day - how could it - the date was August 12th, 1994, and the aircraft an exhibit at the RAF Museum. The 'pilot' was former Unteroffizier Paul Moeller, the other man former Leutnant Hans Wulff. Both had flown He 111s operationally during the Second World War, but this flight of fancy was powered only by their memories and the enthusiasm of a young aviation historian - myself.

Six months previously, a friend of mine, Ron Mason, had mentioned in passing that his brother-in-law was a former prisoner of war, having been a member of the Luftwaffe. Interest level rising, 'was he aircrew?', I enquired. That was not known, but a telephone call was made to Paul Moeller, who lives in Buckinghamshire, and soon I found myself talking to a very rare surviving 'warbird' indeed, for Unteroffizier Paul Moeller had flown He 111 torpedo bombers with I/KG26 'Löwen' in the Mediterranean. Paul was a garage owner who had closed the door on his wartime memories - until that day. Soon he was telling me that on the night of February 1st/2nd, 1944, he and his crew, Obergefreiter Herbert Schumacher, Unteroffizier Willi Boehm and Obergefreiter Rudolf Holzinger, were shot down attacking a convoy and captured. Our conversation was taking place almost 50 years to the day of those dramatic events.

Like Peter Wulff, I have since come to know Paul well. Paul's was a familiar story; after marrying Iris, a member of the Land Army whom he met whilst working on a farm, he settled in England and became a British Citizen. Since the war, however, he had not spoken about his Luftwaffe experiences; not even his grandchildren knew that Paul had been a pilot. Paul and Iris attended the Ramrod Publications and Malvern Spitfire Team enthusiast's afternoon at the Abbey Hotel in Great Malvern a few days after our initial contact; there Paul met a Spitfire pilot for the first time, having expressed a desire to do so, and found himself back amongst airmen with whom he shared a common bond. The Spitfire pilot was Ron Rayner, whose story is also told in this book, and who was flying with 43 Squadron in the same Theatre. I also put Paul in contact with Peter Wulff, and when the pair met shortly afterwards they found that, as I had anticipated, they had much in common; after a day spent together, each felt as if he had known the other all his life. Another bond had been forged out of the experiences of 50 years ago. Paul and Iris have since become enthusiasts themselves, and another dimension has been unexpectedly added to their lives.

I have since been able to further unlock Paul Moeller's memory, and the following is a transcript of a tape which he sent me shortly after our first meeting:-

'I was born in Witten a.d. Ruhr on November 30th, 1922, the son of Paul and Margarete Moeller (née Koch). I lost my father, however, in the "Drift Mine Accident" in 1923. I started school in April 1929, and joined the Flieger Hitler Youth in 1936. I apprenticed as a turner, but in 1937 passed my glider A & B Licence. In April 1939 I also passed the Luftfahrer, or 'C', licence at Dornberg by Kassel. I then passed my medical for flying service with the air force at the Universitäts Clinic in Bonn. I joined the Luftwaffe on November 15th, 1939, and commenced basic training. By January 1940 I was a student at the Luftwaffe Technical School at Munich, and in May I was a Board Mechanic for target towing at Luftdienst Divenow (Insel Wollin). We were using We 34s with Bramo

Fafnir engines, one of the early Junkers aircraft. In August and September we transferred to Wien Stammersdorf for Unteroffizier training prior to joining Flugzeugführer Schule A-B4 at Wien-Schwechat. I then started flying training at Kralup/Molda, north of Prague. At Nürnberg we learned aerobatics, point-to-point touring and night flying. A-B Licence planes were flown, such as FW Stieglitz, Bücker Jungman, Gotha, Bücker Jungmeister, Arado; and later, at Lübeck, the 96b, which had an eight-cylinder Horch engine. We also flew the FW Weihe which had two Hirth engines and the FW Stosser which was a good plane for high flying. In a Stosser I did a 4000 metre high barometer flight as a test for keeping level heights. We also had some Czech planes, such as the Avia B 534 or 504, which was massive for a biplane. It was bigger than the British Gladiator but dangerous - if you got into a spin you had to recover very quickly because after two spins you did not have a chance. I obtained my Flugzeugführer Pilot Licence (No 86119) on September 3rd, 1941. I was then transferred to the Flugzeug Flieger Schule C1 at Sorau, Lausitz. On October 10th, 1941, I obtained my Schleppgenehmigung, a glider towing licence. I then commenced training on Ju 52, He 111 and Do 17s. We started night-flying, long range trips in the Ju 52 and He 111. For example we flew from Munich-Rome-Athens-Salonica-Munich, and then return to our base at Sorau. In June 1942 I was transferred to the Blind Flying School at Copenhagen Kastrup. My radio operator was Willy Boehm who remained with me until we were both later captured. In the autumn of 1942, I went to KG76 at Orleans, but two weeks later was posted to KG26 at Lübeck.

'At Lübeck we assembled as a complete aircrew to fly the He 111. Willy remained the radio operator, Hubert Schumacher was the observer, and Werner Kolzke the mechanic and gunner. With KG26 we were doing a lot of low flying training. At the Ratzeburger Lake near Lübeck we had had stakes 10 metres high in the water for some distance. The poles had markers on the top and we used to fly level with them - if anyone went higher, someone would sarcastically ask if they required oxygen! We also flew low over the Baltic.

'Later we were transferred for a few days to Königsberg in East Prussia where we did more low flying, off Frishes Haff. At night we practised searchlight evasion, mostly for the flak gunners' benefit. About four weeks after the Möhne Dam was hit, I was on leave in Witten a.d. Ruhr, and then went over the Brenner Pass by train to Grosseto in Italy for torpedo training. Aircrews from our unit would board a ship and watch those crews that were flying using dummy torpedoes in practice attacks. We used torpedoes of Italian manufacture, 100 kg and with electronic ignition. "Live" torpedoes were fitted with warheads and supplied to front-line elements of our unit at Cagliari on Sardinia.

'We then experienced the first bombing raid by Allied Liberators, on Grosseto airfield, but there was little damage. The second raid, however, was devastating. Our unit moved to Salon de Provence in the South of France. There all III/KG26 assembled and we flew low level formation training flights and also received radar instruction, all this was in preparation for our first sortie.

'For the first big torpedo raid, in August 1943, 40 He 111s and 20 Ju 88s were assembled. The target was a convoy at Gibraltar. The attack took place 40 km east of Albora, a Spanish island, south of Almeria. On the return flight I escorted a damaged He 111 as far as Almeria before I flew back to base alone. The sortie lasted seven hours and 30 minutes flying time. Back at base the Ju 88s were low on fuel, as always, so had priority to land. De-briefing then took place during the night. Afterwards no-one felt like going to sleep. The following day there was a "Sondermeldung", or special announcement, over the German radio about our attack.

'We also had Italian torpedo planes on our base but I do not recall the Italians ever making use of them. Apparently all of their engines required overhauling before General Badolgio took Italy over to the Allies.

'We flew several sorties against convoys along the North African coast, but there was a heavy raid on our base at Salon de Provence which forced us to re-locate our accommodation. From then on we lived in tents between grapes and peaches. During the height of summer, we had problems getting out of the airfield. We obtained rockets which were fitted to our He 111s between the engines and fuselage. Their running time was 30 seconds, power output being about 500 hp per unit, rate of climb about 25 metres per second. Of course the Heinkel was unloaded and not carrying too much fuel, but it was very exciting.

'Lockheed Lightnings regularly flew over us on reconnaissance flights. We used dispersed airfields like Istres, Orange and Montpellier. To reduce losses we employed rockets on a few planes to deter flak gunners on ships. I think about seven rockets were fitted in place of two torpedoes. I knew of one rocket taking-off on its own, most likely it fell into the Étang de Benre which was an inland lake connected to the Mediterranean itself by a channel south of our airfield. It was probably caused by static electricity or an electrical fault.

'In between sorties we received further instruction in radar. Our favourite practice target was the island used as a prison in Marseille harbour. Because we flew so low there was always the "Sea Schlange" - or Sea Snake - at the bottom of the radar screen and which was actually the radar's reflection on the waves.

'I flew one solo sortie to the North African coast to look for stragglers from the previous night's sortie. This particular plane did not have any "Flammen-Fresser", or exhaust shields, so I was not very pleased. Our electronic altimeter was very good, though, 10 metres per division and I think 150 metres round the clock. Light conditions that night were poor, and during the return flight we had battery problems so navigation was difficult and we had no autopilot.

'Bristol Beaufighters prowled along the North African coast looking for us. When we suspected that we had one on our tail, we kept low and switched on our blind landing equipment to confuse his radar. The main landing signal flashed red in the cockpit and an audible signal sounded in our earphones. Then we flew in a circle to keep out of his radar beam. Continuing then on our course, we would check whether the radar had caught us again, or we would fly a different course, ensuring that, by flying very low, the moon was shining just over the rudder so that the night-fighter had a difficult job as we saw him first.

'There was always talk about invasion. The nearest Allied landings took place at Anzio. We left Salon en route to Anzio - the plan was to fly overland past Rome and then west against the sunset and attack the invasion fleet. West of La Spezia, we flew in a circle to correct our flying time when we were jumped by Thunderbolts and Spitfires. The game was up so we dropped our torpedoes and used maximum boost to get into the clouds and return to Salon. The following night we had a serious briefing by the Waffen SS Commander in the Mediterranean Theatre - he made it crystal clear that we could always have a ground job on the Eastern Front instead.

Unteroffizier Paul Moeller, second left, on leave in Germany.

'February 1st, 1944, was a nice day. A convoy was reported having left Gibraltar the previous night, so off we went again. The raid was timed for 2100 hrs, the moon SE at about 30 degrees elevation. My own position was "tail-end Charlie" on the right-hand side. We flew a course correction whilst still in formation, and during the left-hand turn I lost contact. I continued alone, and when lined up for "Fächerschuss", which means two torpedoes simultaneously two degrees left or right of your line at 800 metres, I was shot at by the escort ships. The whole convoy seemed to be firing at me. The right engine failed completely whilst the other only just rattled on. I released my torpedoes, turned away and prepared to ditch. The water was very calm and I put down on a moonbeam. When I felt the tail-wheel make contact I pulled the stick back with both arms.

The first impression was that I had hit a sandbank - all the rivets screamed on contact. We stopped dead and then floated in a eerie silence. None of us were hurt. The next urgent job was to get the dinghy pack out through the top hatch. The wing was badly holed with sharp edges sticking up. Once we were all safely in the dinghy, we paddled a safe distance and watched our Heinkel, 1H + CL, disappear headfirst forever. Next job we took stock. We set sail, trailing our colour bag, guessing both direction and speed. We had ditched between Cape Ténès and Mostaganem, and about 10 miles off the coast. We saw searchlights from the convoy looking for us so quickly pulled the colour bag out of the water. We had been told that one hour after our raid He 177s would be making another attack with guided bombs. We therefore wanted to get as far away from the convoy as possible. We eventually made landfall in the early hours of February 2nd, 1944.

'Next we started to walk in a westerly direction until we stumbled onto the coastal road. During the morning we came to a group of Arab tents where we had couscous and coffee. Two hours later we heard motor vehicles which turned out to be a truckload of French soldiers, a motor-cyclist, and several policemen on horseback. Thus we lost our freedom'.

On the night in question I/KG26 also suffered another crew all wounded, and also on the same mission, III Gruppe lost two aircraft with eight aircrew captured. Another of their He 111s crashed upon return killing three of the crew, the fourth being wounded.

Paul Moeller continues with his story of captivity:-

'Our next stop was Mostaganem where we lost our possessions, then onto Oran in the Old Citadel in Dark Arrest. Two days later we were collected by a British officer and three privates. They gave us sandwiches and an orange each. Then by Dakota to Algiers and "Quetschmuhle", an interrogation camp. There I received the same threat that had been made a fortnight before, that there were two Russian officers waiting to take me to Russia. We were detained at a nearby camp and the crew was split up. There I met an Me 109 pilot, Kurt Leopold, better known as "Poldi", who had been shot down in Italy. Then to Oran by coastal railway and internment in an American-run prisoner of war camp. Then by Liberty-ship convoy to Norfolk, Virginia, USA, and Camp Picket, west of Richmond. There we refused to work on the camp trucks when we found Russian instructions under the seats. All NCOs, including myself, were then transferred to Camp Reynolds in Pennsylvania. There I made a kite which I flew and promptly an officer came along and forbade me to fly anything above six feet. I then built a replica to look like one I had seen in an American newspaper after D-Day and we had a bit of fun that night. Our next camp was at Aliceville, Alabama, which was very hot and humid. We were joined there by the first prisoners taken in Normandy, and we had a big football match between Normandy and Africa. We were receiving good food, but after the German offensive in the Ardennes commenced that stopped.

Unteroffizier Paul Moeller, extreme right, pictured whilst a PoW in Alabama, USA. He is wearing three badges of importance, at bottom the pilot's qualification badge, the ribbon to the Iron Cross Second Class, and the 'Frontflug-Spange für Kampflieger' in bronze, awarded for 20 operational flights. The man in the centre is Paul's friend 'Poldi', an Me 109 pilot shot down over Monte Cassino. The seated officer on the left is from the Gebirgsjäger, or Mountain Troops, as indicated by the Edelweiss on his left sleeve, and the other is a member of the Panzertruppe.

'By 1945 I was at the Naval Air Station at Jacksonville in Florida. I worked in a garage maintaining the camp transport. On Sunday at 12 noon there was a top 20 programme called LSMFT, which stood for "Lucky Strike means fine tobacco". At Christmas all of our pilots volunteered to fly in American planes against the Russians.

'In March 1946, we travelled by Victory Class ship to Antwerp and by train to a British prisoner of war camp near Brussels. After standing for hours in a queue to fill in release papers we ended up in Tilbury Harbour, England. I have been here ever since!' Paul Moeller's story, however, omits to mention that on October 21st, 1943, he was awarded the Iron Cross IInd Class (Eiserne Kreuz 2 Klass), and on January 15th, 1944, the "Frontflug-Spange" in Bronze for 20 operational flights.

All involved were delighted when Paul Moeller and Peter Wulff attended the launch of 'Angriff Westland' in Yeovil on September 24th, 1994. Their presence was not only to represent the German fighter and bomber crews who had participated in the raids concerned, but, more importantly, to emphasise the peace that now exists between Britain and Germany. This gesture was made more poignant when Mr Roy Madelin, Chairman of South Somerset District Council, invited both former Luftwaffe airmen to walk with RAF veterans through Yeovil during the parade of the following morning, which preceded a church service to remember the dead. On that Sunday morning, however, we were dismayed to learn that the Moellers' car had been stolen during the night. Paul, however, refused to let the problem ruin what was left of the weekend, as he was so determined to march in the parade. The outrage at the theft was shared by us all that morning, but the way in which Paul Moeller accepted the bad news and got on with life impressed me enormously. I am sure that such qualities sustained him greatly whilst he was a prisoner of war.

Paul Moeller back in the pilot's seat of an He 111, if only on a flight of fancy. The summer issue flying helmet and schwimmveste are identical to those he was wearing when shot down and captured on February 1st, 1944.

Chapter Twenty-nine

Hauptmann Herman Kell

Hauptmann Herman Kell.

Making many new friends, some abroad, is a bonus to being a published author. I frequently receive letters from readers overseas, particularly those in the USA and Canada. Occasionally one of these fellow enthusiasts will pay a visit whilst in the UK; the most recent was Derek Boyling, a former 'Brummie' but these last 40 years a naturalised Canadian. Derek was able to visit Worcester on the occasion of an 'Angriff Westland' signing and there was able to meet Ron Rayner, Tony Minchin and Martyn Steynor, all of whose stories are told in this book. Derek told me, however, of his friendship with a former German PoW who had remained in Canada after the war just as Peter Wulff and Paul Moeller had stayed in the UK. This man's name was Herman Otto Kell. Kurt Bühligen, Derek told me, had been Herman Kell's flight mechanic and Kell recommended that Bühligen be sent to train as a fighter pilot - Bühlingen survived the war as one of Germany's greatest fighter aces with over 100 victories, receiving the Knight's Cross, Oak Leaves and Swords. Herman Kell had also shared a room whilst flying He 111s with another famous Luftwaffe airman, Hajo Herrmann; he was awarded the Knight's Cross whilst flying bombers, and later received both the Oak Leaves and Swords whilst a night-fighter pilot playing a key role in Germany's nocturnal defence organisation. Was I interested, Derek Boyling asked, in learning any more about Herman Kell ? The following provides that answer.

'I was born Herman Otto Kell in November 1914, the only child of my poor and good parents, August and Louise Kell, at Nabburg, a small town in Bavaria, Germany. I was brought up in a strict religious background. A death in the family stimulated an interest in medicine, and my dream was to spend a lifetime involved with medical research. I therefore learned Latin in my spare time as a fourth language.

'When I graduated from school in 1933, however, I realised that my parents were too poor to support me through university, so instead I applied to become one of the Reichswehr's 4,000 officers. Due to my humble origins I doubted that I would be accepted - I was the only student from my college ever to be commissioned.

'Reichswehr was the name given to the German Armed Force of 100,000 soldiers and 4,000 officers stipulated by the Treaty of Versailles in 1919. I was accepted under the aegis of Reichspraesident v. Hindenburg, before Hitler came to power. Members of the Reichswehr were actually prohibited from engaging in politics and were therefore the only Germans unable to vote at elections.

'After graduating in the top group during 1935 from the German equivalent of West Point, I volunteered to become an officer in the Luftwaffe, although the air force did not actually officially exist at that time, a German air force having been forbidden by Versailles. My initial flying lessons, therefore, were not from a proper airfield but from a country meadow near Celle.

'By 1936 and aged 21 years, I possessed all pilot's licences and was promoted to the rank of Leutnant. I became the Flugleiter, or airport manager, at Gotha/Thuer. Amongst other things, I was responsible for air traffic and safety.

'In 1937, I was selected by the German Air Ministry, at the age of 22$^{1}/_{2}$ years, to be one of just two Luftwaffe pilots flying officials to and from foreign countries on a weekly basis. The flights were often of 8-10 hours duration over the open sea without radio, weather information or autopilot. We were flying the first all-metal aircraft - the Ju 52.

'On January 1st, 1939, I was the only junior Luftwaffe officer promoted to Oberleutnant. The only other promotions that day were about eight Obersts and Generals.

'I then served first as an Oberleutnant, then as Hauptmann and Staffelkapitän, with 3/KG4 "General Wever". I flew the He 111 operationally in both Poland and Norway and was awarded the Iron Cross 2nd Class on the fifth day of the Second World War. A few days before the blitzkrieg in the west commenced, however, I was ordered back to form a new training school on a deserted aerodrome to prepare new KG4 crews for operations against the enemy. At the start of one of these training flights, an engine failed, I immediately took control from the student and landed the He 111 in a large forest over which we had been flying. The young navigator was killed, two were wounded, but four were unhurt. I was in a coma for two months, but after regaining consciousness I returned to my 3 Staffel on crutches in July 1940.

Bullet damage to the perspex surrounding Herman's pilot's position in his He 111 during the Polish campaign. He won the Iron Cross Second Class on the fifth day of the Second World War.

The wreckage of a KG4 He 111 D-2, Werk Nummer 2117, 5J + AC, in which Herman Kell survived a training crash in Germany, 1940.

'The next order I received was to cause me several lost nights' sleep. It was to devise tactics to lay mines in the Irish Sea harbours with the help of two engineers who supplied me with the technical data required. The giant mines were constructed to descend by parachute. They had to be dropped from a height of 100 metres above the water of the harbour approaches. Anti-aircraft fire could therefore provide a premature end for any such mission. Fortunately I had a brainwave - I flew at 100 metres at just the minimum speed and power to remain airborne. The acoustic guided searchlights were therefore misled, and searched at greater heights whilst I flew over their heads! A test flight over a harbour in the Bristol Channel proved my theory to be sound - we lost not one aircraft on the difficult and dangerous missions.

'On September 6th, 1940, I participated with 3/KG4 in three nocturnal raids against the East India Docks and London in retaliation for the bombing of Berlin. The weather was good. We suffered no losses, but I saw neither any hits nor fires in London proper.

Hauptmann Kell, right, flies his He 111.

'A few days later I received an order to personally fly a solo night raid against an industrial complex on the western edge of Newcastle-upon-Tyne. When I approached the He 111 that I was detailed to fly, and which was not my usual aircraft, I was astonished to see a giant bomb hanging beneath the plane, the like of which I had never seen before. I had trouble actually getting into the plane because the bomb was so big. I flew across the North Sea to Newcastle at about 2000m. Again the weather was good, but I could not find our specific target. In desperation I descended to about 100m or less, and criss-crossed Newcastle for at least 30 minutes without success. The response to the idea of indiscriminately dropping this huge bomb on Newcastle was "No." With the first rays of sunlight, I flew out across the North Sea towards our base in Holland. Once home I expected an unfriendly reception for returning home with the bomb, but fortunately I was wrong.

Hauptman Herman Kell, centre, with his crew and their 3/KG4 He 111.

'On Friday, 13th September, 1940, all night missions were cancelled. An unusually bad weather front covered northern France, the Netherlands and Germany. There was thunder and lightning in every direction. At about 9 pm I received an order for a crew of volunteers to fly a nuisance raid against Victoria Station in London. This came from a high level of authority which was apparently unaware that there are limits to flying in such bad weather! I was the Staffelkapitän, or Squadron Leader, of 3/KG4 so I did not ask anyone else to volunteer and so flew the mission myself. However, I excluded a trainee pilot from our crew, Leutnant v. D., although he felt somewhat aggrieved.

'I was concerned about where I could land upon return, due to the weather, but the Meteorologist was unable to provide the answer. At about 11 pm I switched on the plane's lights whilst I started up, and saw a car approaching from the left. It was the Geschwaderkommodore himself, Oberstleutnant Rath, who had come out in the heavy rain to salute our crew. I had never seen this before.

'I had hardly lifted the He 111 from the runway when I was in turbulent clouds. I had difficulty holding the plane on its course. Strong up and down winds played with our plane at their leisure. Frequently I was unsure whether the plane was flying straight and level, the instrument needles going haywire. When a bolt of lightning illuminated the cockpit, I saw my good old navigator staring at me, the question of whether I could actually maintain control of the aircraft written all over his face - sometimes I was unsure myself. When bolts of lightning hit the plane I often had no answer regarding what to do. Although I had previously flown many times at night and in bad weather, this flight taught me that in addition to ability and experience, sometimes you also need a little luck.

'We finally emerged from the clouds at 6000m to find a cloudless, moonlit night above the Thames estuary, exactly where we were supposed to be; it was so peaceful and quiet it was hard to believe that we were engaged on a war flight. The relaxation was rapidly cut short when we were coned by searchlights. I took evasive action which shook them off momentarily, but after a while I had to accept that it was futile - I did not know then that London's searchlights were guided by radar and not acoustics.

'Orientation above blacked out London was easy due to the recent heavy rain - the wet railway tracks reflected the bright moonlight. Where the glittering tracks joined many others but then suddenly disappeared was obviously Victoria Station. My navigator had actually guided me to this location with his homing device. Suddenly an endless stream of bullets smashed into our aircraft. It was a Blenheim which had attacked from 50-20m, using all his ammunition in one continuous burst. I later learned that the pilot was a New Zealander, Pilot Officer Michael Herrick of 25 Squadron. He had already destroyed two Heinkels and after shooting us down received the DFC. Sadly he was killed in action over Denmark, so after the war I was unable to meet this excellent and courageous young pilot.

'After Herrick's attack the oil pressure of both engines rapidly dropped to zero. I knew that we had no chance. I immediately shut down both motors to avoid both fire or an explosion, but my actions were in vain. Flames spurted out of both engines and engulfed the plane. I called to the mechanic and radio operator in the rear of the plane, telling them to prepare to bale out. There was no answer. I sent the navigator back to check on them. He came back with news that both comrades were dead.

'By now I had changed to a northerly course and we glided down at as shallow an angle as possible, hoping to clear the outskirts of London before hitting the ground. The flames blocked all view of the outside, and prevented the use of all escape hatches except the small one above my seat. I was unsure whether the hatch was big enough to get through with my parachute on, but I had no option. My navigator stood silently beside me, calmly awaiting my decision. At 2000m I guessed that we should be over open countryside. As the hatch was above my seat, I had to jump first to allow my navigator to climb up over my empty seat and out of the hatch. I trimmed the plane for the last time into a steady glide. My navigator and I shook hands and wished each other luck.

'I dived onto the left wing to avoid being hit by the tailplane, and fell into space. As I pulled the ripcord, I saw our burning plane continue its downward glide until exploding on impact with our dead comrades still aboard. Beneath I saw a parachute, but although I called out several times to my navigator I received no answer.

'Suddenly a Blenheim emerged from the night and circled me, uncomfortably close, up on a wing tip. Obviously there was a master at the controls. I pulled some strings of my parachute to drop faster. I hit the ground hard and found myself lying in a field. With the parachute beneath my arm, I hastened to get away from where I had landed. I climbed over several walls, but then the pain from my broken leg caused me to hide beneath some bushes on the banks of a stream. It gave me time to rest and think.

'At first light I saw two anti-aircraft guns about 300 yards away. A soldier went into a wagon. Another came out. I decided to surrender before they all woke up. I left my flying suit at the stream, and approached the wagon to surrender. When I entered the wagon, I pulled my pistol, ready to shoot first if necessary. On the far side of the wagon was a Sergeant, alone. He froze when he saw me enter with a drawn pistol. I told him that it was his lucky day - it was for him to take me prisoner - slowly he recovered his composure!

'He invited me to his table. We had a shallow conversation and he shared with me his frugal breakfast, a cup of watery cocoa with a slice of white bread spread thinly with margarine. I was grateful. He made a 'phone call. When the car arrived he asked me to autograph his record book - I was then surprised to see the name of my navigator already entered therein. I now knew that my fellow crew member had survived. This friendly Sergeant, who never showed any hostility towards me, accompanied me to the waiting car.

'After a short ride the car stopped where a senior officer was waiting. We saluted each other and he took me straight to his personal quarters. He lent me his washing kit and razor. Before I had registered the significance of this he left the room, saying "I do hope that you will not cause me any trouble." I do not know whether he heard my reply: "Sir, you have my word."

'After a while he returned and invited me to breakfast in the Officers' Mess. There I found some 15-20 officers already seated and waiting for me. During the meal I had to answer many questions, but never an unfriendly or hostile question or gesture. I was deeply impressed.

'After breakfast the Commanding Officer went with me to a waiting car. I felt rather bad when I realised that he was unarmed whilst I still had a pistol in my holster. This gentleman in uniform was too noble to ask for my gun.

'In the car he told me that he had been a pilot during the Great War, and that he had been shot down and captured by the Germans who treated him well. I regret that I never found out the name of this exemplary officer and gentleman.

'I spent the next night in an underground cell, probably in Chelmsford. Very early in the morning I was brought breakfast in my cell. Before I could touch it, however, I was led out. A young Lieutenant with four soldiers with fixed bayonets were waiting. I was led through a narrow, dark underground passage. When we emerged we were in a cemetery. It was disconcerting. I watched the young

Lieutenant and resolved to fiercely resist any attempt to shoot me up against a wall. We finally left the cemetery via a gate. I began to sweat and my knees became weak.

'My next "home" was in a bare room beneath the roof of a building in the Kensington Palace complex. During the afternoon I was led into a dark basement room. I sat in a small beam of light. In the half darkness sat a man in civilian clothes at a desk. After providing my name and rank, I was asked a question about my Staffel. My response was, "Sir, I assume that you are or were an officer, and that you are therefore aware that I am unable to answer that question." To my great surprise he replied that he knew who I was and closed my file. He switched on the light and invited me to his desk. We had a friendly, shallow, chat and I was returned to my "room". It was September 15th, 1940, and through my window I saw two Do 17s spin to earth. There were no parachutes. I realised how lucky I had been.

'The next day I was escorted by one officer to PoW Camp, Grizedale Hall in the Lake District. There I joined 286 comrades, including some old friends.

'Shortly before Christmas 1940, we were all shipped to Canada. I spent the next six years there, behind barbed wire, as a "guest" of the strict, but fair, Canadian army under the authority of the exemplary and admirable Colonel Stetham in Ottawa.

'Being a prisoner was not easy, but then again, war was never a recommendable occupation.

'In January 1941, I was instrumental in helping Oberleutnant Franz von Werra to escape. We were on a train travelling from Halifax to Camp W. (100) at Neys, Ontario. I held up a blanket to conceal his exit via a window from which he had removed the screws. Franz of course made it to the USA, which was still neutral at that time, and was later sent home. He was later killed, however, when the engine of his Me 109 failed over the North Sea.

Luftwaffe officers in captivity. Those identified are: Oberleutnant Herman Kell (front row, 1st on left), Major von Massenbach (Observer, Knight's Cross holder, front row, centre), Oberleutnant von Arnim (4/KG4, pilot, front row, 2nd right), Leutnant Hans-Jurgen Bachaus (top right).

Chris Goss

'In the spring of 1946, three interviewers came to our camp at Wainwright/ Alberta to judge and classify every PoW: "White", "Grey" or "Black". The speed of repatriation depended on your classification. One of the interviewers was a Jewess, and of course, as by now the world knew about Hitler's Holocaust, every prisoner prayed not to have to be judged by her. When I entered her office she was reading my file of just a couple of pages after six years as a prisoner. I gave my name and rank, and awaited her questions. She closed my file, remarked that it was lunchtime and invited me to have a cup of coffee with her. I was astonished.

'In an adjacent room, there then sat a German officer and a Jewish lady. They discussed neither politics or the war. Not one unfriendly word passed between them. There was no tension. Clearly peace had overcome. The voice of the Jewish lady was soft, low and slow, but was not free from undertones of sadness. Only a few times did the German suspect a smile on her face.

'After lunch, we returned to her office. At the door she stopped and asked me what classification I really wanted, if I could choose. I told her grey; she said "Then I will give you a grey plus!" That was the most desired classification. We shook hands as I left. I never knew her name, nor did I ever meet that admirable Jewish lady again. With great regret.

'Not long after that, I was repatriated and was reunited with my family in November 1946. My last mission, which had lasted over six years, had finally ended.

'Although the age of chivalry has largely passed, the example of some exceptional human beings whom I met during the war proves that decency and chivalry have still not entirely disappeared.

'I am now aged 80 years, and memories of the war have largely faded away. My memories of the stalwarts of decency and chivalry, however, will never fade'.

I believe that former Hauptmann Herman Kell himself personifies chivalry and honour. He became, after all, a career officer before the Nazis came to power in Germany in 1933, and thus avoided the ideology of the Hitler Youth. He was, in a way, a remnant of the old Imperial Germany.

On September 22nd, 1940, just over a week after Herman's capture, he was awarded the Iron Cross 1st Class. The 'Eiserne Kreuz' was established at Breslau on March 10th, 1813, by the King of Prussia, Wilhelm III. It was designed by the famous Prussian architect, Schinkel, and based upon the King's idea

Enthusiast Derek Boyling poses at the Soldatfriedhof, Cannock Chase, Staffordshire, with the grave of Herman Kell's two crew members who perished when their He 111 was shot down over London. The third airman, Obergefrieter Eduard Koppl, was of 7/KG26, and his He 111 was destroyed over Somerset.
Derek Boyling

of creating an award similar in appearance to the Cross of the Order of German
Knights. Schinkel's subsequent plain but distinctive design became the badge of
courage for Germany's fighting men, spanning two centuries. It is entirely
appropriate that such an honourable soldier as Herman Kell should have received
both classes of this award. A true and chivalrous knight, Wilhelm III would
have been proud of him.

Herman Kell at his home in Ontario, Canada,
pictured in 1995 at the age of 80 years.
Derek Boyling

The last line in 'A Few of the Many', however, goes to another former Luftwaffe
pilot, Major Martin Drewes, a night-fighter ace with 48 victories and holder of
the Knights Cross with Oak Leaves. The following is an extract from a letter
that I received from Martin, writing from his home in Brazil, dated January
14th, 1991, just two days before the Gulf War started and John Peters was shot
down. It is surely a sentiment shared by us all: 'On May 14th, 1941, I was
transferred with another 11 shark-mouth painted Me 110s of our ZG76 to
Baghdad; 50 years ago . . and now . . . I do hope that everything will finish in
peace'.

Acknowledgements

Many people have an input into a book of this nature, including all those with a piece of the jig-saw, no matter how large or small. However, in the first instance I must thank my wife who shared my midnight oil and helped with the large quantity of copy typing that this book required. Anita generally supports my ideas and enthusiasm, so I am fortunate indeed to have such a wife. Little James running around the office shouting "Daddy, Spitfire crashed!" was not an irritation but an inspiration - a bond between father and son.

All of those pilots and groundcrews whose stories are told in this book, and in many cases their wives (or partners) and families, have my sincere thanks for taking the time and trouble to either write or record their memories and search for long-forgotten photographs. I see no point in impassionately listing them all - their names can be found on the contents page. It is sad, however, that two did not live to see this book published, namely Wing Commander PI Howard-Williams DFC and Wing Commander RJE Boulding.

I am honoured that Gulf War veteran and best-selling author Flight Lieutenant John Peters RAF - born the same year as myself - kindly agreed to contribute the foreword to 'A Few of the Many'.

In addition to those mentioned above, the following veterans were also kind enough to offer assistance: Squadron Leader TA Stevens, Flight Lieutenant Peter Wass, former Major Martin Drewes RK & EL, and former Unteroffizier Ottomar Kruse. Miss Margaret Balfour, a former member of the WAAF, has very kindly allowed her personal wartime diary to be extracted and her interest in 19 Squadron is touching.

Unless otherwise indicated, all photographs illustrating 'A Few of the Many' are from my own collection, the majority therefore being obtained from the pilots concerned themselves.

The following friends have also helped with historical and other data: John Foreman (the oracle on losses and claims), Chris Goss, Derek Boyling, Norman Franks, Ernie Hardy, Mark Postlethwaite, Gil Davies, Don Caldwell, Antony Whitehead, Andrew Long, Alan Bray, Dave Malpas, Ray Johnson, Ron & Shelagh Mason, and Steve Brooker.

I wish to thank the following organisations: the Battle of Britain Fighter Association (in particular, of course, the Association's apparently tireless Honorary Secretary, Wing Commander NPW Hancock OBE DFC RAF Retd), the Keeper and staff of the Public Record Office, the Polish Institute, and the RAF Museum and Imperial War Museum.

Allan Smith and his small team at 'Aspect' have once again produced an excellent end result and have made the production of this book, our third together, a pleasure.

Steve Birch, and Glen Griffiths of Ambit Publications, kindly helped with a computer problem.

Finally I reserve a special mention for my close friend Dr Dennis Williams. It is essential to have someone with whom I can share my enthusiasm for wartime aviation and also use as both a critic and sounding board. His efforts as proof reader and editor are beyond the call of friendship, as is his general input into my various projects and productions.

Bibliography

As this book relies largely upon the first-hand account, I have actually had to undertake little new research other than consulting documents at the Public Record Office. However, the following published books would undoubtedly be of interest to anyone wishing to read further about the 1939-45 air war:-

Die Ritterkreuz Träger Der Luftwaffe 1939-45, Volume I, Jagdflieger: Ernst Obermaier and Verlag Dieter, 1966.

RAF Squadrons: Wing Commander CG Jefford MBE RAF, Airlife Publishing Ltd, 1993.

Men of the Battle of Britain: Kenneth G Wynn, Gliddon Books, 1989.

The Battle of Britain Then & Now Mk V: Edited by Winston Ramsey, Battle of Britain Prints International Ltd, 1989.

The Blitz Then & Now Volume II: Edited by Winston Ramsey, Battle of Britain Prints International Ltd, 1988.

Spitfire Squadron: Dilip Sarkar, Air Research Publications, 1990.

The Invisible Thread: A Spitfire's Tale: Dilip Sarkar, Ramrod Publications, 1992.

Through Peril To The Stars: Dilip Sarkar, Ramrod Publications, 1993.

Angriff Westland: Dilip Sarkar, Ramrod Publications, 1994.

Battle of Britain - The Forgotten Months: John Foreman, Air Research Publications, 1988.

1941 - The Turning Point: John Foreman, Air Research Publications, 1993.

JG26 - Top Guns of the Luftwaffe: Don Caldwell, Orion Books, 1990.

Aces High: Christopher Shores & Clive Williams, Grubb Street, 1994.

RAF Fighter Command 1936-1968: Norman Franks, Patrick Stephens Ltd, 1992.